Former corporate lawyer, co-founder of a successful software company and technology investor, David Gillespie is the bestselling author of the *Sweet Poison* books, *Big Fat Lies*, *Free Schools, Toxic Oil*, *Eat Real Food*, *The Eat Real Food Cookbook* and *Taming Toxic People*. He lives in Brisbane with his wife and six children.

Also by David Gillespie

The *Sweet Poison* books
Big Fat Lies
Free Schools
Toxic Oil
Eat Real Food
The Eat Real Food Cookbook
Taming Toxic People

TEEN BRAIN

David Gillespie

First published 2019 in Macmillan by Pan Macmillan Australia Pty Ltd
1 Market Street, Sydney, New South Wales, Australia, 2000

Cataloguing-in-Publication entry is available
from the National Library of Australia
http://catalogue.nla.gov.au

Typeset in 11/18pt Sabon by Midland Typesetters
Printed by IVE

To Lizzie, Anthony, James, Gwen, Adam, Elisabeth and Fin.

CONTENTS

Introduction

I started researching this book because two mothers of teenagers told me to. My wife, Lizzie, said she was barely able to get through a conversation with another mother of teens without hearing about a child in counselling or on medication for anxiety and depression. Then my publisher, Ingrid, said exactly the same thing. Both of them felt something wasn't right. This wasn't how they grew up. They felt something was going on in the world of teenagers that was being hidden by the happy selfies on Facebook and Instagram, and they both wanted me to start digging to see if their hunches were right.

Before I started, I really wondered why I was bothering. Surely, I thought, everything that could possibly be written about parenting teens had already been done, and done better than I could ever do. Sure, there seemed to be more fuss in the media about teens overusing their phones, but it seemed to me to be the perennial intergenerational problem of 'teens these days'. Yes, it was a minute-by-minute fight in our house to keep the kids away from their school-mandated iPads. And yes, the presence of those devices in the house had introduced a whole new level of sneaky behaviour and teen angst. But I put all that down to normal growing pains.

Then I started reading the research on the significant changes in reward pathways in adolescence. I wondered why I'd seen nothing much in the press about that well-established biological reality. And I wondered why I saw even less about why that might be a problem in an age when billions are being spent by tech companies to encourage teenagers to become addicted to their products.

I knew software is engineered to addict. When it comes to non-business-related software, addictive products sell. Non-addictive products die a fast death. This is especially the case when every product in the category is 'free'. I'd worked long enough in the industry to know how product management and marketing work. But I didn't know that teens are particularly susceptible to addiction. I knew it was always a struggle to prise a screen from our teenagers' hands, but I tended to have a vaguely dismissive, 'What harm can it really do?' approach. And yes, I felt devices in schools were a significant distraction likely to impair performance, but I had no sense of how uniquely destructive to teen wellbeing they could be.

In short, I was happy to drift, uncomfortably, through allowing teen access to devices and accept, uneasily, the assurances that while they might be distracting, it was for the best or at least would do no permanent harm. That was until the union-of-the-mothers-of-teens told me to have a good hard look at it. In a nutshell, here's what I found:

1. The biology of puberty makes the teen brain uniquely fragile. It makes teens susceptible to addictions that can last for life and usher in mental illness.
2. Parenting is much more permissive and parents need to harden up to save their kids.
3. Unfettered access to screens is driving an epidemic of addiction, depression and anxiety, the likes of which we have never witnessed before.

What I found was frankly terrifying. In less than a decade we've totally changed the future of the human race, and we've done it without so much as a backward glance. Think that's an overreach? Bear with me while I explain.

Humans are brainy

Humans have the longest pregnancy of any mammal. Before you hit Google and start screaming 'Elephants!' and 'Whales!', hear me out. We, well women, produce what software developers call 'minimum viable product' after nine months, but the job is by no means done by then. A newborn human may as well still be in the womb for all it can accomplish on its own. It can't walk, feed itself, talk, swim or even do a crossword. Compare that to a baby horse. Sure, a foal is a little unsteady on its feet . . . for a minute or two. But a one-day-old could outrun even the fastest adult human. This a pretty handy feature for an animal that would be choice number one on the all-you-can-eat buffet for most carnivores. If anything, human babies would be an even tastier morsel.

So why do we risk pushing a thoroughly defenceless newborn into the cruel world without even so much as a pocketknife to protect it? We do it because if we didn't, we wouldn't have our most powerful evolutionary advantage, our brain. Humans dominate this planet as the apex predator, but you wouldn't know it to look at us in our native state. We don't have fangs or armour or talons or venom. We're not particularly strong for our size. And we only have middling capabilities when it comes to our senses of sight, smell and hearing. Any number of predators could take us in a one-on-one fight without even breaking a sweat. But what we do have is the most sophisticated brain on the planet. In the braininess stakes, it's us and daylight second, third and fourth. The technical hitch is that this relatively gigantic brain needs to be contained in a relatively gigantic head, and that head needs to pass through a relatively small birth canal with very non-negotiable hips hemming it in. The solution evolution came up with was minimum viable product.

Big as it already is, compared to everything else on the planet, babies are born with only half a brain. After birth is when the real growth occurs. And it doesn't stop till the kid hits their mid-20s. It's tempting to think of a child as a mini-adult. From the outside, they certainly look like one. Especially when you dress them up in business suits and other adult-wear. It's even more tempting during and after puberty to think of them as adults. Because that's exactly what they look like. They have all the gender differentiating bits and pieces and they are approximately adult-sized. But regardless of how they look, these are not adults or mini-adults; the hardware in their heads is still undergoing massive change and the software that drives it is being rewritten on an hour-by-hour basis.

Our gigantic brain gives us two primary strengths: we learn things rather than requiring that they be genetically programmed by instinct, and we cooperate well in large groups of humans. Because we're born very prematurely, it takes us a while to get our motor skills up to scratch, but by the age of two we're physically pretty much where every other animal starts out. However, our brain is just getting warmed up. Unlike other animals, we can learn abstract things like how to read, write and do maths, and those things in turn set us up for even more complex learning.

Before puberty we sort out all the basics. We get walking nailed down, learn how to use tools to save effort, get to know what sorts of things are dangerous and what sorts of things we enjoy, get all the language stuff sorted, learn how to not get killed by other humans, and generally get ready to become adults. At this stage we're still prototype humans. We have some external hardware that enables us to tell potential adult males from potential adult females, but we're not capable of reproduction and we haven't developed most of the part of our brain that will be critical to our survival as adults. We mimic our elders and sometimes even convince them we actually have a clue what we're doing, but in reality we have very little self-control, or ability to plan complex actions or run proper simulations of consequences that would enable us to think strategically. We're reactive and impulsive but that's okay, because all the adult supervision of our actions is supposed to be done by, well, adults. We're a human-shaped template ready to be formed into a fully functional, fully independent adult.

Puberty

Puberty is when making an adult begins. Some obvious stuff starts to happen on the outside, but that's far from the only thing going on. Males and females become clearly differentiated and capable of producing other humans. They also quickly approach the proper size for adults. But in their heads, much more complex things are happening. Males turn into large, hairy, smelly beasts with no impulse control and a desire for danger and sex. Females create a body with all the fat storage necessary for creating the next generation of human brains and an unquenchable desire for the approval of others. Your teenager might have the same name and look vaguely like the kid you had before puberty, but they have about as much in common with that kid as a butterfly has with a chrysalis.

For about a decade from the commencement of puberty, the last chunk of the human brain is under construction. During that phase we're learning how to be an adult. We're learning how to do a proper risk assessment; how to adjust our behaviour according to the results of that risk assessment; how to plan strategically; how to control our impulses, delay gratification and regulate our emotion; how to extend our attention span, working memory and focus; how to care about someone other than ourselves; and how to interact appropriately with other adults. Building a critical bit of the brain inside a living body is a pretty spectacular trick akin to an engineer building an aircraft while in flight. So as you might imagine, some compromises need to be made to get the job done. The biggest compromise is that our teenage brains become completely open to addiction, which can then lead to depression and anxiety and a bunch more unpleasant stuff. The brain-under-construction is on a hair-trigger, and it takes real skill and determination from the adults in the room to make sure it doesn't crash and burn.

None of this is new in an evolutionary sense. Humans have been doing this puberty thing for at least 10,000 generations and largely getting it right. Puberty was just a phase, and as long as the boys didn't kill themselves with their exaggerated exuberance it turned kids into functional adults without too many problems. We managed that largely because, until very recently, highly addictive behaviours and substances were not terribly available to humans at all, let alone during the most vulnerable years of their brain development. Before the Industrial Revolution, unless you were very, very wealthy, the only addictive substance you were likely to encounter was alcohol, and it certainly wasn't being wasted on teenagers.

Roll forward to the 1960s, and the range of addictive substances had substantially increased. Sugar is cheap and was incredibly effective at increasing sales, so it was increasingly embedded in almost every part of the food supply, starting with breakfast cereals but very quickly moving out into just about everything. After they set themselves up with a stomach full of sugar, a teenager could get cigarettes and booze – it wasn't easy but it was possible – and if they knew the right people and had some money, they might even get access to some weed or even heroin. Gambling was still difficult to access, but there were moves to open it up to kids as newsagents began to have access to gambling products.

As the decades rolled on, access to most of these things became steadily easier for most teenagers. And all of that had its effect on the kids who were teenagers during the last half of the 20th century and the first half-decade of the 21st century. Teen violence, crime, smoking, alcoholism, drug addiction, depression, anxiety and pregnancy all climbed steadily. Suddenly, being prone to addiction in our teenage years was a bit of a problem. And it was a problem our biology was unprepared for. Until then, it hadn't really mattered, but now it was causing significant harm, not just to the kids but also to the society having to cope with the rising menace of delinquent teens. It was bad and getting worse quickly, with no solution in sight.

The rise of the online world

And then, in 2007, the world changed. Just 13 years after the release of Netscape, the world's first user-friendly tool for accessing the internet, Apple released the iPhone, a device that allowed every teen to carry the internet in their pocket. The personal internet devices had an almost immediate impact. Trends in bad things that required a teen to be physically present dropped like a stone. Teen pregnancy, alcohol consumption, illicit drug-taking, violent crime and physical bullying have all gone off the statistical cliff. All the obvious ill effects of exposing teens uniquely vulnerable to addiction had disappeared, and society breathed a collective sigh of relief. We didn't know why, but somehow magically things had self-corrected.

But as the parents of kids who became teens after 2010 are now discovering, there's no such thing as a free lunch. Teen anxiety, depression, self-harm and suicide have suddenly become much, much worse. The personal device has simultaneously killed off a range of dangerous and addictive behaviours that were relatively hard to come by, and replaced them with a different set that can be accessed 24/7 for free.

In 2010, Apple followed up the iPhone with the iPad, and was able to convince schools that having the internet in your pocket was actually an educational necessity. Less than a decade later, our world is awash with addictive behaviours and our schools are the dealers. No one needs to commit crime to get the money needed for a hit. And now you don't need to steal your big brother's ID to acquire booze, meet a shady person in a sketchy place to buy your next hit, or have unprotected sex with the footy captain to join the cool kids. Now you just need to tap your phone or tablet and the next hit is free. These free hits aren't blunt instruments like the addictive substances of the 1980s. They're not a pill that gives one person an incredible high but barely affects the person next to them. No, the new tools of addiction are purpose-built for the target audience and refined by market forces to be as effective as possible in addicting your kid. Massive product variation means there is a highly addictive gambling, gaming, porn or social media app designed explicitly to excite them.

Modern parenting styles

At exactly the same moment in history a tide of child-centred parenting swept over the Western world. We convinced ourselves that baby knows best and started demand feeding. Trained appropriately to respond 'How high?' every time a child said 'Jump', we extended that notion into every aspect of child rearing. Suddenly, saying no to a child was the worst possible thing a parent could do. A future full of precocious, attention-seeking, spoiled adults was fast approaching. But it was okay, because just in time Apple invented the electronic pacifier, and technology companies convinced us and our schools that having an addicted but quiet child was actually educating them. We wouldn't accept that explanation from a heroin dealer, but we've taken it hook, line and sinker from technology companies.

Buckle up for the proof

I've made some pretty outrageous claims in that little tirade, so now I expect you to expect me to prove them. And that's exactly what this book is about. I spend the first half looking in detail at exactly what's going on in a teenage brain, how it's different from those of both children and adults, and why it matters. This is all solid science and at times it gets complicated – but don't worry, I have heaps of dodgy analogies that helped me understand it.

And here's the thing: complicated science often boils down to simple intuitive actions you already knew, but now you know why they'll work – and that makes all the difference to whether you'll implement them. My first book, *Sweet Poison*, could have been written with crayon on one piece of paper because the takeaway message was 'Don't eat sugar'. It wasn't a new message. It wasn't an irrational message. But it was one that everyone, including me until then, ignored because dietitians told us fat was the problem.

The detail in this book about what's going on in a teen brain is complicated but worth understanding, because once you do, you'll see why these five simple rules are just about all we need to know about raising teenagers in an age of ubiquitous addictive technology.

The rules

1. Parents make rules and kids follow them.
2. Access to personal electronic devices (and all other addictive substances) is severely restricted.

3. Rules are clear and unequivocal.
4. Breaches of rules are punished – consistently.
5. All teens need eight hours' sleep a night.

If you're thinking that's even more obvious than 'Don't eat sugar', you're probably right. But if you want to gain the knowledge that will give you the confidence to follow them, then read on. You won't regret it. Before I wrote this, I was as I suspect you are – 'Yes,' you say, 'I know I need rules, but sometimes it's very hard.' Now I know why I need them, I've become extremely non-negotiable on that point. I hope it has a similar effect on you, because your kid needs you to step up.

PART I

THE ADOLESCENT BRAIN

HOW THE HUMAN BRAIN WORKS

Scientists have known the rough numbers on brain growth for the better part of a century, but the recent widespread availability of advanced imaging technology means we're starting to have very detailed insight into how the human brain develops.

We begin growing our brain in the third week of gestation, and the job is pretty much complete by the time we're 25. Yep, you read that right – our brain doesn't finish growing until a fair while after we could be called an adult in most Western countries. In other words, we're not playing with a full deck until well into our third decade, and this has important implications for how we parents should interpret (and respond to) teenage behaviour. Bear with me for a bit – we'll get down to the nitty-gritty of your teens soon enough.

The embryonic brain

From the sixth week of gestation, neuron production gets under way, and this is completed by about halfway through our mother's pregnancy. By that point we pretty much have all the neurons we'll ever have, about a hundred billion of them. Neurons are our information-processing cells, but rather like telephones, until they can connect to each other they're not much use. A typical neuron can make more than a thousand connections to other neurons and looks a little like broccoli with a very long stringy tail. The head is thousands of relatively small input connectors called dendrites, and the tail is a large output connector called an axon. The axon can grow to relatively enormous lengths and connect the neuron with other neurons in far-distant parts of the brain.

'We begin growing our brain in the third week of gestation, and the job is pretty much complete by the time we're 25.'

The connection point is called a synapse, and the long-distance connections are called pathways. An example is perhaps our most important and earliest developing pathway, the thalamocortical pathway (pathway from the thalamus – Greek for 'chamber' – to the cortex – Latin for tree bark, here used for the outer layer of the brain). It transfers sensory information from our eyes, ears, muscles and skin to the neurons that need to react to it via the thalamus, a relay that sits at the top of the brain stem.

These pathways and many other connections form the information-processing networks that are responsible for everything we know about the outside world, and all our thoughts, feelings and actions. An adult brain has more than 86 billion neurons and 60 trillion (yes, trillion – that's 60,000,000,000,000) neuronal connections. We spend the rest of our gestation shuffling neurons to the right parts of the brain and establishing immense connectivity between them.

The baby brain

Between birth and 18 months, the brain triples in size to about 75 per cent of its adult size. It then grows a little more slowly to about 90 per cent adult size by the age of six, and hits full size around 11. But these measurements can be a little deceptive. While the brain volume stops expanding at 11, the increasing complexity of neuronal connections continues well into puberty. Inside the brain, massive reorganisation is taking place during these high-growth phases.

When I was a kid, there was a popular toy called PinPression. It was a large square of thousands of blunted pins that could move through tight holes in a board. When you placed anything on the pins they'd depress around the shape of the object, leaving behind a magnificent 3D model of the object made of raised pins on the other side of the board. Just after birth, the connectivity levels in the brain (which influence our ability to learn new things) vastly exceed those of adults. We're like the pin toy with a blank field of pins ready to be pressed down by what we find in the world.

'Between birth and 18 months, the brain triples in size to about 75 per cent of its adult size.'

As we encounter the real world, we begin to prune back that connectivity. We're not eliminating neurons, just the connections between them, the synapses, that don't get used. The more we experience something, the more connections are reinforced and the more hardwired it becomes. Stuff we don't use gets thrown away. There's no point keeping junk we rarely use. Our growing brains have a very definite use-it-or-lose-it approach, and that's worth remembering when it comes to deciding which experiences we choose to expose young children to.

Our slow march to maturity

We're super learning machines, and what we learn is heavily influenced by what we encounter in that time of massive connection growth and changeability (often called *plasticity* – like plasticine, it can be moulded around the shape of what it encounters).

YOUR BABY SPEAKS MANDARIN AND RUSSIAN AND FRENCH

Babies are born with the ability to distinguish the distinct sounds of all languages, but by six months they can no longer recognise sounds that aren't spoken in the language of the people around them. The brain starts out as a blank pin toy for language that's pressed up against the language in your household. Everything it hears programs it to be able to speak that language. And this is significantly enhanced by the fact that many adults speak simplified and phonically enhanced 'motherese' – baby talk – to babies. Every other language-like connection it had is thrown in the bin. This, of course, makes it much more difficult for us to learn a new language when we're older. Our brains ditched most of the bits that would have helped.

This occurs at a minute-by-minute timescale. Every minute a child is forming millions of new connections, keeping some and chucking the rest according to what they encounter. They're on learning overdrive. They're pressing the pin toy up against everything they find, thousands of times a day. This is the period where we acquire language, walking, talking, social interaction, how to use chopsticks and, well, pretty much everything we would need to be a functional adult in the types of societies most humans lived in until the Industrial Revolution.

In the last two decades, brain-imaging technology has developed to the point where we can now accurately map exactly which

EXPERIENCE MAKETH THE MAN – AND THE WOMAN

Experiments on other mammals tell us that a very different type of brain develops depending on the environment a young animal is exposed to. Animals raised with their littermates in large free-roaming enclosures with interesting and changing landmarks develop a much wider range of brain structures and functions than matched animals raised in a standard laboratory cage.

Importantly, these differences in structure are permanent once the growth phase is over in our mid-20s. At birth the brain is like a chunk of marble ready to be carved into a statue by childhood and adolescent experience. Whether you end up with a statue of David or of Homer Simpson depends entirely on how good the sculptor is. For us, that sculptor is the environment we expose our kids to.

That's worth thinking about next time your little petal wants to sit in a corner with their iPad rather than going outside and frolicking with their friends.

part of our brain grows when, and the implications for childhood and teenage behaviour are fascinating. We don't build a brain the way we build a house. We don't start with a plan and build it from the outside in, we start with Buckingham Palace and demolish the rooms we don't use. Then we thoroughly renovate the rooms we decide to keep.

The studies tell us our brains perfect themselves one bit at a time, maturing in a very definite order of progression. First, a newborn sorts out movement and sensors (legs and eyes, etc.). After a year or so we've pruned back our motor and sensory connections and optimised them for the world we encountered, so we're well adapted to navigate and receive raw data from that world. Then, in early childhood we move on to spatial orientation and coordination, attention, speech and language. And during late childhood, puberty and into our 20s, we finish off with the higher order stuff: impulse control, decision-making and social skills. The detail in these phases matches the evolution of our species. So as we added on a new capability, it was chucked onto the end of the queue of brain development. (No doubt hipsters have an extra bit at the end of their brain development associated with being able to detect a better-quality espresso.)

'Our brains perfect themselves one bit at a time.'

Adaptive cooperation

The most recently evolved part of the human brain is the prefrontal cortex (the front cover of the brain). It's responsible for planning, complex thinking, personality expression, decision-making and moderating social behaviour. The prefrontal cortex runs all our simulations of the future and uses them to control our actions now.

As far as we know, we're the only mammal that can predict future events and act on information that isn't currently in our environment.

We use this simulation capability to help us plan actions and control our responses. We also use it to read other people's minds. Well, not literally, but close enough. We spend enormous computing cycles on anticipating the responses of other humans. We're constantly putting ourselves in the shoes of others and incorporating our predictions about them into our thought models. Doing this accurately has been the key to our evolutionary survival.

We can, based on past behaviour, predict whether a person can be trusted, and we can use that knowledge to act cooperatively on a scale no other animal could ever achieve. Yes, ants and bees work cooperatively, but their cooperation is hard-coded into their DNA. A worker bee can't come up with a new plan if the food sources disappear. And a soldier ant can't decide to become a worker if more hands are needed. Yes, elephants and chimpanzees live in groups and help each other, but those groups are limited to related individuals. Intergroup cooperation is nonexistent. Humans are uniquely able to cooperate with strangers, and to adapt that cooperation on the fly according to changes in circumstances.

This capability for adaptive cooperation and the ability to plan joint action has meant that even though we're individually a hopelessly puny predator, as a group we're very hard to beat. Unfortunately, the downside to this ability to predict the future is that we spend an awful lot of time worrying about it. And it doesn't take much to turn this worry into disabling anxiety – but more on that later.

At the start of each phase, our synapse connections in the relevant area of the brain are at the highest they'll ever be. Then experience carves out the detail by pruning back those connections. In the prefrontal cortex, for example, our peak number of connections is at around the age of four. We cut that back by about a quarter by the time we're 11, and then we almost halve that again by the time we're in our early 20s. That last bit is when we get down to the serious business of creating an adult brain capable of living in, and cooperating with, a community of humans. A critical element of the sculpting that occurs in this phase is done by our reward pathway.

The reward pathway

We have a reward system to reinforce behaviours that promote the survival of our species. Without it we wouldn't eat, reproduce or run away from danger – and that can be a little career-limiting if your plan is to survive more than one generation. The trouble with our reward system is that it operates on three assumptions that were fine during 99 per cent of our evolution but are now very dangerous.

The first assumption is that rewards aren't that common. Our environment won't offer much food or sex, and we'll probably have to work pretty hard to get either of them on our terms. The second assumption is that our environment will provide lots of danger, so we need to be very sensitive to hormones released in response to it. And the third is that there are no short cuts to rewards. The only way to have our body produce our reward system hormones is in response to seeking and then receiving rewards that help us survive.

REWARD SYSTEM HORMONES

Dopamine is our go-juice. A squirt of dopamine sharpens us up. We think more clearly and our muscles work better on dopamine. It motivates us to chase a reward or, if necessary, to run away fast from danger.

Serotonin is our chill pill. Once we successfully get the food or sex we were chasing or survive the danger that was making us run away, we get a squirt of serotonin that calms the excitement caused by dopamine and relaxes us. It makes everything seem better and makes us generally feel safe and at peace.

Dopamine

The part of our brain responsible for these hormonal responses is called the reward pathway (well, actually the mesolimbic [mid-brain] pathway, but let's keep it simple). When we see, think of, or interact with things that are good for our survival – like sex, water, food, social acceptance, looking after babies and winning – a relatively small group of neurons in the lower centre of our brain (the ventral tegmental area [VTA], if you must know) generates electric current. That current travels down the axon – the long tail of the neuron – and stimulates the release of an 'I want that' chemical messenger called dopamine. Reward pathway axons terminate in the prefrontal cortex, our executive-decision-making control room. Dopamine converts the sensory experience of noticing something into desire for that thing. It makes us want stuff. Without it, we'd ignore food, our babies, mates and friends, and never derive the evolutionary benefits of interacting with them – such as staying alive, reproducing and cooperating.

Our driving force

Dopamine is often called the pleasure hormone but that's not quite right. It's certainly inherently pleasurable, and we love how we feel when we get a squirt of the excitement and anticipation it produces, because it's associated with the pleasure we feel when we obtain the thing we need. But it's really our motivation drug. It makes us approach certain things. We can't eat food or mate with a partner if we don't approach them. Evolutionary theory tells us that animals that chase rewards are more likely to survive and reproduce than those that don't. Animals whose dopamine-producing neurons have been deactivated don't seek food and will starve to death if getting it requires any effort (such as moving). But they'll still eat and enjoy it if the food is placed in their mouths.

'Dopamine is often called the pleasure hormone, but it's really our motivation drug.'

Dopamine keeps us alive by motivating us to get off our bottoms and chase things that are good for us. Once there, we then let the executive function in our prefrontal cortex make a decision about whether to proceed further. Not all things are equally attractive. The amount of dopamine released is directly proportional to our degree of attraction to the reward. More dopamine equals stronger desire for the thing that produces those higher levels of dopamine. It also works in reverse. When we encounter danger, dopamine is used to fire up our stress response. And this makes us run in the opposite direction or, if that's not an option, put up a fight. When we successfully escape or avoid the danger, we experience a rewarding flood of relief.

How we know

In the 1950s, psychologists proved this by implanting electrodes deep in the brains of lab rats that would directly stimulate the production of dopamine when the rats pushed a lever. The rats didn't get any other reward, just the dopamine surge. The poor little sods went nuts, pushing the lever up to 2000 times an hour and, in later experiments, completely ignoring the presence of food, water, a female in heat (for male rats) or the need to feed newborn pups (for female rats).

We know this also holds true for humans because of an ethically dubious experiment performed on a 24-year-old homosexual man in the early 1970s. This involved planting an electrode directly on the VTA and giving the man, called B-19, the ability to activate it. In each three-hour session, he would press the button up to 1500 times. The paper described the result: 'During these sessions, B-19 stimulated himself to a point that . . . he was experiencing an almost overwhelming euphoria and elation and had to be disconnected despite his vigorous protests.'

A similar experiment was accidentally performed in a woman as part of an attempt to cure chronic pain with electrode implantation. The electrode ended up too close to the VTA and the woman wanted to activate the electrode constantly, to the exclusion of everything else. She even developed chronic blistering on the finger she used to turn the dial up to maximum. She would beg her family to take it away but would quickly want it back again.

Control through hormonal interplay

But there's a difference between the way our reward system works in real life and those experiments. Those trials showed that when dopamine is directly stimulated to massive levels, we lose control of our reward-seeking impulses. In real life this is usually prevented by the supervisory part of the human brain. Dopamine is transmitted to the prefrontal cortex, which then decides what to do about it based on input from other areas such as our appetite control system. In the 1930s, psychologists proved that rats learned really quickly that pressing a lever produced something they want, such as food or water. But a rat's desire to do so was moderated by whether or not it was hungry. Scientists are not yet clear on the detail, but how much we desire something depends on how rewarding we find it once we get it, and this is in turn related to the release of the reward part of the system, a neurotransmitter called serotonin.

'How much we desire something depends on how rewarding we find it once we get it.'

Serotonin and GABA

We like the way dopamine makes us feel sharp, edgy and ready for reward, but it isn't inherently rewarding. Serotonin is our reward. Once we start consuming the thing we were chasing, our serotonin levels go up. It, in turn, increases the levels of a dopamine suppressor called GABA (γ-amino-butyric acid). GABA is always present and acts as a braking system on dopamine. Think of GABA as the brakes in a car and dopamine as the accelerator. Our brain is a terrible driver, because in our normal state we have the brakes and the accelerator both pressed down about halfway. The result is that nothing is happening. To make something happen we can increase dopamine (press down on the accelerator) or decrease GABA (release the brake) or both. When we chase a reward, the accelerator gets pushed down but the brake is still half on. When we get the reward the brake gets pushed to the max and the accelerator comes off.

GABA dials down the stimulating effect of the dopamine and allows serotonin to make us feel calm and contented. We stop chasing and start enjoying. Serotonin is always present in the background (and is in large part responsible for our overall mood through its control of GABA and therefore dopamine), but when we achieve something we need, we get a spike in serotonin (and therefore GABA) levels and we feel great.

A delicate hormonal symphony

All of this is moderated by how much we really need the thing we were chasing. It's a complex and finely balanced system of chemical feedback loops, and scientists are a long way from understanding exactly how it works. But the result is that exciting impulses induced by dopamine surges are generally well controlled in real life by the higher order part of our brain. We get just enough dopamine to stop us being the mouse that lies there waiting for food to be placed in its mouth but not so much that we're pushing the dopamine button 500 times an hour.

The object of our desire must also stimulate sufficient dopamine to motivate us to expend the energy required to get it. Our brains are constantly balancing the energy required to fulfil a desire against the strength of that desire. And the strength of the desire is in turn moderated by how rewarding it was the last time we did it. We might not be prepared to cross the room to eat raw broccoli, but we might be prepared to jog to the shop to get ice cream (we'll come to exactly why later). It also records negative outcomes from things we thought we might desire but that didn't produce a reward. If we take a big bite of something that looks good but tastes putrid (like the 'chocolate' cake iced with Marmite in *The Vicar of Dibley*), we're much less inclined to chase it again.

Sometimes there's no energy cost and a powerful surge of desire, so we can just keep stimulating dopamine with no effort whatsoever. This is what happened to B-19, who would hit the stimulation button every seven seconds for three hours straight, and the woman who developed calluses from dialling the stimulation electrode up to maximum. Getting the dopamine hit required virtually no effort, but it also produced no real reward and so didn't create the impulse-repressing releases of serotonin and GABA.

We do, however, become acclimatised to the storm of constant dopamine by dialling down our responses to it. As a result, we need to keep hitting it harder to get the same sense of excitement. This makes us want to repeat the surge in dopamine just to feel good again. This is why B-19 and the woman became uncontrollably addicted to the dopamine hit they could produce by hitting a button or turning a dial. And why humans can become addicted to certain substances and behaviours.

Summary

- The human brain takes 25 years to mature.
- The most important part of that process occurs with the onset of puberty and is enabled by the reward system.
- We have a reward system to reinforce behaviours that promote the survival of our species.

- The motivator in our reward system is dopamine. It keeps us alive by getting us off our bottoms and chasing things that are good for us.
- The object of our desire must stimulate sufficient dopamine to motivate us to expend the energy required to get it. Our brains are constantly balancing the energy required to fulfil a desire against the strength of that desire. And the strength of the desire is in turn moderated by how rewarding it was the last time we did it.
- Sometimes there's no energy cost and a powerful surge of desire, so we can just keep stimulating dopamine with no effort whatsoever. When this happens, we will become addicted to whatever is producing the dopamine hit.

ALCOHOL AND OTHER DRUGS OF ABUSE

We really like the way dopamine makes us feel, so we'll always chase things that increase the release of dopamine. And because of the self-reinforcing feedback nature of dopamine (the more we get, the less it works and the more we want), unfettered access to a good supply of it can quickly develop into addiction. If that addiction develops during puberty, it will be laid down as part of the hardwiring of our brain and will be very difficult to change – for the rest of our life.

We can potentially become addicted to anything that provides us with a hit of dopamine. But some substances cheat. We learn pretty early on that we feel much better with a full tummy than with an empty one. That cements a pathway that produces dopamine to make us get up and get food, while serotonin and GABA act to reward us for eating it and suppress the desire to keep eating it. The same goes for sex. Dopamine tells us to chase it and the serotonin reward follows (and GABA suppresses the desire to give it a go again – well, for a little while anyway). But some substances provide a shortcut to rewards by chemically manipulating our reward system.

Alcohol

One of the oldest of these shortcut substances known to humans is ethanol, the active ingredient in alcohol. Ethanol is made by the fermentation of sugars found mostly in fruit in our natural environment. As a species, we've been enjoying a tipple since we first encountered overripe fruit. So, forever. And because we like the way it made us feel, we haven't been happy to leave it to chance. We've been turning sugar into ethanol on purpose since at least the beginning of settled farming in around 10,000 BC.

It turns out we're really quite keen on alcohol, and that's mostly because it doesn't play by the same rules as normal food. We like water too, but only if we're actually thirsty. We don't just drink alcohol to quench our thirst. We drink it because it directly stimulates the production of extra dopamine. It uses a chemical trick to provide us with a super-hit of our go-juice, and this makes us seek it out. It also chemically enhances our serotonin and GABA production, and delivers a much bigger reward than garden-variety thirst-quenching.

Cannabis

Cannabis, also known as marijuana (among other names), is made from the leaves of a flowering herb that grows abundantly in Central Asia. Like alcohol, cannabis has been with us for a very long time. The Ancient Greeks were writing about the buzz it gave them as early as 440 BC. It contains chemicals called cannabinoids that are known to be addictive.

We do make our own cannabinoids. These endogenous (homemade) cannabinoids or endocannabinoids are neurotransmitters just like dopamine, GABA and serotonin. Our endocannabinoids play many roles in our body, but relevantly they reduce stress and anxiety and make us feel calm and generally happier. They're an important part of how we adapt to a stressful situation. Without them, the stress would just keep building. We can force ourselves to release our own little happy pills by putting ourselves under stress. And that's exactly what endurance

WHY MARIJUANA CAUSES THE MUNCHIES

Cannabinoids like those found in marijuana stimulate the appetite by supplementing our homegrown endocannabinoids. Endocannabinoids stimulate appetite, but the amount we produce is inversely proportional to the amount of leptin in our bloodstream.

Leptin is a hormone produced by our fat cells. The more fat cells we have, the more leptin is produced. The more leptin in our bloodstream, the less endocannabinoids we produce and the lower our appetite. But inhaling some externally produced cannabinoids ramps up our appetite, hence 'the munchies'. Cannabinoids also directly increase our preference for sweet tastes. So those munchies are likely to include lots of sugar. If your plan is to gain weight, then smoking weed is an excellent way to do it.

athletes do. The 'runner's high' is caused by an increase in endocannabinoids caused by the stress of distance running.

Marijuana has exactly the same effect as a long-distance run, only more intensely. It floods our brain with cannabinoids, which increase both dopamine and GABA levels. This in turn makes us want to do it more, provides pain relief and makes us feel calm and at peace with the world. We like that feeling. Some of us like it enough to run a marathon to get it. Others would prefer to smoke a joint. Either way, it's addictive, and like alcohol it's an addiction that if first laid down during puberty is much more likely to last for the rest of our lives. If that addiction is to marathon running then okay (I guess), but if it's to marijuana then that's not so good.

SUGAR ADDICTION

The reason we'd walk over hot coals for chocolate but wouldn't cross the room for broccoli is that chocolate contains an addictive substance – sugar. All food is addictive in a sense. We seek food if we're hungry. But normal food stops being appealing once we've had our fill. At that point GABA is released and dopamine is suppressed. In rat studies this has been repeatedly proven not to be true of sugar. Rats have an unlimited capacity to continue releasing dopamine in response to sugar. The pattern of dopamine release looks much more like an addictive drug than a food. The effect is milder than illicit drugs but still clearly defined, with identical chemical pathways being activated.

If you're inclined to say bring me a human study and I'll believe it, I challenge you to say no the next time someone offers you chocolate.

How addictive substances work

The details vary, but all addictive substances behave in approximately the same way. They'll all stimulate excess dopamine production and they'll all, to a greater or lesser extent, deliver rewards via the GABA system. All will also provide some level of pain and anxiety relief, and so some – for example, marijuana, codeine, morphine and amphetamines – are regularly used as medical treatments. One of the most powerful addictive substances, MDMA (aka ecstasy) is being successfully trialled for use as a treatment for post-traumatic stress disorder and anxiety in terminal illness.

The gateway effect

Once we're addicted to one thing, we're much more likely to become addicted to something else that produces a similar or more powerful version of the same effect. This 'gateway effect' is well documented in relation to smoking. One of the more recent studies showed that smokers were 7.3 times more likely to use marijuana, 7.5 times more likely to use cocaine, 13.9 times more likely to use crack cocaine and 16 times more likely to use heroin than people who'd never smoked. Once we're addicted, we're an addict, and much more susceptible to anything that produces high levels of dopamine.

'Once we're addicted to one thing, we're much more likely to become addicted to something else.'

The gateway effect happens because our brain actively adjusts to the presence of increased dopamine output. Substances that increase dopamine cause us to express a higher level of Delta FosB, a transcription factor (see box opposite) that acts as an addiction switch controlling cell behaviour in the reward pathway. Delta FosB is turned

TRANSCRIPTION FACTORS

A transcription factor is a protein that controls the rate at which parts of our DNA are 'transcribed' so that proteins can be made in the parts of our cells that assemble proteins. Those proteins in turn control how our cells behave. Transcription factors are effectively switches for our DNA. They turn genes on or off according to the circumstances. They ensure that only the necessary genes are activated at the right time and in the right amount in every cell in our body.

One of the many things transcription factors do is help us adapt to our environment. Heat shock factor (HSF), for example, turns on genes that help us survive at higher temperatures, while hypoxia-inducible factor (HiF) helps us respond to low oxygen in our environment.

An important one to remember is *Delta FosB*, which helps us remember to respond to rewards but is also our on-the-fly adaptation to a high-dopamine environment.

on by every rewarding behaviour, and its release is cumulative. Overexposure to dopamine adds more and more Delta FosB. This can happen just by experiencing the reward frequently. So having sex and eating often can produce greater concentrations of Delta FosB and produce addictive symptoms – if you can manage to overcome the satiating effects that would tell you to stop. The other way to ramp it up is to consume substances that directly increase dopamine production. All illicit drugs, all morphine-derived painkillers, many antipsychotic drugs, alcohol, nicotine, caffeine and sugar do this to a greater or lesser extent.

Once Delta FosB is turned on, we'll compulsively seek anything that will give us a dopamine hit. And the more Delta FosB that's activated, the more we'll seek that hit. Delta FosB is our long-term reminder to seek rewards. Without it we might forget we like food or sex – and that would be very bad for our survival as a species. The problem comes when we dial that reminder up to maximum and ordinary desire becomes craving. Once activated, Delta FosB remains active in the brain for months after the triggering substance or behaviour has been removed. Experiencing something desirable frequently will cumulatively add to our Delta FosB, or we can artificially get a pile of it quickly by taking addictive substances. Once it crosses a threshold (which varies from person to person), normal desire becomes craving. If we avoid the things that would add to our pile of Delta FosB, the amount of it available will gradually fall. This slow decline of unrequited craving for dopamine is what we call withdrawal.

There's evidence that the gateway effect means we're not choosy about how we get the dopamine hit driven by Delta FosB activation. We know, for example, that rats dependent on morphine, alcohol or cocaine will all consume less of the addictive substance if they exercise. Cocaine-addicted rats will switch to sugar given the choice. And humans addicted to nicotine are less likely to relapse if they exercise.

The biology of quitting

Substituting a 'hit' with a behaviour that has fewer side effects and then slowly reducing the amount delivered can be a useful way of weaning an addict away from a more dangerous addiction. This is likely to be why smokers significantly increase their coffee

TIME CURES ADDICTION

Annabel is a single mum coping with her 11-year-old son, Peter, who is addicted to *Fortnite* (see page 47). Left unsupervised, he would play the game 24 hours a day and probably wouldn't bother eating or sleeping. Trying to limit his access usually ends in a fight – and those fights are getting harder for Annabel to win. She says that since he discovered *Fortnite*, it's like a drug dealer moved into her house and it makes her son behave like he is possessed. The grumpy and aggressive stranger in her house tells her when he will eat, when he will go to bed and whether he will do his homework. She describes her son as a full-on addict and says he shows no interest in any of the things he used to like as a child, or anything else at all.

A week ago, after a particularly vicious fight, Annabel completely banned the game and hid the Xbox controller. She says Peter's mood was very nasty for the first few days but a week in, she can't believe the change in him. It's like she's got her little boy back. He's asked to buy the ingredients for making slime, so he and his younger sister can mix up a batch. He reads books – not *War and Peace*, but books. He even invited his *Fortnite* buddies over for a game of Monopoly, a game he has never shown any interest in before, mainly because he has never been bored enough to even contemplate playing any board game. He still talks about the game and watches other people play it on YouTube, but he is significantly less aggressive, edgy and obsessed.

IS VAPING ANY SAFER THAN SMOKING?

Cool kids don't smoke anymore, they Juul. With its aura of adolescent coolness, Juul is by far the most popular vaping product in the United States, but vaping in general is fast becoming an addiction of choice among kids. Australia has a complex set of laws that for the moment are keeping vaping levels low, but like most things, if you really want it you can get it.

E-cigarettes deliver nicotine, marijuana or sometimes just flavouring in a liquid that the device heats so it can be inhaled as a vapour. They were initially invented to provide a way for smokers to wean themselves off cigarettes and away from the dangers of inhaling the carcinogens contained in smoke, although there is emerging evidence that the vapour is no less harmful than smoke. We know almost nothing about the long-term effects of inhaling the heated vaping liquid, let alone the flavours and dyes, and given the massive acceleration in use, that's a very real concern. We're effectively in the position science found itself when smoking first became a mainstream activity. We simply don't know how bad it might be, but the early evidence is very worrying.

In the United States, where it's no more legal for a child to vape nicotine or marijuana than to smoke them, the 2017 Monitoring the Future survey of US youth revealed that the teenage vaping trend is very real and has overtaken smoking as a means of access to addictive substances. The survey found that 11 per cent of 12th-graders (final-year high school students) reported having vaped nicotine in the previous 30 days compared to 9.7 per cent who had smoked. Eight and a half per cent of 10th-graders had vaped compared to

5 per cent who'd smoked, and 3.5 per cent of 8th-graders had vaped but just 1.9 per cent had smoked. In addition, 4.9 per cent, 4.3 per cent and 1.6 per cent of 12th-, 10th- and 8th-graders reported having vaped marijuana in the past 30 days.

Recent detailed studies of that data, and the relationship between adolescent vaping and smoking, have come to the conclusion that vaping should be regarded as a gateway to smoking. Young vapers become smokers later in life.

and sugar consumption while quitting. Their brains are after a dopamine hit and they'll get it elsewhere if the ciggies aren't forthcoming. No, they don't study neuroscience and find substitutes; their brains just go with things that make them feel good.

Science is used explicitly to attempt this in the nicotine patch industry. Nicotine is the addictive substance in cigarettes, but it can be delivered without the side effects caused by having to smoke burning herbs to get it. The studies show that nicotine consumption during quitting works. A smoker is between 49 per cent (gums) and 102 per cent (sprays) more likely to stop smoking if they use nicotine while quitting. Note that they stop smoking. This doesn't mean they stop using nicotine, just that they change the delivery vehicle.

A major analysis performed in 2018 found that of people who were dual users of cigarettes and e-cigarettes (vapers), just 12 per cent had quit smoking a year later, whereas 43.5 per cent had become exclusive smokers. Some treatments use a nicotine substitute like varenicline or bupropion, but there's no evidence that these are any easier to quit than nicotine, and they can produce side effects such as nausea, insomnia, abnormal dreams, headache and constipation. To actually break the addiction to nicotine, a smoker will either need to slowly reduce the supply of nicotine or quit cold turkey and go through withdrawal. There's no easy path.

Summary

- We quickly learn that we feel much better with a full tummy than with an empty one. That cements a pathway that produces dopamine to make us get up and get food, while serotonin and GABA act to reward us for eating it and suppress the desire to keep eating it. The details vary, but all addictive substances behave in approximately the same way. They'll all stimulate excess dopamine production and they'll all, to a greater or lesser extent, deliver rewards via the GABA system.
- Once we're addicted to one thing, we're much more likely to become addicted to something else that produces a similar or more powerful version of the same effect. This is called the addiction 'gateway effect'.
- Delta FosB is a ratcheted set point that determines how much dopamine we need in order to respond to stimulation. It is turned on by every rewarding behaviour, and its release is cumulative, but time without exposure to dopamine allows it to reset to normal levels.
- Substituting a 'hit' with a behaviour that has fewer side effects and then slowly reducing the amount delivered can be a useful way of weaning an addict away from a more dangerous addiction.

ADDICTIVE BEHAVIOURS

Stick with me a little longer as we cover the basics – I'll show how all of this is relevant to our teens very soon.

We don't need to actually consume something in order to begin desiring it. We get excited by the smell or sight of food, and the sight of precursors to sex (such as nudity). The mere possibility that a reward might be on offer is enough to get our dopamine levels rising. Without the dopamine, we wouldn't be prepared to expend energy to get the reward.

When we know we'll get a reward given a certain cue, the profile of dopamine release looks like the graph overleaf.

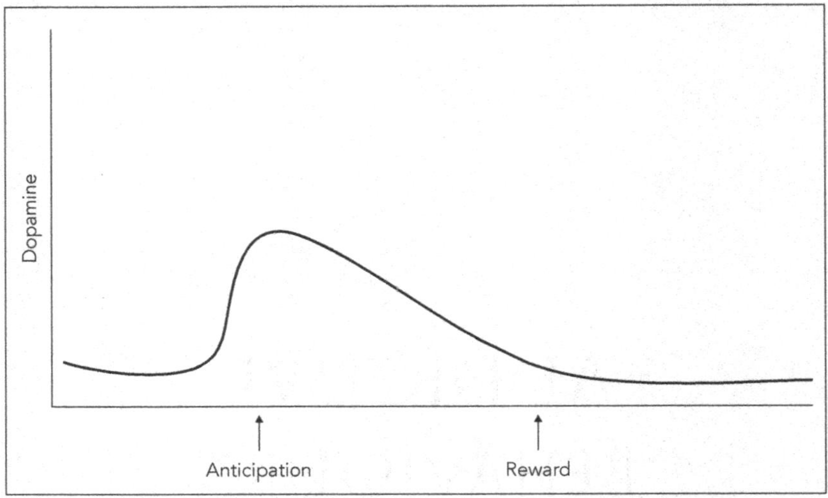

But if the reward is uncertain, the dopamine release looks more like this:

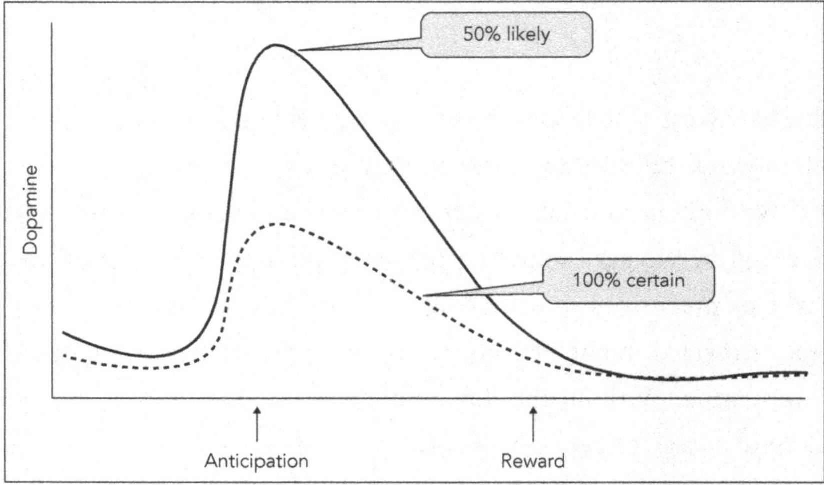

Introducing a significant chance of not getting the reward massively increases the dopamine hit from potentially rewarding behaviour, in much the same way artificial stimulants like alcohol and cocaine do. Seeking food or sex only really has a chance of moving from desirable to addictive if we can continuously press the desire button with a significant chance of not obtaining the dopamine- (and desire-) suppressing effects of receiving the reward. In normal society neither is really possible. It would be a very unusual set of circumstances where you could see or smell food all the time but never be able to consume it when you were hungry. You're also unlikely to frequently encounter a lot of desirable nudity (or other behaviour) suggesting sex is on offer, on the bus, at work or at school (well, certainly not at any bus, workplace or school I've ever experienced).

Porn

The pornography industry has tapped into this lack of sex in the workplace and provided a dopamine-stimulation service for as long as humans have had the ability to draw pictures. Pornography wasn't invented by the internet. Much as it did for music, the internet just made porn a lot cheaper and easier to distribute and consume. Porn provides all the stimulatory effects of dopamine release, and while a self-administered reward might sometimes be available, there's not always a one-to-one relationship between stimulation and reward. Porn permits humans to continuously hit the dopamine button in a way that simply isn't available in real life, just like the woman who had calluses from dialling the electrode stimulation to maximum.

Needless to say, a high volume of repeated dopamine hits will very quickly dial up our Delta FosB, and voilà! We're addicted. We experience cravings and we'll go through withdrawal if we stop. Naltrexone, a drug used to treat alcohol and drug addiction, is also effective in reducing sex addiction, so it's not unreasonable to conclude that the same pathways are being activated.

Food porn

Showing you yummy food when you're likely to be hungry is exactly the method used by the fast-food industry to drive you into their stores. Pay attention to when ads for pizza and burgers are shown on TV – that's right, at dinnertime. And note that the advertisements focus on close-ups of delicious steaming hot food. This is all designed to make your reward pathway fire up enough to get you off the couch and into their store, or at least to the ordering app on your phone.

But apart from in the advertising industry, food porn has never really taken off, because we can sit there eating a cupcake while we watch *MasterChef*. This is the equivalent of watching real porn after you've just had sex. You've been rewarded and GABA is actively suppressing dopamine. You might find it interesting, but you won't find that it generates desire (unless, as we'll see, you're a teenager without GABA brakes).

Danger porn

But dopamine is a double-edged sword. It isn't just stimulated by things we find attractive, it's also generated in response to danger.

As part of our stress response (see box opposite), the cortisol levels in our bloodstream ramp up. Cortisol increases dopamine release in the same way alcohol and cannabis do. Oddly, yes, this means we can become addicted to danger. The reward in that scenario is the relief of surviving. Once the danger passes, cortisol

'DANGER, WILL ROBINSON!' HOW OUR STRESS RESPONSE WORKS

When we sense danger, our brain sends an immediate signal to our adrenal glands. They respond by pumping a hormone called adrenaline (aka epinephrine) into the bloodstream. Adrenaline increases our heartbeat and blood pressure so that more blood is pushed into our muscles and other vital organs. We breathe faster to increase oxygen supply, and that extra oxygen is sent to the brain to increase alertness. Our sight, hearing and other senses become sharper.

Adrenaline also tells the body to release fat and blood glucose from storage so that more energy is available to all parts of the body. This all happens before you're even consciously aware of danger. It's an automatic and instant danger-response module used to save your life. Think of it like your brain instantly jamming the pedal to the metal at the first sign of danger. If the threat is something like an oncoming car, your stress response will make you jump out of the way before you could even begin formulating a plan of action.

The stress response makes you react quickly and then will immediately subside. But if the danger is ongoing, a secondary response will kick in. Our brain will instruct the adrenal glands to release cortisol to keep us revved up – not adrenaline-level high alert, but still ready for action. Cortisol is our mobilisation hormone; we get a squirt of it when we wake up (to get us out of bed) and whenever we exercise, as well as while there's a continuing threat. It keeps our accelerator depressed for as long as is needed to get us past the danger. Once that longer lasting danger is gone, cortisol levels drop and we calm down.

levels drop, serotonin and GABA kick in, and we feel as relaxed and rewarded as if we'd just had a great meal or great sex.

If you crave activities where death or serious injury is a very real possibility *every* time you take it on, you're addicted to danger. 'Extreme sports' tend to involve vehicles, such as aircraft (skydiving), boats (waterskiing) or motorbikes (motocross) or pit the individual against overwhelming forces of nature like ice (ice climbing), giant waves (big wave surfing) or gravity (BASE-jumping and bungee jumping). And while they sometimes also involve an exertion-generated dopamine surge, they always have the overlay of life-or-death situations for that extra-sharp 'high'.

Mix the availability of extreme sports with a teenage boy's lack of impulse control (see page 85) and sense of invulnerability and you have a potent cocktail of potential harm. It is probably best to keep adolescent boys, in particular, away from sports that could kill them, but more on that shortly.

Computer games

Most of us aren't tempted to put our lives at risk often enough to become addicted to a cortisol high. But just as the porn industry developed around simulating sexual desire without actual sex, there are ways to fool our body into reacting as if there's danger when in fact there's none. We can imagine danger and it can make our body react as if it's real. A well-written horror story can immerse us to the extent that we actually feel the danger encountered by the characters. A well-told fireside ghost story can terrify us. And a horror movie can do it even more effectively. But the very best way to simulate danger is to use what I like to call danger porn – the computer game.

FORTNITE

The latest highly addictive example of danger porn is the hottest internet first-person shooter game ever. *Fortnite* pits 100 online players against each other in a fight to the death with an array of powerful weapons they find after being parachuted, unarmed, onto a deserted island at the beginning of the game.

As a player, your immediate priorities are to find weapons before anyone else and build fortifications by breaking down existing buildings on the island. The winner is the person whose character is still alive at the end. It's kill or be killed, and combat is face to face, but unlike other shooter games, the world and characters look like well-drawn cartoons. And while there's plenty of up-close-and-personal death, there are no gory blood spatters. It's been described as a cross between *The Hunger Games* (the killing survival bit) and *Minecraft* (the building bit).

Launched in September 2017, *Fortnite* was acquiring 10 million new users a month by the end of that year. By mid-June 2018, there were 125 million *Fortnite* players. It's creating YouTube millionaires as well. It had the most YouTube uploads relating to gameplay in January 2018. In just one recent two-day live-broadcast event, 42 million people tuned in to watch others play the game. The biggest *Fortnite* broadcasting star is 'Ninja' (Tyler Blevins), who has said he makes more than US$500,000 a month streaming his 300 hours a month of live gameplay to his 10 million subscribers.

Sixty-eight per cent of *Fortnite* players are aged between 10 and 30 and 72 per cent of those over 18 are male. The game is free to download and play, but users can spend money on improvements to their characters such as victory dances ($8), character body types ($8) and 'skins' (for between $8 and $20) that allow a player to customise the look of their in-game character. These enhancements don't improve a player's chances in the game, but it makes them look cool. Those micro-purchases amount to around US$300 million in revenue a month to the game-makers, and that number is growing very fast.

Fortnite incorporates everything the gaming industry has learned about how to make danger porn addictive. It has high-quality graphics, advances quickly and, just like gambling, has an element of luck. It also involves a strong social element. Gamers can play in teams of up to four players and cooperate in building defences and finding weapons. Even if you're exhausted and need an hour's sleep before work or school, if your team needs you, you'll go one more round. There's all the urgency of a common mission and threat that a team of hunters would experience in real life.

The near-miss phenomenon

Many computer games have survival of your character as their central premise. This can vary from something as simple as *Pac-Man* to something as sophisticated and bloodthirsty as first-person combat-simulation games such as *Fortnite*, *Call of Duty*, *World of Tanks* and *Halo*. Good games make players invest in the survival of their avatar or character. They then place the character in ever more dangerous situations. The player isn't really fighting off ghosts or in military combat, but their brain behaves as if they are. Adrenaline and cortisol levels rise, and that increases dopamine. And just as with porn, in a well-written game the reward – the relief of surviving – is only forthcoming some of the time. Playing teaches the gamer how to survive longer, and when players die they don't feel like they lost but that they nearly won. This is called the 'near-miss' phenomenon, and it's used very effectively in the design of gambling machines.

A near miss is an unsuccessful outcome that's close to the desired outcome. It's no more rewarding than any other loss, but it gives the player the illusion of control. When a horse comes second or two cherries are displayed on a poker machine instead of the three needed for a payout, a player receives a much bigger shot of dopamine and is much more likely to play again even though they lost just as badly as if their horse came last or they got no cherries. Most computer games don't allow your character to survive indefinitely, but the really addictive games use the near-miss phenomenon and in-game credits and scores to motivate us to keep coming back for more. Hit the (simulated) danger button often enough and you'll become just as addicted to the game-induced dopamine surge as the lady with the callused finger did to dialling up the dopamine-stimulating electrode.

JUST ONE MORE ROUND

Steven's 13-year-old son, Sam, hasn't yet hit puberty but it hasn't stopped him becoming a *Fortnite* addict. He can still be talked out of playing if a game of footy with Dad is on offer but it has quickly become Sam's go-to time-filler. Steven has very strict limits on use – no access during the school week and one hour a day on weekends and holidays – and he enforces them by keeping the Xbox controller in his desk drawer at work during the week. Even so, he says it's always a struggle to get Sam to stop when the time is up. He plays in an online team with his friends using headsets to talk to each other. He aggressively protests that he can't just leave the game in the middle of a mission – his team needs him! And it means that the one-hour time limit is more theoretical than actual and that Steven has to sit there watching the game lest another mission 'accidentally' be started. At least, Steven says, it isn't as bad as a story he heard from a reliable source at the footy club. They say they saw their neighbour rush into her backyard, Xbox in hand and hurl it into her swimming pool. The machine hadn't even hit the bottom before her teenage son, fully clothed in his school uniform, dived in after it.

Gambling

Books, movies and computer games aren't the only way we can simulate danger. We can also do it at the newsagent, pub, horse-racing track, casino and, increasingly, anywhere we can access a betting app on our phone – so, just about everywhere. Gambling takes all the danger-simulating aspects of computer games and horror movies, and adds real-world focus and incentive. Gambling literally asks us to invest in the survival of our chosen player, be it a horse, a card or a little ball on a roulette wheel. It's the imitation danger of the computer game but without all the expensive programming.

Gambling can add risk and, sometimes, reward to any situation that normally wouldn't be anywhere near as life-and-death interesting. I can enjoy watching a good game of footy, but if I've put money on it, I'll be much more tightly focused on the outcome.

Even if there's no real money riding on the result, just the pleasure of winning drags us in. Go on, admit it, you care a lot more about the result of the Melbourne Cup if you're in the office sweep than if you're not.

Real-world consequences significantly magnify the extent to which we engage in the game and therefore our cortisol responses to it. Gamblers have exactly the same cortisol responses as people in danger, but the reward isn't forthcoming on every attempt, and the repeated cortisol-driven dopamine stimulation can lead to a state of addiction. Increasingly, there's crossover between computer games and gambling, which makes our teens more vulnerable to gambling addiction than ever before. Computer games have in-game currency that can be translated to real-world money, and gambling apps have borrowed some of the gamification techniques of computer games. You no longer need to play a boring old poker machine; you can become a character who has real money riding on whether they win or lose. Or you can participate in gaming tournaments with hundreds of millions of dollars up for grabs for the best players.

Approval porn

Humans dominate this planet because we work well together in groups. Making sure we actually bother to interact with other humans is therefore just as important to our survival as having sex (and babies) with them. Loner predators with no claws, fangs or poison don't tend to survive long in our natural environment. So we're hardwired to find social interaction with other humans rewarding.

We like to be liked by others, so we're constantly scanning our in-group for signs that we're liked. We'll actively seek out things we think will mean we're liked more, and we'll avoid things that might mean we're liked less. We call this peer pressure, and it drives us to ensure our behaviour is consistent with that of the others in our group. We don't seek conformity because we want to be like everyone else but because we want them to like us.

In evolutionary terms this makes perfect sense. Our survival in nature depended on our ability to work with others. We'd work better with others if we valued what they valued. And the group values would in turn be driven by what helped them survive in their environment. If being good at finding food is valuable to the group, then every member of the group will value that characteristic in others. And every member of the group will seek approval by being even better at finding food.

'We like to be liked by others.'

The approval-seeking mechanism wired into our brain drives us to cooperate for the greater survival of the group by making us compete for approval. The flip side also works for the benefit of the group. We avoid behaviour that will result in being disliked by others. Groups will generally disapprove of behaviour that harms other members of the group, and so that kind of behaviour is automatically controlled by our little 'like' addiction.

Naturally with something as good as oxytocin (see box opposite) on offer, dopamine spurs us into action to obtain it. Mice whose oxytocin is genetically disabled completely ignore each other and are happy to be isolated, but normal mice always prefer to interact with each other. They also become depressed when isolated. The same mechanism in humans is why solitary

OXYTOCIN: THE LOVE HORMONE

Oxytocin is our super reward for bonding with others. It stimulates dopamine release, ensuring we desire the thing producing the oxytocin response. It also stimulates serotonin, suppresses our anxiety hormone, cortisol, and makes us feel terrific. Anytime we feel good about being close to another person, it's oxytocin providing the hit. It's released when we orgasm, and when women give birth and breastfeed, so it's critically important to reproduction and maternal behaviour.

Oxytocin effectiveness varies in direct proportion to oestrogen levels in women. They'll find being near potential mates much more interesting when oestrogen is at its peak just as they begin the post-ovulation (luteal) phase of the menstrual cycle.

It's also released just through ordinary social interaction, and it doesn't even have to be social interaction with a human. Just petting a dog for five minutes will increase oxytocin levels – in both the human and the dog. Just remember that if you ever struggle to understand the phenomenon of fur babies – people treating pets like they're children.

The reward pathway in women is significantly more sensitive to oxytocin than in men. This means women are significantly more sensitive to social cues than men, and find social interaction more rewarding than men do. In teenage girls, this sensitivity is dialled up to 'maximum', making them desperate for the approval of others and extraordinarily vulnerable to technologies that exploit that need (see page 220).

Oxytocin also increases envy and gloating. When we think someone is doing better than us, that feeling of envy will be magnified by oxytocin, and that's also true when we think we're doing better than others. Oxytocin gives us schadenfreude – it makes us feel happy when bad things happen to other people. It also makes us more territorial. We're much more likely to act aggressively towards people who are not in our in-group when we're high on oxytocin.

confinement is such an effective punishment. Given a choice, we'd rather be with people than alone. Yes, we'd like to be having sex with (some of) those people, but just being near them is intrinsically rewarding thanks to oxytocin.

The people we most want to be near are the ones we think like us. Social approval is what makes us like hanging out with others. We like the feeling that they like us. The more approval we sense, the more oxytocin and serotonin are released and the better we feel. The oxytocin also sharpens our perceptions of social interaction – we become better at telling what people think of us – and increases our bonding with the group we perceive to be our in-group. On oxytocin we're more loyal to our group and more likely to be aggressive towards people we think are outsiders. Oxytocin keeps us bound to the people we like and who we think like us.

Teenagers are uniquely susceptible to the power of oxytocin. Adolescence is a phase when the addictive power of oxytocin is magnified enormously. No one is more concerned with obtaining the approval of others than a teenager. No one is more tightly bound to their group, or more sensitive to the wishes of their peers. And no one is more

'The more approval we sense, the better we feel.'

vicious in excluding those who might not conform to those pressures. Young women are even more powerfully affected because of their enhanced sensitivity to oxytocin: woe betide a girl who decides the in-group is not for her.

Social media

Remember how when you were a teen you used to walk down the street handing out polaroids of your half-naked self to strangers and asking for their approval? No, neither do I. But that's exactly what social media encourages adolescents to do. It exploits their natural human instinct to seek approval and leverages that with a teenagers' lack of impulse control.

SEEKING APPROVAL

Mary's 14-year-old daughter, Gracie, has an iPhone and did have an Instagram account, but as soon as her mum started following her, she ditched it. Most of her friends don't bother with Instagram much anymore either. They still share and comment on each other's photos but they do it on platforms where they are less likely to encounter their parents, such as Messenger and Snapchat. Mary can't remember the last time she saw Gracie without her iPhone in her hand, but at least she can't take it to school anymore. Her school recently banned them because a boy was caught showing his mates porn (involving a horse) while waiting in the tuckshop line – or so the gossip goes.

Mary has seen some of the photos Gracie's girlfriends post. If they are clothed it isn't in much. They are very much fishing for compliments and Gracie is very careful to ensure she's giving the right feedback to the right friends about their photos. The tendency to post explicit photos has Mary on high alert. She is hypervigilant when it comes to letting Gracie into private spaces with her phone. So much so, that she recently burst into the bathroom after she heard the sound of a phone camera. There she found a fully clothed Gracie with iPhone in hand. Gracie swears she was taking a photo of her hair, so she could look at it more closely.

We can simulate sex with porn and we can simulate danger with computer games and gambling, but it's taken a while for technology to get to a level where social feedback can be simulated just as effectively. Before the internet, the only real way to do it was to actually meet people in real life and impress them enough that they liked us within the constraints of socially acceptable behaviour – so no naked polaroids. That's a very time- and energy-consuming pastime, and one we were unlikely ever to become addicted to. We'd like it, yes. And we'd desire the company of others, yes. But we wouldn't crave it or go into withdrawal if it wasn't forthcoming. The advent of the pervasive use of the internet has, however, finally made it possible for social interaction to become an addiction. Welcome to the era of approval porn.

'The internet has made it possible for social interaction to become an addiction.'

Approval porn is software that allows you to simulate being in a large group of people and having them like you. If you wanted to make addictive social software, it would need a couple of key ingredients. A reasonable number of people would need to be using it, because rather like a telephone, if no one else is using it, it's pointless. It must allow you to tell people about yourself and good things that are happening – remember, in real life the point of social interaction is to gain approval. For it to be addictive, there must be an element of chance as to whether you'll get the approval. And it must provide a means of communicating that approval to you.

Farming the likes

Facebook and Instagram fit the bill perfectly: they're pervasive; it's easy to post stories and images; and 'likes', views and comments provide instant feedback. But most importantly, all of this can be done very quickly and repeatedly. Every time a like rolls in on your latest announcement or photo, your social-interaction system gets ready for the oxytocin reward you'll obtain from bonding with a real person. That means you'll get a little shot of dopamine. And then the next like gives you a little bit more.

Posting new stories or photos so you can get the 'likes' is exactly the same, biochemically, as B-19 hitting the dopamine button, or drinking alcohol, watching porn, playing a computer game or placing a bet. They're all artificial dopamine stimulants. Because it's much easier to farm the 'likes' on a platform like Facebook or Instagram than in real life, the probability of becoming addicted is much, much higher. One way to make any social media software non-addictive would be to create a version without likes and comments. But don't hold your breath waiting for that to happen, because it would be an instant commercial flop. It would be like porn without the nudity or gambling without the risk of losing.

We don't even like what we like

When researchers have tested the effects of social media on real teenagers, the results have gone exactly as you might expect. In one recent study, scientists at UCLA's Semel Institute of Neuroscience and Human Behavior gave 32 teenagers who didn't know each other access to a simulation of Instagram. Each teen was shown 148 photos on the app, including 40 images each teen had submitted. Each photo was shown for 12 minutes and the teenagers' brains were scanned with an fMRI scanner while they were looking at the photos. Each photo also showed a number of likes. They weren't real likes, they'd been assigned by the researchers. When a teenager saw a large number of likes against one of their own photos, their reward pathways lit up like a Christmas tree. They really enjoyed the fake like-love.

In a second arm to the study, teens were encouraged to 'like' photos they enjoyed. But once again there was a trick: for each photo, half the teens saw a lot of likes already and half the teens saw it had very few likes. The same photo shown with lots of likes was much more likely to be liked by the teenager, even if they didn't know any of the people who'd presumably already liked the photo. If everybody else said it was good then they were significantly more likely to click the 'like' button. Likes beget likes, even when the likes are from strangers. (Oh, by the way, after the experiment, the researchers told the kids the likes were fake. They're not animals – they couldn't have teens go out into the world believing some of their photos weren't liked much.)

Taking the concept of meaningless 'likes' a little further, comedian Zach Brousard had people post photos of themselves being proposed to by, or proposing to, paid actors. The people were either in committed relationships (with people who weren't the actor) or too young to be believable. Even so, the 'likes' and congratulations flooded in – even from people who knew them well. We clearly don't think much before we hit the 'like' button. So, if you're feeling like a little like-love, post a photo of you getting a proposal. It's guaranteed to give you a dopamine hit.

We're constantly seeking the social approval, and likes provide a fast-acting simulation of that. No, it's (mostly) not real. But it's good enough to fool our dopamine system. Just as porn, computer games and gambling are good enough to fool it too. And teens are particularly vulnerable to its charms.

Social envy

Apart from the addiction to dopamine hits from likes, social porn comes with another nasty little downside. Remember that oxytocin increases envy and schadenfreude as well as social bonding. Artificially hyping up teenagers on a drug that makes them envious and more likely to enjoy the misfortunes of others is unlikely to end well. It means they can be simultaneously high on the likes and dissatisfied with their lives because others are doing better (as judged by the number of likes they receive). And if the likes don't come, they're on the express train to depression and anxiety (more about that later).

Yes, all of this is possible in real-life social situations, but the volume and accuracy of the measurement available via social media is massively greater. You don't get real-time, minute-by-minute assessments of your social likeability in real life. And you definitely don't get them when you're lying in bed alone late at night worrying about your social life. But when your phone is right there with you, confirming your worst fears, things can escalate very quickly.

Shopping

Social media is the latest in approval porn, but it isn't the only kind. Before Facebook supercharged our desire for approval, we had shopping.

A key element of our approval-seeking mechanism is that the behaviour must be important to our in-group, the people whose opinion we value. I'm not a rocket scientist. I never hang out with rocket scientists. So I don't care what rocket scientists think about what I know about rockets – which, frankly, could be written on the back of a postage stamp. I'm a lawyer and I know a lot of other lawyers, so their professional approval of my legal work is very important to me. But it's not just about our skills in our chosen profession. There are some social groups where being a lawyer is perceived as being a good thing and others where you might as well be a banker (i.e. completely ostracised), so I'm more likely to seek out the former than the latter.

And this is equally true of any skill or attribute. Acquiring useful abilities is, more than a little bit, driven by how we think others whose opinions we value will react to us having that ability. Becoming a good hunter, a good cook, a good mother or even a lawyer just for the buzz of being socially accepted seems like a lot of work for a very small reward, but without that reward-system-driven, dopamine-fuelled desire, none of it would happen. We'd all just lie there like the lab rats with the disabled dopamine system waiting for food to be put in our mouths.

There are, however, shortcuts to approval. Yes, you can post a photo and farm the likes. You could even take a photo of your law degree and farm both the likes that come in from your parents. But if you want to go a little old-school and you have access to the money (or credit) to make it possible, then owning things your in-group approves of can give you an instant boost without all that unpleasant skill-acquisition nonsense.

From trade to money to credit

Before the agricultural revolution around 10,000 BC there were no shops. If we wanted to farm the likes, we had to acquire the necessary skill. If our group valued eating meat, then we had to be good at hunting to be liked. And if our group valued peacock feathers, then we had to be good at finding them to be liked.

Around 10,000 BC we invented farming and shortly thereafter, trade. Initially this didn't change much. If I wanted to buy your peacock feather because my group liked them, you had to need whatever it was that I was growing. But we sorted that out pretty quickly by inventing money. Now I could buy your peacock feathers using the money I got from selling my grain to someone who did want it. If peacock feathers were something valued by my in-group then I was effectively buying 'likes'. Still, I had to do an awful lot of farming to get the money for those peacock feathers, and so it never really took off as an addictive behaviour. Rewarding yes, addictive no.

It took us a while to think of it, but we eventually invented money-for-nothing, otherwise known as credit. From about 3500 BC until the early 19th century, the use of credit was fairly limited, mostly because a key aspect of credit is trusting that the person you lend money to will have the ability to pay it back. The only people getting credit were people the lender knew or knew were incredibly rich. So if I wanted to get the peacock feathers now and pay for them later, I needed to know someone rich who was prepared to trust that I'd repay them. Lending happened, but not often by today's standards.

The Industrial Revolution massively increased the number of humans living in one place. As towns and cities rapidly expanded, the likelihood that a shopkeeper personally knew every customer rapidly diminished. By the early 19th century, credit reporting – records about the creditworthiness of strangers – became a thing. Credit reporting meant a shopkeeper could extend credit to strangers and be reasonably confident of being repaid.

At first this was largely restricted to fancy clothes. If you needed credit for food, you weren't a good credit risk anyway. But if you had a little more capacity, the first thing on most people's list was something to help them farm the 'likes' of their friends – a new dress or suit. By the early to mid-20th century, an array of consumer goods started to enter the market – the Model T Ford, washing machines, refrigerators and TVs. Increasingly, because of standardised creditworthiness reporting, these status-improving items could be bought on payment plans. Someone wanting to farm the 'likes' of their friends could own a car or a TV now and pay it off later.

At first credit checking was a slow and laborious process that really sucked the desire out of an impulse purchase. If you had to wait a week for the credit check to be done, there was lots of time for people to talk you out of buying that new dress. But after the Second World War, the widespread use of telephones dramatically increased the speed of credit checks. It still wasn't fast and it was still based on whether you'd paid back your last loan, but that easier credit eventually supercharged the postwar consumer-spending boom. During the last half-century, the invention of credit cards, computers, sophisticated repayment-likelihood algorithms and an ever-increasing array of cheaper and cheaper consumer goods all worked together to make credit easier and easier to get on the spur of the moment.

The way we shop now

Now, if we see something we think our in-group will admire, we can have it instantly. Shopping with a loaded credit card is the real-world version of farming 'likes' on Facebook. The credit card gives us the means to instantly appear to own the things we know our friends will desire. We don't have to work for five years to buy a new BMW with cash; we can have it now for $1 down and a $1 a day. The payment plan is long, and at the end we'll have nothing of value, but all our friends will admire us for having a BMW throughout that time. If we want the latest handbag, now we can reach for the credit card and turn up at the party with it on our arm (to what we imagine will be the delight of all our friends). If we can get it on sale then so much the better. Or if we're so popular on Instagram or YouTube that the manufacturer sends it to us for free so we can talk it up in our posts, we've really made it. That way we get the approval associated with its real value but at a discounted or zero cost. The thought of shopping for goods others will desire is addictive in exactly the same way as the thought of posting a picture and getting loads of likes.

'The thought of shopping for goods others will desire is addictive.'

You might be thinking there's not a lot of chance involved in shopping. You either buy something or you don't, and the only potentially chancy bit is whether your credit card will bounce. Since we know that means dopamine levels will be lower than if chance were involved, we should be less likely to become addicted. The chance of getting a bargain in a sale does increase the addictiveness of shopping, but if you really want to mainline shopping with an element of chance, there's no better place than the internet. It's not that buying online is any chancier, it's that we get a double dopamine hit. The first comes as normal, with the purchase of something we know all our friends will love. And the second comes when the package actually turns up on our doorstep.

Around 80 per cent of shoppers say they're more excited when their online purchases arrive in the mail than when they buy the same thing in a shop. In Australia we only vaguely know when that delivery might occur. On any given day there's a distinct element of chance as to whether it will turn up or not. That uncertainty will produce a much stronger dopamine hit when the package actually arrives. Random delivery adds the spice to online shopping that can make it really addictive.

Summary

- We don't need to actually consume something in order to begin desiring it. We receive a dopamine surge from simulations of rewarding behaviours.
- Porn is a dopamine-inducing simulation of sex. Computer games and gambling are dopamine-inducing simulations

of danger. And shopping and social media are dopamine-inducing simulations of being liked by others.

- The danger is that all of the above can be consumed much more frequently than the real thing. And this has never been truer than in a time when they are easily available via the phone in our pocket or the tablet device in a school bag.

Depression and Anxiety

Anxiety is a normal part of our stress response to danger. We perceive danger, adrenaline floods our system and our brain and body are on edge, ready for action. If the danger persists, cortisol triggers dopamine release and holds us in the action-stations state. From a biochemical perspective there's no way to distinguish anxiety from that normal, second-phase, cortisol- and dopamine-driven response to a stressful situation. We don't have to be faced with mortal danger to feel normal anxiety. Any stressful situation – a mean boss, a high workload, a tight deadline, an exam, relationship troubles, public speaking, big bills or sick children – will provoke a normal stress response. The dopamine surge helps us cope by sharpening up our thought processes and physical responses. And when the stress passes, serotonin and

GABA reward us with relief and dampen down our dopamine.

Unfortunately, the particular state of the teen brain makes it particularly vulnerable to both anxiety and depression, as we'll see in the next chapter.

'We don't have to be faced with mortal danger to feel normal anxiety.'

Anxiety

Anxiety is worrying about bad things that might happen more than their risk profile would suggest we should. This results in increased dopamine and reduced serotonin. Serotonin is our reward, and the lack of it is our punishment. In either case, dopamine is in play as our motivator. It works just as effectively as a motivator to stay away from bad things as it does to approach good things. Dopamine excites us and makes us approach good things so we can get a rewarding surge of serotonin. But bad things drop our background serotonin levels and make us stay away from the unpleasant person, situation or experience. When bad things deplete our serotonin, this cascades through to lower GABA, which in turn takes the brakes off dopamine. Because it drives our 'stay-away' reflex, more dopamine than normal keeps us away from the bad thing causing the serotonin drop. But the extra dopamine will also put us on edge – it's still dopamine and it still puts us on high alert, whether we're chasing a reward or running from danger.

Anxiety becomes a diagnosable disorder when it either doesn't go away after the danger has passed or when we overreact to things that wouldn't normally trigger a significant stress response. Post-traumatic stress disorder (PTSD) and obsessive-compulsive disorder (OCD) are examples of anxiety that doesn't go away. General anxiety disorder (GAD; worrying every day about things that wouldn't normally be stressful), social anxiety (an intense fear of being criticised or embarrassed), agoraphobia (a fear of being trapped in a situation with no escape) and panic disorder (panic attacks) are examples of conditions where our stress response is on a hair-trigger.

HOW COMMON IS ANXIETY?

Anxiety is the most common mental disorder in Australia, one in seven people aged 16–85 having suffered from some form of diagnosable anxiety within the past 12 months. The breakdown of those conditions was:

- PTSD – 44.4 per cent
- social anxiety – 32.6 per cent
- agoraphobia – 19.4 per cent
- GAD – 18.8 per cent
- panic disorder – 18 per cent
- OCD – 13 per cent.

(Total exceeds 100 per cent as people can suffer from more than one type simultaneously.) Women are approximately twice as likely to experience anxiety as men. Prevalence drops by a third between our mid-40s and our mid-50s and halves again by our mid-60s.

Depression

Closely related to anxiety, depression is a disorder where the sufferer is unable to recover from bad things when they do happen. Depression is an inability to experience pleasure. We all feel sad at times and that's normal. Bad things happen and they'll depress our mood. There's nothing rewarding about discovering you have cancer or hearing that a loved one has passed away. When bad things happen our background serotonin levels will drop and we'll

MAJOR DEPRESSIVE DISORDER

Often referred to as clinical depression, for a diagnosis of major depressive disorder the criteria listed in the fifth edition of the *Diagnostic and Statistical Manual of Mental Disorders* (DSM-5) specify that at least five of the following symptoms of depression must be present concurrently for a minimum of a two-week period. At least one of the symptoms must be the presence of either depressed mood or loss of interest or pleasure. These symptoms must cause clinically significant distress to the person and they must interfere with their normal functioning at work, at home or in social settings. They must not be attributable to a medical condition, substance abuse or bereavement.

1. *depressed mood*
2. *loss of interest or pleasure*
3. weight loss when not dieting or weight gain of more than 5 per cent in a month
4. insomnia or oversleeping nearly every day
5. slowing down or speeding up of thought and physical movements nearly every day
6. fatigue nearly every day
7. feelings of worthlessness nearly every day
8. inability to concentrate nearly every day
9. recurrent thoughts of death nearly every day.

struggle to take pleasure in anything. The magnitude isn't the same, but the identical mechanism is at play every time something negative happens. Even if it's as minor as someone criticising us, we'll suffer a dip in serotonin.

Eventually we recover after something bad happens. Our neurotransmitters return to normal state and we once again can feel happy. Sadness only becomes a problem when it continues out of proportion to the event that triggered it or when there's no obvious triggering event. We call this disorder depression. From a biochemical perspective, we're not getting sufficient reward – serotonin – to lift our mood back to normal.

Anxiety and depression often occur together

Because both conditions result in serotonin levels that are too low, the biochemistry predicts that anxiety (worrying about bad things more than we should) and depression (being unable to recover from bad things) are likely to occur together – and that's exactly what happens. Several recent studies have found that anywhere between 57 and 77 per cent of people with major depression also

HOW COMMON IS DEPRESSION?

According to the Australian Bureau of Statistics, one in 25 Australians aged 16–85 have suffered some form of diagnosable depression in the past 12 months. As with anxiety, women are twice as likely to experience depression as men. And again, just as with anxiety, prevalence drops by a third between our mid-40s and our mid-50s and halves again by our mid-60s.

suffer from an anxiety disorder. These people are hypersensitive to a bad thing happening, and that hypersensitivity translates into anxiety about it happening again.

When everything is working normally, the combination of neurotransmitter reactions should keep us safe and happy. Good things will make us approach and will give us a reward that will chill us out and make us feel good. Bad things will make us go in the other direction and make us alert to avoiding the same thing if we ever encounter it again. In both situations we'll quickly revert to equilibrium, having added to our knowledge of good things and bad things. But it's all very finely balanced, and it doesn't take much to knock it about.

STRESSED OR DEPRESSED?

Tom has three adolescent daughters. His oldest is now 23. She was in her teens before anyone was letting kids play with iPhones. The middle daughter, Christine, is now 20 but was the first teen in Tom's family to have screens on tap 24 hours a day. She got her first phone when she was about 12 and, since nobody had any experience with portable internet devices, she was allowed to use it whenever and wherever she liked. It turned out that meant all the time and everywhere. Whenever her parents would try to take the device away, she would become angry and sometimes physically violent. This was all overlaid on a personality that liked to be in control and resisted change at the best of times.

When she was about 15, Christine attempted self-harm. It wasn't a very successful attempt – because she tried to use Tom's disposable twin-blade razors, which ended up giving her a shaved arm and some nicks – but it was enough to drive Tom to book an appointment with a psychologist. The psychologist signed the family up for weekly sessions, diagnosed Christine as being depressed and prescribed antidepressants, which she dutifully took. Tom feels that after the diagnosis Christine used the 'depression' as an excuse for her behaviour. She knew her parents were worried about her fragile state and wouldn't push too hard on anything. After six frustrating months of no real progress, Christine ran away from home, leaving a note that simply said: 'Life sucks.' Tom immediately called the police. A helicopter and dog search later, they tracked her down loitering near some train tracks. The police took her to the nearest hospital for a psychiatric assessment. The psychiatrist immediately determined that Christine wasn't depressed and recommended she be slowly weaned off the antidepressants. He also diagnosed her as having an extreme form of anxiety caused by changes in routine. She likes her life to be highly predictable and organised.

Tom and Christine have not looked back since that diagnosis. They both now understand what upsets her and neither of them has the vague cloud of a 'depression' diagnosis hanging over them. Christine now has a very detail-oriented job and a dog that she adores like her child, and she spends a lot less time on her iPhone. Tom is certain that if Christine had been a teenager a decade earlier none of this would have happened. He firmly believes her personality would have been the same but she would have had time out to be bored and gain perspective. He says with social media there are no breaks. He also says that more than 60 per cent of the parents of teens among his friends are experiencing similar problems and many of their children are currently seeing psychologists.

DRUGS FOR DEPRESSION AND ANXIETY

Anxiety and depression are obviously very closely related. We know that high dopamine levels cause anxiety. And we know that low serotonin levels are associated with depression. So drug treatments for anxiety and depression have traditionally focused on these pathways.

Anti-anxiety medication such as Valium (diazepam), Xanax (alprazolam), Serapax (oxazepam) and Ativan (lorazepam) immediately reduce anxiety by instantly increasing the effectiveness of GABA – the great dopamine suppressor that's severely lacking in teens. They calm the sufferer down but don't necessarily *make* them happy.

Antidepressants, such as Prozac and Lovan (fluoxetine), Zoloft (sertraline), Aropax (paroxetine), Cipramil (citalopram) and Luvox (fluvoxamine), increase the effectiveness of serotonin.

Because many sufferers are diagnosed with both anxiety and depression, many of these drugs are prescribed simultaneously. But these are very blunt instruments that often affect many systems besides the ones targeted by the drug. Anti-anxiety drugs are addictive and antidepressants can double aggression and suicide risk in teenagers (but not in adults).

Addiction

Addiction ramps up dopamine but not serotonin levels. Imbalance between dopamine (our on-edge, ready-for-action neurotransmitter) and serotonin (our feel-good, chill-out neurotransmitter) makes us much more prone to anxiety. It also progressively increases the amount of dopamine (see Delta FosB, page 34) we need to obtain a rewarding serotonin hit, leaving us open to the risk of too little serotonin over the long term and therefore depression. From a diagnostic perspective, it's difficult to tell the difference between a drug addict and someone suffering from depression. They both exhibit a lack of interest in activities they once enjoyed, are irritable, have feelings of hopelessness, lose appetite, sleep less and lack motivation.

Even worse, some forms of addiction will explicitly decrease serotonin levels. Danger porn (extreme sports, gaming and gambling) works by using the serotonin decrease and dopamine surge associated with fear. And approval porn carries an inherent risk of depressing serotonin. What if the photo you post gets no likes? Or everyone hates the dress you just bought?

It's little wonder then that the statistics show very strong relationships between anxiety, depression and addiction. Gambling addicts are 18 times more likely to suffer psychological stress, more than four times more likely to abuse alcohol and more than twice as likely to be depressed as people without a gambling problem. Equally, people suffering a mental illness are 20 per cent more likely to abuse alcohol, 27 per cent more likely to be addicted to cocaine and 86 per cent more likely to be smokers.

'Statistics show very strong relationships between anxiety, depression and addiction.'

Addiction is a malfunction of our reward pathway that causes our need for dopamine to be constantly ratcheted up at the expense of our ability to be satisfied by serotonin. Once that pathway is out of balance, we can then become more prone to anxiety and depression. That doesn't mean this is the only way this can occur, just that it's much more likely when our reward pathway is pushed out of whack by addiction.

When we constantly expose ourselves to something that produces dopamine at high levels, we can become addicted to it. But without stimulation buttons, we have to work very hard at it, because our impulse-control module will be constantly working against addiction, making sure we only pursue something for as long as we need it. We chase food until we're full. We chase sex until we're satisfied, and we chase the approval of others until we get it. Once we get the reward or the danger has passed, serotonin and GABA kick in to suppress the dopamine. Addiction is a malfunctioning reward system caused by overexposure to dopamine and a failure to control dopamine-driven impulses. All of this applies to humans of any age and either sex. But on top of this we need to layer the special hormonal environment of being pubescent, as we'll see in the next chapter.

Summary

- Anxiety is a normal part of our stress response to danger. It produces a dopamine surge which helps us cope by sharpening up our thought processes and physical responses. And when the stress passes, serotonin and GABA reward us with relief and dampen down our dopamine.
- Anxiety becomes a diagnosable disorder when it either doesn't go away after the danger has passed or when we overreact to things that wouldn't normally trigger a significant stress response.
- Closely related to anxiety, depression is a disorder where the sufferer is unable to recover from bad things when

they do happen. From a biochemical perspective, we are not getting sufficient reward – serotonin – to lift our mood back to normal.

- Addiction is a malfunction of our reward pathway that causes our need for dopamine to be constantly ratcheted up at the expense of our ability to be satisfied by serotonin. Once that pathway is out of balance, we can then become more prone to anxiety and depression.

TEENAGERS, IMPULSE CONTROL, ADDICTION AND DEPRESSION

The bad news is that the impulse-control part of what I just said only really applies to fully formed adult brains. An adolescent's impulse-control module is still under construction. Crucially, this is the bit they're working on from puberty through to their mid-20s, and this can be very bad news for their ability to avoid addiction, anxiety and depression.

The challenge for parents is to provide a safe environment for learning but not to make it so safe that nothing can be learned. We don't let babies crawl around on the freeway, but we also don't freak out if baby falls down 100 times while trying to figure out how to stand in the safety of our living room. We let the experimentation happen but make sure they have a safe place to fall. Similarly, teenagers want to try everything that adults do and more.

The job of the adults in the room is to allow enough experimentation for them to learn but not so much that they do themselves permanent harm. We don't let toddlers play with carving knives and we should be very careful with the social equivalents for teenagers. There are many 'knives for toddlers' in the teenage world. We should avoid putting teens, particularly boy teens, in a situation where their lack of impulse control and poor decision-making could be lethal – for example, leaving a loaded gun within reach or allowing them to drive a powerful car.

The biology of puberty

Puberty is the phase of mammal development that turns essentially sexless children into adults capable of reproduction. Before puberty, the only real physical differences between human children is in their sex organs. Girls and boys are the same size and possess similar physical skills and capabilities. The sex hormone programming before birth has set them up as boy or girl templates ready for completion during puberty, but until then, the differences are largely cosmetic.

'Puberty turns essentially sexless children into adults capable of reproduction.'

GABA, the substance that dampens down dopamine, is a multipurpose suppressor of stuff (that is, of course, the technical term). It's the reason we don't enter puberty straight after birth. Until the age of about 11, it suppresses the release of gonadotropin-releasing hormone (GnRH), the hormone that in turn stimulates the release of follicle-stimulating hormone (FSH) and luteinising hormone (LH).

SOCIAL GENERATIONS

We're all used to people being tagged as millennials or baby boomers or gen X, but what exactly does that mean? There are no precise definitions, but these labels are a convenient shortcut for groups of people who share a similar date of birth and similar cultural experiences. The rough boundaries for recent generations in Western culture (North America, Europe, Australia and New Zealand) are set out below, but the start and end dates aren't hard and fast:

- **baby boomers** – people born from the mid-1940s to the late 1950s
- **gen X** – people born from the early 1960s to the early 1980s. (Born in 1966, I'm a gen X.)
- **millennials** – also called **gen Y** – people born from the early 1980s to the mid-1990s. (Our eldest, born in November 1995, is on the border between millennial and gen Z.)
- **gen Z** – also called **iGen** and **post-millennials** – people born from the late 1990s to about now. (The rest of our kids, born between 1997 and 2003, are card-carrying gen Zs.)

Anyone who's a teenager or in their early 20s today is part of generation Z, the generation after the millennials.

FSH and LH are the hormones that cause the development and activation of mature reproductive organs in all mammals (including us). These hormones instruct our reproductive glands (gonads) – ovaries in girls and testicles in boys – to release the sex hormones that cause us to develop to sexual maturity. Males release much more of the androgens (see box) and as a result become bigger,

A CRASH COURSE IN HUMAN SEX HORMONES

Androgens are the primary male sex hormones. The major androgen is testosterone, responsible for the development of male reproductive organs and promoting increased male muscle and bone mass. Androgens are not exclusively male hormones. Women have them too, but generally circulating at much, much lower levels. While a woman has 0.8–10 nanograms of bioavailable testosterone in a decilitre of blood, a teenage boy has 107–430 nanograms per decilitre. Testosterone levels vary throughout the day, and can be 50 per cent higher in the early morning than in the afternoon.

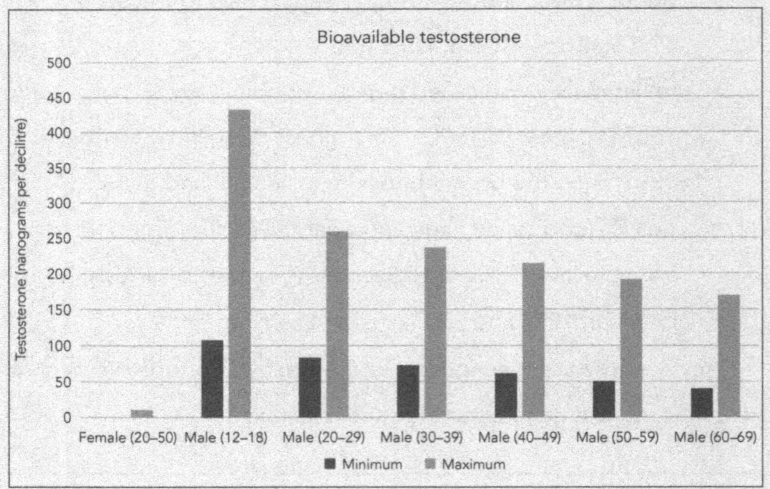

Oestrogens are the primary female sex hormones. Puberty is kicked off in boys and girls by the production of testosterone, but in girls the testosterone is quickly converted into oestrogen hormones by the ovaries. Oestrogens are responsible for the gender and sex-specific characteristics of women, but they're also present at low levels in men. While a man has 10–40 picograms of oestradiol (one of the primary oestrogens) per millilitre, a premenopausal woman has 15–350 picograms per millilitre.

Androgens are responsible for muscle and bone mass, hairiness and body odour in both genders. But since a girl with very high testosterone will still have 10 times less than the very lowest level in a boy, the effects in girls will be significantly less.

more muscular, smellier, hairier and more aggressive. Females convert testosterone to oestrogens, and those female hormones drive the development of breasts, wider hips and increased fat storage. All of this extra female machinery is focused on just one thing – babies. The extra fat storage is needed to assemble a new human brain, a truly massive consumer of relatively rare types of fat. The wider hips are to accommodate giving birth to that massive brain, and the breasts are for more fat storage and making sure the kid is well fed after birth.

We have all the hormone machinery in place to enter puberty from birth, but GABA keeps everything on hold for the first decade of life. Then, for timing reasons that are still not entirely clear, GABA effectiveness drops to about a third of the childhood levels in early puberty, climbs to about half those levels by mid-puberty and slowly climbs back to childhood levels by the time brain development is complete in our mid-20s. Teens are operating a brain with a brand-new and very powerful motor, with many more connections than an adult brain, but with brakes that only work at half, or less, power.

IS PUBERTY STARTING EARLIER?

The average age of onset of puberty for girls has dropped by about a year (from 11 to 10) in the past half-century. And there's some evidence that the trend to earlier onset in girls is accelerating. The average for boys has stayed at about 12 years. The evidence isn't conclusive, but it's likely that obesity is the cause of the acceleration in girls. Oestrogen, a primary driver of sexual characteristics in girls, is manufactured from testosterone by the ovaries, but it's also made by fat cells. The more body fat a girl has, the higher her levels of oestrogen. It's likely that higher average childhood body weights are resulting in excess oestrogen production and that this is driving earlier onset of puberty in girls.

Impulse control

This depressed GABA effectiveness in puberty – or braking-system failure, as I like to think of it – has important implications for impulsivity and self-control. Studies in humans have been able to directly measure the relationship between GABA levels in our brains and our levels of impulsivity, self-control and reaction time. The lower the GABA level, the more impulsive we are. We also think less about our actions, and as a result our responses are significantly faster. None of these things was related to how smart the subjects were or how good their memory was. It was solely determined by the GABA levels in the parts of the brain associated with supervising

'On low GABA, as in puberty, we act on impulse, make poor decisions and overreact.'

our decision-making. On low GABA, as all humans experiencing puberty are, we act on impulse, make poor decisions and overreact. Sound like any teenagers you know?

SEED OILS DESTROY SPERM COUNT

Around one in six Australian couples meet the World Health Organization definition of infertility (unable to conceive after 12 months of unprotected sex). And in about half of those cases it's because the male is infertile.

Omega-6 fat is the dominant fat in the 'vegetable oils' used in every processed food. These oils come from seeds (like canola or rapeseed, soybean, sunflower, safflower, rice bran and grape). We've known for some time that in experimental animals, high omega-6 fat consumption lowers sperm count and significantly impairs the quality of those that remain. But a 2009 study in humans has taken that research one step further.

In that study, 82 infertile men were compared with 78 (proven) fertile men. Detailed profiles of the fatty acid make-up of each man's semen were prepared. The results were unequivocal. Infertile men had a significantly higher ratio of omega-6 to omega-3 (15 to one versus six to one in fertile men). And critically, the higher the omega-6, the lower the sperm count. The amount and ratio of omega-6 also dramatically and negatively affected the other two primary measures of sperm quality, the motility (ability to move) and morphology (the shape).

This study didn't relate the condition of the sperm directly to diet, but other studies have shown that the fatty acid make-up of semen reflects the dietary intake of fatty acids.

Female impulse control is variable

Boys and girls have equally low average levels of GABA during puberty, but those in girls vary significantly during a typical menstrual cycle, while in boys they remain steady. In girls, GABA is higher than in boys during the follicular phase of the menstrual cycle – the half between the end of the last period and ovulation. This is because a large amount of FSH and LH are required in order to ovulate, and so GABA spikes during this phase. GABA then drops suddenly and is lower in girls than boys during the luteal phase, the half of the menstrual cycle between ovulation and when the period starts. This decrease in impulse control is

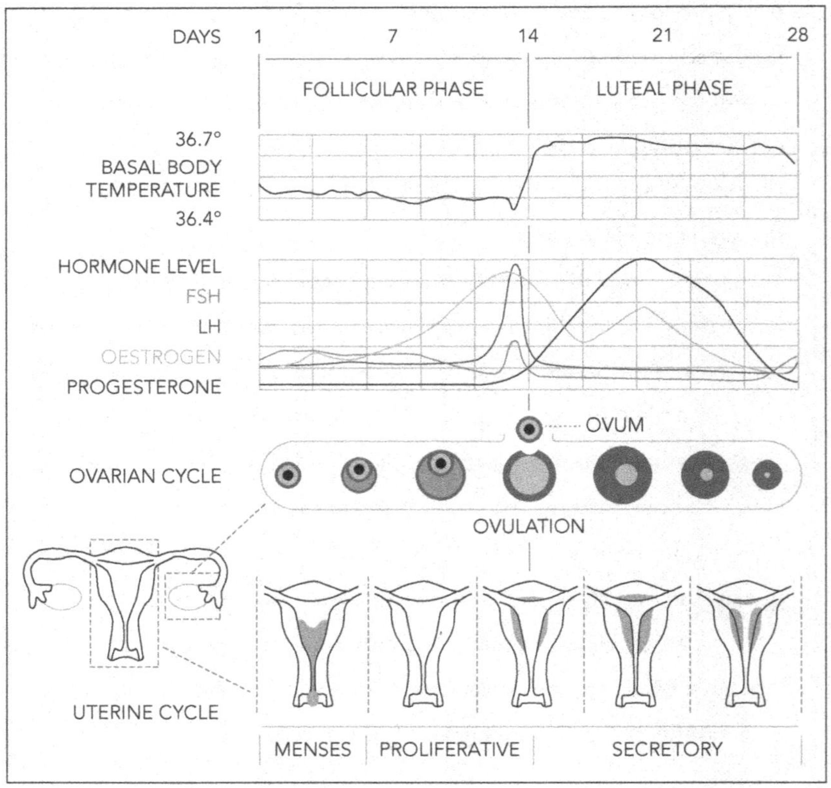

equally true in adult women, but because of the lower starting point for GABA, the impact is much more pronounced in teenage and young adult women. Teenage girls will have especially poor impulse control and make worse decisions while ovulating. It's little wonder then that many women report feeling cravings for chocolate during this phase of the cycle.

Male impulse control is non-existent

Testosterone complicates the picture a little. It increases GABA effectiveness, so you might think it makes boys less impulsive than girls. But the increased effectiveness only occurs in the parts of the brain associated with avoidance. These are the fear and anxiety centres that are supercharged by dopamine when we encounter danger. Normally these anxiety centres would make us avoid danger and be more careful, but add testosterone to the mix and this avoidance response is damped down by the increased GABA. While that makes boys less anxious, it also seriously messes with their impulse control. Just like teenage girls, teenage boys are operating in a state of reduced impulse control anyway but add testosterone into the mix and that becomes massively magnified when confronted with a dangerous situation. Men taking testosterone supplements often report that they feel 'pumped and invincible'. This is the testosterone talking, and given the massive surge in testosterone experienced by teenage boys, this is roughly how they feel all the time.

Males and danger

Making humans who consider themselves invulnerable is of course why females bothered inventing males in the first place.

TESTOSTERONE

In 1881, a Mauritian neurologist, Charles-Édouard Brown-Séquard, was among the first to describe the effects of a hormone we now know as testosterone. The 72-year-old professor told the Société de Biologie in Paris that he had come up with a 'rejuvenating therapy for the body and mind'. He'd injected himself with a liquid extracted from dog and guinea pig testicles and reversed the effects of ageing.

He reported that the injections increased his physical strength and intellectual energy, relieved his constipation and even 'lengthened the arc of his urine'. His contemporaries thought Brown-Séquard was delusional and that the only thing working on him was the power of suggestion. But it turns out he was right. Testosterone, a substance that was yet to be properly isolated or named, can have all of those effects and many more besides. And Brown-Séquard's observations make him one of the early founders of modern endocrinology.

The Bible got its biochemistry seriously wrong when it said Eve was made from Adam's rib. All humans start out female. Then, between weeks six and 13 of gestation, a dose of testosterone turns the Y chromosome carriers into the variant we know as males. Without that testosterone, all humans would remain the primary sex: female.

That initial surge sets male brains and bodies up for the second, truly massive surge they receive during puberty. The result is a more heavy-duty variant of human. It's stronger, bigger and more likely to do dangerous things. Oh, and because it doesn't bear children, it's dispensable. In short, it's the perfect human for sending out into the world to do risky stuff, like hunt woolly mammoths, while the real humans, females, stay safe and work together to raise the next generation. This is why males are three times more likely to die from injury than females from puberty onwards.

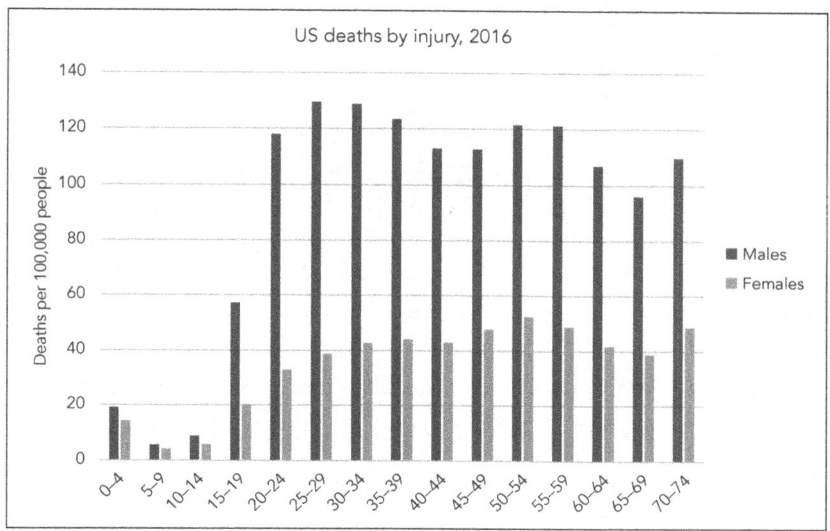

The male lack of impulse control also explains the surges of crime and violence that occur in adolescent males. In 2015, three out of every five arrests for violent crime in the United States were males aged 15–29. An adolescent male is four times more likely to be arrested for a violent crime than an adolescent female. The graph of violent crimes by age and gender (below) is strikingly similar to the graph of testosterone levels by age. Female violent crime also peaks, at much lower levels, in the same period, because while they might not be high on testosterone, their lack of GABA still means their impulse control is impaired.

'An adolescent male is four times more likely to be arrested for a violent crime than an adolescent female.'

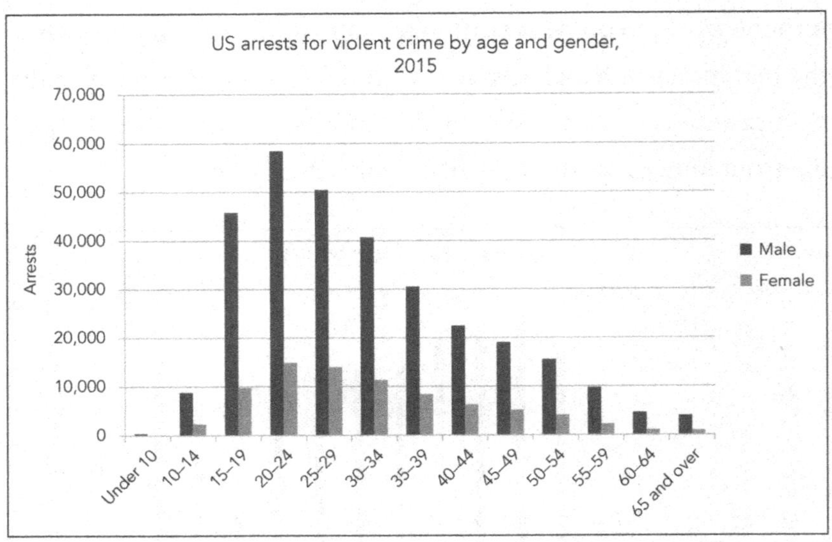

Over the past decade, crime of all types in under-18s has been plummeting. Boys are still much more likely to commit crime than girls, but across all categories crime is down 40–50 per cent. Crimes in over-18s have generally stayed about the same or, in the case of female property crime, significantly increased over the same period. There isn't an official explanation for this sudden change in teen crime, but I suspect that smartphones and tablet devices can take the credit. There are now much easier ways to get a hit of dopamine than holding up a bottle shop. And those easier ways can be done from the comfort and privacy of your own bedroom. Very few teens are arrested for refusing to 'like' their 'friend's' photo on Instagram.

'Over the past decade, crime of all types in under-18s has been plummeting.'

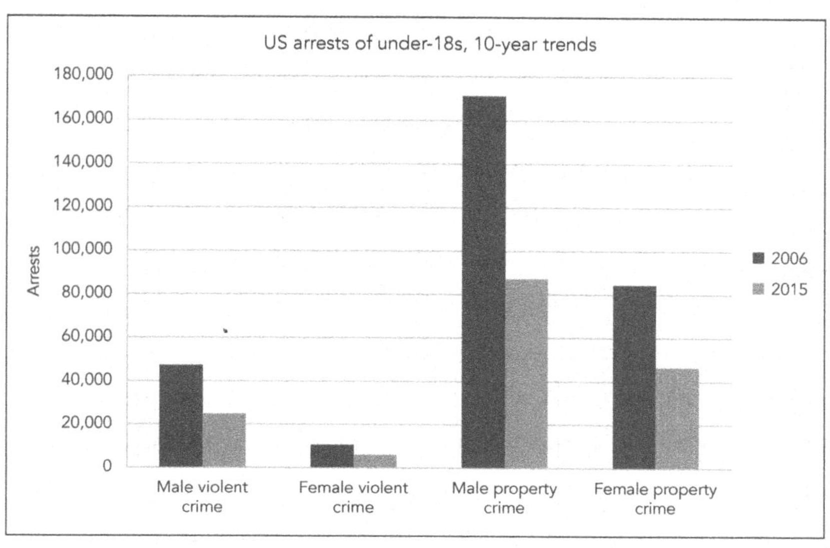

Substance addiction in young people

Having generally low GABA levels on the reward side of the system (as all teenagers do) is very bad news for our ability to deal with addiction. Remember that we depend on GABA to suppress our dopamine-fuelled chase for rewards, so serotonin can go to work and make us feel good once we get them. During puberty, not only are we very low on GABA, but we're in the process of training our reward pathways for future behaviour. We're making fast, frequently bad decisions. We're also taking risks with new experiences so we can learn what we find pleasurable and what to avoid. Our brain is, minute by minute, locking down the pathways that will determine our decision-making for the rest of our lives.

This phase is like the one we went through with our motor-sensory systems when we were toddlers. We tried out new physical skills, like crawling, walking and standing. Sometimes they weren't

'We're much more likely to become addicted at this age and much more likely to retain the addiction forever.'

the smartest thing to do in the circumstances, but we kept pushing the limit because we felt better when we accomplished greater mobility. We also tried shoving everything we found in our mouth to see if it was food-worthy. Sometimes we were right and sometimes we were badly wrong but we learned quickly.

During puberty the adult-supervision part of our brain is doing exactly the same thing, but this time it's not sensations and movement being learned. This time it's survival skills, reproduction, social interaction and impulse control. In this context, the removal of our GABA 'brakes' makes evolutionary sense. Teenagers are preparing to leave the protection of adults. But while they're still in that relatively safe space, their brains are wired to take more risks and try new things. Just like the toddler learning to walk and eat, they'll learn quickly which behaviours are rewarding and which are dangerous.

Potentially addictive behaviours are therefore top of the list to avoid. Because of the low GABA state of the pubescent brain, we're much more likely to become addicted at this age and much more likely to retain the addiction forever.

Alcohol and drugs

Adolescents have plenty of dopamine and not much GABA. Alcohol increases dopamine and fires them up to seek out more alcohol (and drink as much as possible), but the suppression part of the equation is much weaker. While an adult has a happy buzz on after a few tinnies, the teenager is still hunting the reward. A higher dose means more dopamine and greater reinforcement of the behaviour (see Delta FosB above). So we'd expect that the earlier we're exposed to alcohol, the more likely we are to become addicted to it and stay addicted to it throughout our lives. And that's exactly what the research tells us. Teens are much more likely to be addicted to alcohol, and early starters are more likely to stay addicted.

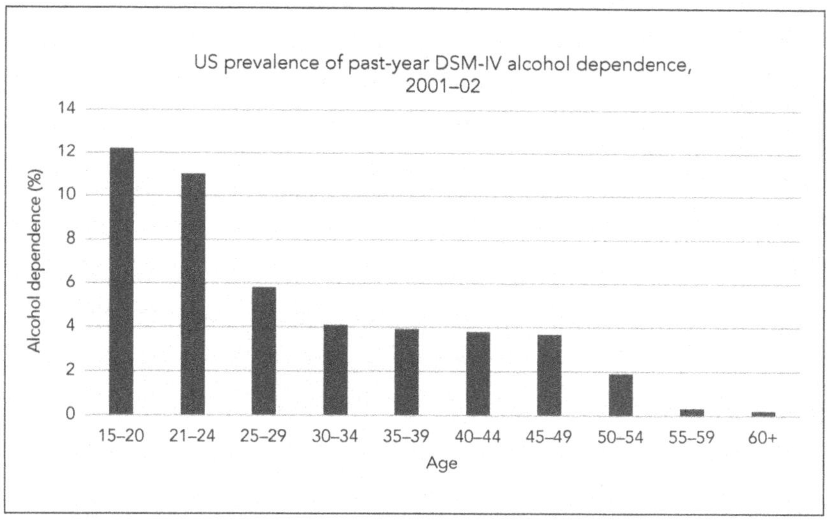

In the United States in 2002, 12 per cent of people aged 15–20 had suffered from a diagnosable alcohol dependence disorder within the previous 12 months. People in their early 20s weren't much better off, with 11 per cent affected. But adults in their late 20s were less than half as likely to be alcohol-dependent, and incidence continued to drop every half-decade after that. The statistics tell us that by the time we hit 60, just 0.2 per cent of us are alcohol-dependent.

The studies also confirm that the earlier kids start drinking, the higher the likelihood that they'll become addicted to alcohol.

In one of the largest recent studies researchers looked for the best predictors of alcohol abuse in adulthood. Sex, race and family income made no difference at all. But the age at which a person first became drunk was a very strong predictor. A child who first started drinking in their mid-teens was on average twice as likely (and could be up to five times as likely) to become dependent on alcohol (within two years) as someone who waited until their 21st to have their first big night on the booze.

An even more striking finding from that research is that early alcohol exposure massively increases the risk of becoming addicted to cannabis. The researchers asked about cannabis because it's the second most used drug by teens after alcohol. They found that a child who first starts drinking at the age of 15 is on average 7.4 times (and up to 20 times) more likely than the average person to become addicted to cannabis within two years. Once again sex, race and family income made no difference. This is the gateway effect (see page 34) in action. Once we set up an addictive response in the brain, anything that activates the same dopamine rush (or better) will do.

Sugar: addictive and in everything

The most highly available addictive substance is, of course, sugar. It's added to almost all modern (i.e. processed) foods. Food with added sugar sells much better than food without it, because sugar increases our dopamine levels and makes us desire and approach it. If they could get away with putting cocaine in food (as they did for Coke before 1903), they would, but pesky do-gooder nanny-state types have some sort of problem with that, so sugar will have to do.

The result has been a massive increase in the amount of sugar consumed by the average teenager over the course of the past century. Between 1978 and 2004, sugar consumption among US teens increased by 40 per cent. As with many other addictive substances (see page 89), gen Z's have started to appreciate the danger and have dialled it back. Their consumption of sugar has fallen since 2004, but it's still 20 per cent higher than in 1978. As with all other addictive substances, the peak life phase for consumption is puberty.

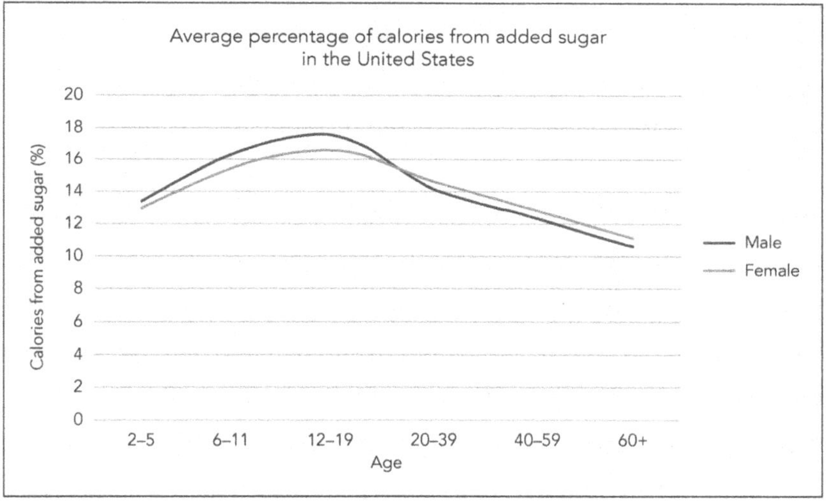

Sugar increases testosterone

Sugar makes us fat and insulin-resistant, and ultimately makes us diabetic. It's well established that people who are obese or have insulin resistance or type 2 diabetes have extremely low levels of sex hormone binding globulin (SHBG). One of SHBG's jobs is to keep testosterone out of circulation. By binding to testosterone, SHBG controls the amount of free (and therefore active) testosterone in our blood. Having low levels of SHBG results in there being much more free testosterone in our blood.

For a long time researchers have believed that insulin resistance, the precursor to type 2 diabetes, is the cause of the low levels of SHBG. Low SHBG is such a reliable indicator of insulin resistance that SHBG testing is being proposed as a good early sign of the development of type 2 diabetes.

A 2012 study has shown that isn't exactly right. It turns out that insulin levels don't directly affect the level of SHBG, but the presence of fat around the liver affects both the insulin level and the SHBG level. One sure way to create a fatty liver is to consume large amounts of sugar, because the fructose half of sugar is (directly and immediately) converted into fat (by our liver).

The best way to prove that is to try feeding a healthy person high quantities of fructose and see if they develop fatty liver, insulin resistance and low levels of SHBG. Because volunteers for that kind of fun might be a bit thin on the ground, researchers have had to resort to rats as the model. You can't use any old garden-variety rats. To be certain, you need to use rats that have been bred with the human gene for the production of SHBG. Before you get out the rat-breeding equipment (whatever that might be), you might like to know it's already been done.

In 2007 a group of Canadian researchers tried feeding these transgenic rats glucose and fructose (the two halves of table sugar) to see what happened. They found that both sugars suppressed SHBG production but fructose was twice as effective (glucose 40 per cent, fructose 80 per cent suppression) and fructose was especially quick, doing its damage after just three days. This SHBG effect was caused by the accumulation of the fats created as a result of processing the fructose.

The fructose in sugar directly increases the amount of circulating testosterone. The last thing a teenage boy needs is more bioactive testosterone, but if you want him to be more aggressive and impulsive, then feeding him sugar is the way to go.

Polycystic ovary syndrome

For females of any age, increased testosterone as a result of sugar consumption is very bad news. It leads directly to the constellation of symptoms we see in the current epidemic of polycystic ovary syndrome (PCOS). Due to the still-massive sugar consumption by teens, as many as one in five Australian females of reproductive age now have PCOS. Exact data on the numbers affected are hard to come by, because up to 70 per cent of PCOS cases have not been medically diagnosed.

The symptoms usually include acne, the appearance of male patterns of hair growth (and male baldness), and irregular or absent periods. But the big impact is on fertility. PCOS is the primary cause of female infertility in Australia today. The reason doctors suspect the syndrome goes largely undiagnosed is that pretty much the only time it's tested for is when a woman seeks fertility treatment.

Gen Z are doing a lot less drugs

Every year, the US National Institutes of Health conducts a survey called Monitoring the Future, to gauge teen attitudes to, and use of, illicit drugs. It asks a standard set of questions and is completed by a representative sample of about 45,000 school students from the 8th, 10th and 12th grades across the United States. They've been doing this since 1975 and dutifully publishing the answers to the same set of questions every year, which makes it an extraordinary resource for accurate data about teen drug use, allowing us to compare attitudes across generations using real data. We don't need to rely on adult recollections, which invariably amount to 'things were better in the good ol' days'. The good news is that gen Z don't do drugs to get their kicks. Well, a lot less of them do than any previous generation. The only real exception is cannabis.

I had a pretty protected upbringing. I knew kids who could get drugs but I never really got close to it myself. I knew kids who drank a lot but, once again, it wasn't a big part of my adolescence. Even so, compared to my kids, I was a raging party animal. Schoolies week, for example, was not the bubble-wrapped Sunday School service it is today. Teenagers drank heavily (at least) and roamed the bars and streets of the Gold Coast with impunity. Today everyone is corralled, tagged, red-frogged and counselled – and the kids don't mind that much (as long as Snapchat still works). Don't get me wrong, none of this is a bad thing – but even compared to my own sheltered adolescence, kids these days are drug and alcohol wallflowers.

Alcohol

The latest release of the data tells us that teen alcohol use has been plummeting since 1991. Less than one in five of today's 12th-graders have been drunk in the month before the survey compared to almost one in three 25 years ago. And just one in 50 modern 8th-graders had been sozzled in the past month compared to one in 13 in 1991. Binge drinking, defined as having more than five drinks in a row, has also dropped dramatically from

41 per cent of 12th-graders having done it once in the fortnight before the survey in 1982 to just 17 per cent now.

Cigarettes

Cigarette use has fallen even more sharply. In 1976, 39 per cent of 12th-graders had smoked within the month before the survey. By 1992 that number had dropped to 28 per cent, before climbing back up to peak at 37 per cent in 1997. But the resurgence was short-lived, and smoking has dropped every year since. Now just 10 per cent of 12th-graders and less than 2 per cent of 8th-graders have had a ciggie in the month before the survey.

Cannabis and illicit drugs

Marijuana use has seen no such fall-off. Sure, it's not the heyday of the 1970s when more than half of all 12th-graders had smoked marijuana in the year before the survey (damn those hippie baby boomer grandparents), but after a sharp drop in use that bottomed out at just 20 per cent in 1991, it's bounced around just under 40 per cent since 1997.

A lot fewer kids use heroin, but unlike with weed, the rates of decline have been significant. As for most drugs, use peaked in the mid- to late 1990s but has been dropping steadily ever since. In 2000, 1.5 per cent of 12th-graders admitted to having used heroin in the past 12 months. Now it's just a fifth that many (0.3 per cent). The trends for and numbers of users of ice (crystal meth) and crack cocaine have been almost identical.

Club drugs (variants of MDMA often called ecstasy) were being used by one in 10 12th-graders in 2001. But once again, gen Zs are getting their kicks elsewhere – just 3 per cent had used one in the 12 months before the survey. This is an important fact to keep in mind the next time you see a politician freaking out about drug-crazed teens. The reality is that kids using hard drugs is much less common now than it's ever been.

Attitudes to riskiness

The survey also tries to get behind the numbers by asking students whether they see taking the drug as being risky. Today's teens think crack, heroin, ice, cigarettes and drinking are risky, but that smoking marijuana isn't. In line with its continued strong use, the percentage of 12th-graders who see taking marijuana regularly as being a 'great risk' has dropped from 80 per cent in the early 1990s to less than 30 per cent now. Meanwhile, the percentage who see smoking as a 'great risk' has grown steadily from just over 50 per cent in 1975 to just over 75 per cent now, while the perceived risk of drunkenness has risen steadily from the mid-30 per cents to the mid-40 per cents today. Heroin, crack and ice have always been seen as risky by about three-quarters of 12th-graders.

This is compelling evidence that messages aimed at communicating the personal risks of a behaviour do affect the likelihood that a teenager will try something potentially addictive. Boundaries matter and will make a difference, but only if they're consistently communicated, which highlights the importance of parental rules. If everyone thinks something is risky, addiction to that thing is much less likely to develop. Although, of course, there'll still be the testosterone-driven difference, no matter how low the overall number, simply because boys don't see risk the same way as girls do.

Boys and girls are different

Boy and girl teens are equally likely to abuse sugar and regulated addictive substances such as cigarettes, alcohol and prescription amphetamines, but boys are twice as likely to abuse an illegal substance such as cannabis, cocaine or ecstasy. With their testosterone-fuelled lack of appreciation for risk and danger, boys are also twice as likely to become addicted to behaviours that involve more risk.

> **'Boys are twice as likely to become addicted to behaviours that involve more risk.'**

Young men and women are about equally likely to play poker machines, Keno and Lotto where the stakes and the risks are small. But males are twice as likely to bet on the gee-gees or dishlickers, four times more likely to play table games in a casino and nine times more likely to bet on sport. Very low-risk options such as raffles, sweepstakes, bingo and scratch tickets operate more as stress relief than danger porn and so, since males have much less anxiety (see below), these tend to be favoured by females.

Young males and females have the same low-GABA state capacity for addiction but in the male, testosterone-fuelled fearlessness drives them to experiment with the riskier options. To the male brain, these aren't particularly risky options. To the female brain, not juiced up on testosterone, they are.

The US Centers for Disease Control and Prevention (CDC) has been conducting a series of 1700 surveys since 1991 looking into risky behaviour in teens. This comprehensive series now includes answers from more than 3.8 million high school students and gives an excellent insight into changes in violence and injury, teenage pregnancy and sexually transmitted infections, as well as corroborating the results on drugs and alcohol covered in the Monitoring the Future surveys. Gen Z kids are physically safer than any generation before them. They never leave their bedroom so they drink less, date less, are less likely to become pregnant, and are less likely to take illicit drugs, be in a car accident or be the victim of violent crime. They even eat less sugar than gen Y.

But their mental health is a different kettle of fish altogether. Rates of depression, anxiety and eating disorders in teens are at levels never seen before.

Depression and anxiety in young people

Until the 1960s, the experts regarded depression as an adults-only disease. The consensus was that children were considered too immature to experience depressive disorders. Teenage symptoms of depression and anxiety were regarded as part of 'normal' teenage mood swings. Now, however, it's abundantly clear that far from being impossible during puberty, that's the age when depression and anxiety are most likely to be experienced.

Because of their overactive reward systems, teens are at least twice as likely as an adult to become addicted and, depending on the substance, the rates can be much higher than that. Depression and anxiety are much more likely when there's addiction-related reward-system malfunction (see page 22). This is especially so if you happen to be female, because girls don't get the benefit of anxiety-suppressing testosterone coursing through

'Rates of depression, anxiety and eating disorders in teens are at levels never seen before.'

their brains and, just for fun, have even lower levels of anxiety-suppressing GABA available for about half of every month.

Depression and anxiety in Australian teens

In Australia, we're very fortunate to have access to one of the most thorough long-term studies into children available anywhere in the world. The Growing Up in Australia study has been tracking a representative group of 10,000 children from every state born in 1999 and 2000. Every two years, the researchers pose a series of questions to the same children and their parents. And the answers provide a large and very accurate dataset about gen Z Australians. Because it's an Australian Government study, the participants are all cross-referenced to government databases such as Medicare, the Census and NAPLAN education testing. As data goes, it doesn't get much better than this. It's like the popular series of British documentaries, starting with *7Up*, that filmed a group of children every seven years of their lives, but this study is very big and has very accurate data.

The latest release of the Growing Up in Australia study found that, based on children's answers to a survey designed to establish depressive symptoms, 18 per cent of the 14–15-year-old boys and 32 per cent of the girls in the study displayed significant depressive symptoms. It also found that 13 per cent of the 14–15-year-old boys and 34 per cent of the girls in the study displayed higher than normal anxiety levels.

Another survey of more than 6500 Australian families with teenage children published in 2015 reported that the comparable numbers for symptoms of major depressive disorder (see box, page 69) among 16–17-year-olds were 8 per cent for boys and

20 per cent for girls within the last 12 months. The same survey also used a common test of psychological distress to gain some insight into symptoms of anxiety in those teenagers. The results were similar to those of the Growing Up in Australia study. It found that almost 18 per cent of boys and 36 per cent of girls aged 16–17 showed high or very high signs of psychological distress.

Similar US studies have found that 6 per cent of boys and 17 per cent of girls aged 12–17 had experienced a major depressive episode in the past 12 months. They also found that 38 per cent of girls and 26 per cent of boys aged 13–18 had experienced anxiety at some time. No, that doesn't mean US kids are less depressed than Australians, just that the sample was broader. The age range includes younger ages where depression rates are much lower, so the overall numbers are also a little lower. In the Australian survey only 3 per cent of boys and 7 per cent of girls aged 11–15 reported symptoms of depression.

These are big, well-conducted surveys, and the results vary quite a bit because of the nature of the diagnostic tools being used and the ages of the children, but I think we can safely say that in children who have begun puberty, about one in five girls and one in 15 boys are likely to experience symptoms of depression to a significant degree, and about twice that number will experience symptoms of anxiety within any 12-month period.

Adult rates of depression in Australia are significantly lower. About one in 30 men and one in 20 women will experience a major depressive episode within the next 12 months. The numbers are even smaller for children before puberty, with just one or two in 100 showing signs of major depression and no difference in rates between boys and girls. Anxiety in prepubescent children is about

THE GROWING UP IN AUSTRALIA DEPRESSION SURVEY

The survey used was developed in the United States and is based on the DSM-III symptoms for diagnosing depression. The maximum score is 26 (two for each of the questions). A respondent with a score of eight or more was classified as having significant depressive symptoms.

Child Self-Report

MOOD AND FEELINGS QUESTIONNAIRE: Short Version

This form is about how you might have been feeling or acting **recently**.

For each question, please check (✓) how you have been feeling or acting ***in the past two weeks***.

If a sentence was not true about you, check NOT TRUE.
If a sentence was only sometimes true, check SOMETIMES.
If a sentence was true about you most of the time, check TRUE.

Score the MFQ as follows:
NOT TRUE = 0
SOMETIMES = 1
TRUE = 2

To code, please use a checkmark (✓) for each statement.	NOT TRUE	SOME TIMES	TRUE
1. I felt miserable or unhappy.			
2. I didn't enjoy anything at all.			
3. I felt so tired I just sat around and did nothing.			
4. I was very restless.			
5. I felt I was no good anymore.			
6. I cried a lot.			
7. I found it hard to think properly or concentrate.			
8. I hated myself.			
9. I was a bad person.			
10. I felt lonely.			
11. I thought nobody really loved me.			
12. I thought I could never be as good as other kids.			
13. I did everything wrong.			

one in 14, and about 70 per cent of that is separation anxiety. Anxiety numbers peak in the teens, with about one in three children showing symptoms. This drops back to about one in five by our 30s and then one in 10 once we turn 60 (see graph opposite).

It turns out that far from being non-existent in our teenage years, our lifetime risk for depression and anxiety is at its absolute highest during the phase when we're most susceptible to addiction.

MANY PARENTS HAVEN'T GOT A CLUE

The 2015 Australian survey also compared the results from the children's self-reports to those of their parents' reports about the child. If the parental figures were used, the numbers dropped dramatically. Based on parent reports, just 5 per cent of 16–17-year-old boys and 11 per cent of girls the same age were depressed. Many parents also said their kids were depressed when those kids didn't think they were. If we add those numbers to the others, we find that about a quarter of 16–17-year-old girls and one in 10 boys display symptoms of depression.

This suggests that parents don't really know what their kids are feeling. The survey asked questions aimed at quantifying that. Just 7 per cent of kids without depression said their parents didn't know what they were feeling versus 15 per cent of those with depression. Similarly, 40 per cent of children without depression said their parents knew a lot about their feelings, but just 14 per cent of depressed kids said the same thing. It's clear that many depressed children firmly believed their parents didn't know what they were going through and, based on the results of the survey, about half the time they were probably right.

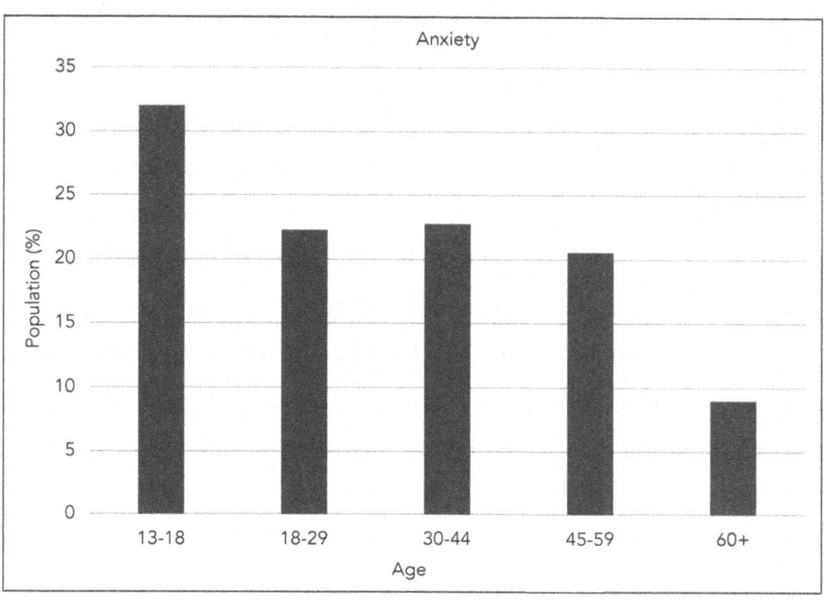

LEAVING CAN BE HARD TO DO

Our eldest daughter, Gwen, started preschool in 2005 and she was not a fan. Day after day, Lizzie would take her to the school and Gwen would get teary at the prospect of Lizzie leaving without her. It was wrenching for Lizzie, and she didn't know what to do. On the one hand she wanted to leave because she knew Gwen would settle down when she did, but on the other hand she didn't want to walk out on a crying child.

The teacher solved it by taking Gwen's hand and leading her away. On every occasion after that, Lizzie knew to just hand Gwen to the teacher and leave. This worked just as well for the mini-separation happening at dance class. Gwen got over her separation anxiety within weeks, and both were stronger for having done so. They weren't easy weeks for Lizzie (or Gwen) but we haven't had a problem with separation anxiety since – Gwen is now living in Europe for a year on exchange.

Teen depression and anxiety are on the rise

The studies also tell us that these figures have been increasing steadily in teens for at least a decade. In 2004, just one in 20 boys and one in eight girls were affected according to the US study. This represents a one-third increase in boys and a 60 per cent rise in girls in just a decade. Similarly the Australian study reported that depression in 12–17-year-olds almost doubled in girls in the 16 years between 1998 and 2014, and increased by 60 per cent in boys in the same period. Depression in children aged 6–11 didn't change at all in that time. There was also no change in the rate of depression in people over 20. Anxiety is increasing even faster. Australian research tells us that anxiety among 18–24-year-olds more than doubled between 2010 and 2014, and a very large UK study has reported that anxiety in children aged 6–18 more than tripled between 2003 and 2011, the majority of that increase occurring in the 15–18-year age group.

The US researchers also found that other factors normally associated with anxiety and depression, such as alcohol and/or drug abuse and family income, couldn't account for the persistent rises. The massive recent acceleration in anxiety and depression is a gen Z–only thing, and it only affects teenagers. The increase can't be blamed on sugar, alcohol, nicotine, drug abuse or violence, because the trends for all of these things are heading in the other direction. So something else must lie at the heart of the epidemic of teen anxiety and depression, and there's good evidence that this something is being home-delivered by the modern equivalent of a textbook – the tablet device. Even worse, your local school principal is the pusher.

Electronic addiction

Now that gen Zs have hit their teens and early 20s, we're getting to know them a little better. And what we're finding is very strange indeed. Gen Z aren't like any generation that's gone before them. They're the first generation that have grown up with artificially augmented intelligence. Gen Z don't need to know how to get from A to B because their map app will tell them. They don't need to know what seven times four is because their phone will tell them. And most importantly, they don't need to retain a single fact because Google, founded in 1998, is always just a tap away. The oldest members of gen Z were born at the same time as Google and the commercial internet. None of their generation has experience of life without instant access to the entirety of human knowledge. They simultaneously know everything, and nothing.

'Gen Z aren't like any generation that's gone before them. They simultaneously know everything, and nothing.'

The devices permanently attached to their hands are loaded with addictive programs, and that's not by accident. It's a noisy world out there in the app-development market, and the crowd is growing bigger every day. There are well north of 3 million apps available, and if you want your clever little app to be one of the few that are frequently used, it better have some addictive characteristic or you'll swiftly become roadkill on the digital superhighway.

Making programs addictive has spawned an entirely new academic field – behaviour design – focused on the manipulation of desire. In other words, how to trick our reward system into making us use the app. Needless to say, it borrows many of its techniques from the hard-won experience of the gambling industry. Cost of entry is low or free, rewards vary in size and timing, and there's a strong element of chance as to whether a reward will be received.

All the 'porns' are represented. Danger porn sits there in the guise of games and gambling apps. Approval porn hides under social media and online shopping icons and, of course, there's the oldest of the electronic dopamine stimulators, actual porn. The average teenager's tablet computer is a cornucopia of highly addictive simulators of things we know are addictive (when taken in excess) in the real world. There's unlimited danger, sex and social approval on offer. It's little wonder the average teen would struggle to leave their device alone for even the shortest time. No, gen Z don't smoke, drink, take drugs or even eat sugar as much as their parents did. They don't need to. They can get a dopamine surge anywhere, anytime, just by looking at their phone.

What boys and girls do online

Because testosterone and oxytocin are in play, gender plays a part in which variety of 'porn' a child is likely to become addicted to. Boys are attracted to danger porn in the form of video games, because testosterone drives them to seek danger. And due to their consistently low GABA levels, they'll be better at games that require fast reactions. Action-based video games deliver simulations of that kind of danger. In 2016, more than three-quarters of all video games sold were either first-person military simulators, other action games that emphasise physical reaction time, role-playing military fantasy or sports simulations.

In Australia, teenage and 20-something males dominate the video-game statistics. A teenage boy spends almost twice as much

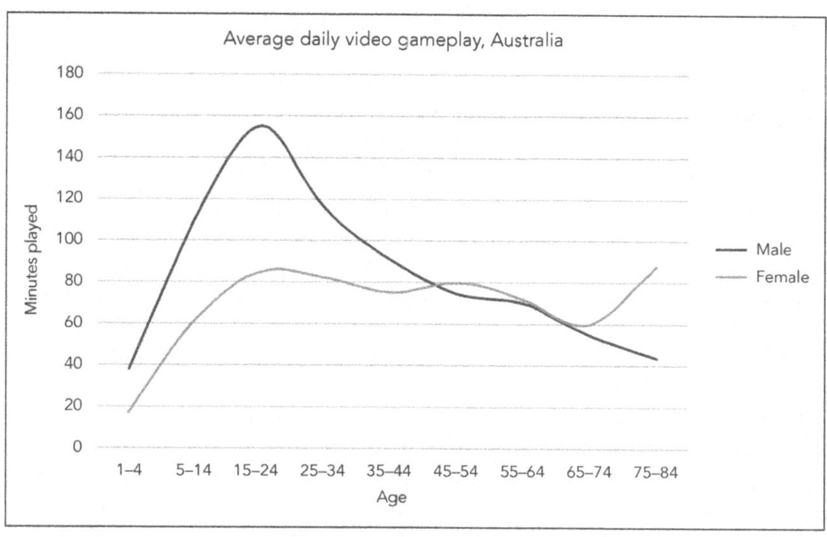

time as a teenage girl playing video games. Women get their own back in their late 70s, but Granny isn't playing *Call of Duty*, she's trying to stay sharp by playing games pitched as memory and cognitive-skills enhancers.

Girls prefer interaction with programs that focus on social reward because they find oxytocin, the love drug (see page 53), significantly more rewarding than boys do. Girls are more than twice as likely to use social media apps as boys. And just as with video games, rates of use have been increasing rapidly.

That's not to say that games are exclusively for boys and social media are exclusively for girls, just that the usage patterns follow what the neurotransmitter and hormone structure of the teenage brain would predict. Boys will favour danger simulators and girls will favour social approval simulators.

Lizzie has always been well ahead of the science on gaming and social media. While I took the attitude that a little bit of *Minecraft* or

RuneScape or YouTube wouldn't hurt anyone, Lizzie quickly realised that not only were they massive time-sinks, but that the kids started behaving like addicts needing a fix whenever she said no. It took me longer than it should have to read the science set out in this chapter, but it confirms Lizzie's intuition in spades. And now I am (mostly) part of the solution rather than part of the problem. It isn't easy in a house full of school-mandated iPads, but together we work hard to try and keep our kids off technology designed to addict them.

Many of our kids are addicts

In 2016, the Australian computer game business was worth $2.96 billion and growing by a fifth every year. In the United States it was US$30.4 billion and growing at a similar rate. Detailed UK studies tell us that use of social networking apps has more than doubled among teenagers in the past seven years (see graph below). The massive acceleration in the use of both tells us clearly that the manufacturers are doing their job. They're addicting our

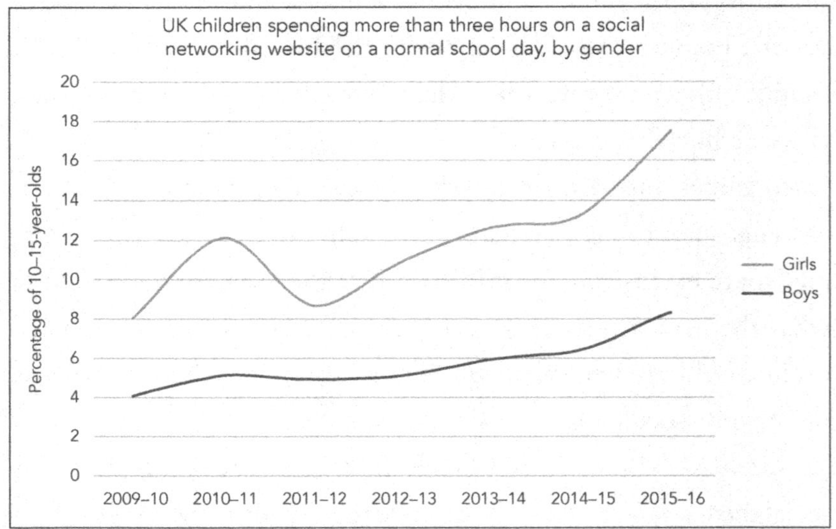

kids to the socially acceptable equivalent of the dopamine button that could be endlessly pressed by the lab rats, B-19 and the poor woman with the callused finger (see page 25).

The good news is that this addiction is coming at the expense of more traditional addictive behaviours like consuming sugar, smoking, drinking and abusing drugs. The bad news is that it's still addiction, and the massive recent rises in anxiety and depression in gen Z tell us it's happening a lot more than the old addictive behaviours. This of course makes sense. A rate-limiting factor on all addictive behaviour is how easy it is to obtain. All kids eat sugar because it's not restricted at all. More kids smoke and drink than take cannabis because, despite laws to the contrary, smoking and drinking are highly accessible for teens but cannabis is a little harder to get. Many more use cannabis than cocaine, once again partly because it's a lot easier to access. But there's no limit on access to social media (other than a largely notional requirement that you must be 13) and the only restriction on gaming is an unenforced and largely unenforceable rating label (e.g. MA15+).

Before the release of the iPhone in 2007 kicked off the modern era of constant access to a personal computing device, there were some physical constraints on accessing addictive software. If you wanted to play computer games or update your Myspace page, you needed an expensive computer, usually connected to a fixed-line internet service in your parents' home. And you were usually rationed in use, if not by parental concern, then at least by competition for time on the machine (and the need to use the telephone that shared the connecting line). If you wanted to share a photo of your latest shopping triumph, you needed to use the family camera, then transfer the photo to the home computer, then upload it, all within viewing range of your parents and beloved siblings, so you weren't going to be posting too many nude selfies (even if there was somewhere to post them).

I might as well have just recounted tales of Elizabethan England for all the relevance any of that has to a gen Z. They've had access to computing devices that have been about their person at all times since before they hit puberty. They've never known any other reality. Now there's nowhere and no time you can't play a combat game or farm the 'likes'. Boy-focused danger porn and girl-focused approval porn are there for the taking all the time. Sexual addiction is still a little more restricted. It's still not acceptable to watch hardcore porn on the bus, but the portability of the device means it's still more accessible than ever before.

'Gen Z have had computing devices about their person at all times since before they hit puberty.'

Putting smartphones and tablet devices in the hands of GABA-impaired, addiction-primed teenagers is the addiction equivalent of them having a dopamine button in their pocket at all times. It's telling indeed that Steve Jobs, the inventor of the iPad (released in 2010), wouldn't let his own kids (then aged 12, 14 and 19) use it. He knew something most dealers of addictive substances know – you don't get high on your own supply, and you certainly don't let your kids do it. According to a recent report in the *New York Times*, it is now standard practice for Silicon Valley parents to contractually require nannies to keep phones, tablets, computers and TVs turned off and hidden at all times. There are even messaging groups where sharp-eyed parents can post reports of nannies seen using devices near their charges.

Not only are the addictive devices now in every pocket, but most Australian schools have made it all but mandatory to possess one. The latest statistics from the Victorian Education Department, for example, tell us there are 10 computers for every nine government secondary school students (not counting teacher or administration computers). This means the average class of 27 kids has 30 computers.

It's a far cry from my school days (the 1980s), when we were lucky in having one classroom of 30 computers to service a school of 1600 students and, believe me, the most interesting thing you did on those was write a program that printed 'Hello World'. Even if, like Steve Jobs, you don't want to let your kids anywhere near an iPad, you'll be under enormous pressure to get one for them anyway, because their school will insist very firmly that it's vital to their education. From an addiction perspective, this is the equivalent of stocking the school canteen with ciggies and insisting that all students smoke in class and purchase a couple of vodka shots with lunch every day.

This addiction is bad enough in itself, but it can lead to greater problems that can ruin, or even end, a teen's life.

Summary

- GABA is an important part of how we avoid becoming addicted to rewarding experiences. It works by suppressing dopamine. If GABA levels are lower, we are much more prone to addiction.
- During puberty, GABA levels are significantly reduced, making all adolescents much more susceptible to addiction.

- Once those addictive pathways are laid down during puberty, they become paved addiction highways for the rest of our lives.
- Gen Z are the first generation to have experienced 24/7 access to portable digital devices. As a result, rates of addictive behaviour that requires them to be physically present, such as drugs, smoking, drinking, sex and physical danger, have declined massively. But electronic simulations of those things have sky-rocketed and, along with them, the rates of anxiety and depression.
- Paradoxically, our teens are physically safer but mentally more fragile than any previous generation.

THE CASCADE OF TEEN DISEASE

As we've seen, teenagers have impaired GABA. This makes them especially vulnerable to becoming addicted to anything that increases dopamine, because GABA normally suppresses dopamine. Being addicted massively increases the likelihood they'll become anxious and depressed. Gen Z is the first generation ever to be handed a dopamine generator, in the form of personal computing devices, and told they can use it whenever and wherever they wish – in class, in the bath, at church, while waiting for a burger, at work, on a date, on the toilet – anywhere.

Given the combination of unlimited dopamine (and the addiction risk it carries) and impaired teenage GABA-driven ability to control that dopamine, it's no surprise we're experiencing a wild explosion in teen anxiety and depression. The real surprise is that

'It's no surprise we're experiencing a wild explosion in teen anxiety and depression.'

it's not worse than it already is. But the story of dysfunction doesn't end there. As with most things in the human body, pushing a system out of balance will cascade through to other disease states. Eating sugar increases testosterone, which causes increased aggression in males and infertility in females (see page 93). Increased depression appears to be responsible for increases in self-harm and suicide. And while there is an association between anxiety and eating disorders, it is not clear yet which is driving which, or if indeed it is just the case that depression and anxiety are simply symptoms of eating disorders. Either way, we know both disproportionately affect teenagers and in particular, teenage girls.

Eating disorders

Eating disorders are a class of disease that largely affects young women and girls, indicating once again the special susceptibility of the teen brain, but can also occur in boys and men. The three main disorders are anorexia nervosa, bulimia nervosa and the more recently described binge-eating disorder. While our knowledge of the causes of and cures for any of these is in its infancy, new brain-imaging technologies are starting to provide some vital clues.

Eating disorders are generally preceded by symptoms of anxiety. We know from a large study of Swedish medical records that more than 70 per cent of people diagnosed with an eating disorder have also been diagnosed with at least one of anxiety, depression or substance abuse. A similar study in the United States found that almost all (97 per cent) of those with eating disorders also suffered from at least one other psychiatric disorder. And other US studies confirm that about two-thirds of the time a person with an eating disorder also has symptoms of at least one anxiety disorder. These studies have also demonstrated that the anxiety precedes the eating disorder and that the anxiety continues after the sufferer re-establishes more normal eating patterns.

How eating disorders are diagnosed

The official manual of psychiatric diagnosis, DMS-5, recognises three main eating disorders: anorexia nervosa, bulimia nervosa and binge-eating disorder. All of these conditions go beyond the dieting or overeating behaviour we all exhibit at various times, becoming frequent, obsessive and extremely psychologically distressing.

Anorexia nervosa

Anorexia nervosa results in significant weight loss because of self-imposed starvation or overexercise or both. Sufferers refuse to eat sufficient food to maintain a normal body weight. When it comes to anorexia in teens, the relationship with anxiety is becoming very clear. A recent UK study of teenagers found that 94 per cent of those diagnosed previously met the criteria for an anxiety diagnosis.

The term anorexia was first used by one of Queen Victoria's doctors, Dr William Gull, and no, he wasn't talking about the famously rotund leader of the British Empire. The physician first described the disease in an Oxford address delivered in 1868. He said it occurred mostly in women between the ages of 16 and 23, and was 'characterised by extreme emaciation'. He noted that it was really a default diagnosis arrived at by eliminating all other known diseases. He had no idea what the root cause might be.

He knew force-feeding could be used to keep the patient alive but it didn't cure them. Gull said his anorexia patients sometimes recovered (after many years) and sometimes starved to death, but he wasn't confident that any treatment he recommended made any real difference.

Dr Gull called the disease apepsia hysterica (meaning failure of digestion in females) but a few years later noted that a French professor of medicine had independently described the same disease in a paper published in 1873. Dr Charles Lasègue had called the disease anorexia hysterica (from the Latin *an* – 'without', *orexia* – 'appetite' and *hysterica* – 'from the womb'). Gull liked the term anorexia but felt that anorexia nervosa (*nervosa* is Latin for 'a habit of the mind that affects the body') was better because 'hysteria' restricted the disease to women and by then some men had also been diagnosed.

Because it can be diagnosed without any newfangled medical instruments, we have unusually good long-term data on anorexia.

ANOREXIA: DIAGNOSTIC CRITERIA

The diagnostic criteria for anorexia nervosa haven't changed since Dr Gull's time:

- persistent restriction of food intake leading to significantly low body weight
- an intense fear of gaining weight, or behaviour – such as intense exercise – that prevents weight gain
- disturbance in perception of own body weight or shape, and lack of recognition of the seriousness of low body weight.

Those data tell us it's rarely diagnosed in women over the age of 24 or in men. It also tells us that the numbers of 15–24-year-old women affected in Western countries have been steadily climbing (at the rate of 7 per cent a year) since at least the 1930s. Studies in the Netherlands suggest that diagnosis of anorexia among young women more than doubled between the mid-1980s and the mid-1990s, but there was no significant change in the (small) numbers of younger or older women or men of any age affected. More recent studies using hospital admissions suggest the rate of anorexia is climbing among adolescent girls but large population-based studies are yet to be performed. It is not at all clear on current data that rates of anorexia are growing and this is a contrast to the rapidly increasing rates of adolescent anxiety. It seems that anxiety is likely to occur with anorexia, but could not be said to be the cause.

As you might expect, insufficient food results in the body optimising for starvation. This means it shuts down all unnecessary activity to focus on life preservation. Anorexia results in a complete cessation of menstruation in most girls and, because the brain consumes about a quarter of our energy needs, significantly impairs cognitive ability. The long-term effects are even more devastating, with recent research suggesting long term damage to heart muscle could be responsible for up to half of all deaths due to anorexia.

Most people recover from anorexia in the sense that they eventually eat sufficiently again. But the disease can also have a disastrous long-term impact on bone density. The peak growing season for our bones is exactly the age when anorexia can strike. The significant malnutrition associated with the disease usually produces osteopenia, a reduction in bone density that is a precursor to osteoporosis. In an effort to counter that potentially permanent inhibition in bone growth, many doctors now prescribe oral contraceptives for anorexia sufferers. The theory is that as anorexia also shuts down periods, the contraceptive will simulate ovulation and infuse the body with additional reproductive hormones. Unfortunately, there's no evidence that the treatment is effective at reducing osteopenia (or anorexia). The only effective 'treatment' we have is to get sufferers to eat again willingly, regain weight and regain normal periods.

The definition of recovery from anorexia is that the patient reaches and maintains a normal weight. If the patient is female then menstruation should also return to normal. Anorexics have about a 33 per cent chance of recovery within 7.5 years.

Anorexia is the rarest eating disorder. But still, one in 200 Australian women are likely to suffer from it at some time during their life. It has the highest mortality rate among psychiatric disorders, with one in 20 sufferers not surviving. This is almost six times the rate of premature death in the healthy population, 2.5 times the rate for schizophrenia and double the rate for bipolar disorder. That average of six times the normal death rate hides an even more alarming statistic: the risk of death for women who are first diagnosed under the age of 15 is three times normal, but it rises to 10 times normal if they're first diagnosed between 15 and 19, and skyrockets to 18 times normal for a diagnosis between the ages of 20 and 29. Age at diagnosis is, so far, the only reliable predictor of mortality risk. Of the premature deaths due to anorexia, one in five take their own lives and the remainder die from heart failure complications of starvation.

'Anorexia has the highest mortality rate among psychiatric disorders.'

Bulimia nervosa

'Bulimia is about twice as common as anorexia but much less likely to result in death.'

Bulimia (from the Greek for 'ravenous hunger') is an eating disorder in which the sufferer binge eats and then induces vomiting or takes laxatives to purge the food in an attempt to prevent weight gain. Because anorexics may also purge as part of their disease, the weight at diagnosis is the primary criterion used to distinguish bulimia from anorexia. Generally, underweight purgers are diagnosed as anorexic and normal-weight or overweight purgers as bulimic. The disease was first described in 1979, more than a century after anorexia, as a 'morbid fear of becoming fat'.

It's about twice as common as anorexia but much less likely to result in death. Mortality among bulimia sufferers is about a third that of anorexics but still approximately twice that of a comparable group of non-sufferers. As with anorexia, bulimia mainly affects young women, but the rate of recovery is about double. Around 74 per cent of bulimics will recover within 7.5 years. Unlike those with anorexia, people with bulimia are usually normal or above-normal weight and usually have a history of being overweight.

Binge-eating disorder

Binge-eating disorder is the latest eating disorder to be added to the official manual of psychiatric diagnosis. It appeared for the first time in the DSM-5 (released 2013). Binge-eating disorder is what it sounds like: bulimia without the purges. Sufferers are usually overweight or obese and binge eat but don't purge afterwards. It's more than 10 times more common than anorexia and bulimia put

DIAGNOSING BINGE-EATING DISORDER

For a diagnosis of binge-eating disorder, these criteria must be satisfied:

- Repeated episodes of binge eating – consuming within two hours or less more food than would be considered normal – paired with a feeling of loss of control.
- The episodes involve at least three of: eating faster than normal, eating until uncomfortably full, eating large amounts when not hungry, eating alone, feeling bad afterwards.
- The sufferer exhibits marked distress.
- The episodes occur, on average, at least once a week for three months.
- There's no compensatory behaviour such as purging, or any other associated eating disorder.

together. Unlike the other disorders, it affects males and females equally and isn't specific to any age group. It's diagnosed in about 40 per cent of people seeking treatment for obesity.

The key element distinguishing binge-eating disorder from the pigging out we all do occasionally (go on, admit it, that ice cream bucket was full yesterday) is the frequency (the fourth point in the box). This isn't just every now and then, it's at least once a week for a continuous period of at least three months.

As you might expect, just like bulimia sufferers, binge-eaters are unable to control the amount of food they eat. Unlike bulimics, they don't force themselves to purge as a result. It could be that bulimia and binge-eating disorder are part of the same spectrum of disease, with bulimia simply being a more severe version of binge-eating disorder that seems to disproportionately affect young women at the same stage of life as those affected by anorexia. But I'm not entirely convinced that this disorder should be lumped in with anorexia and bulimia. The first two largely affect young women, but binge-eating disorder affects almost everybody. To me it looks like ordinary old garden-variety addictive behaviour that could be explained by the massive amounts of sugar in our food supply (see page 92).

Purging disorder

Under current diagnosis guidelines, purging (vomiting or taking laxatives) is classed as a separate eating disorder but also may or may not be present with each of anorexia, bulimia or binge-eating disorder. If you think that sounds confusing you'd be right; even the scientists investigating these conditions have trouble teasing out one from another, and there are no reliable statistics on the prevalence of purging. The best they can say at the moment is that they all have similar risk factors. The only significant difference is that females who purge are almost twice as likely to be addicted to drugs and alcohol as women who have never had an eating disorder and four times as likely if they are also bulimic. In other words, they are significantly more likely to display addictive behaviours. My two-cents worth is that the purging is an anxiety-related, conscious attempt to stop weight gain resulting from an inability to stop 'over-eating'. It's likely linked to the anxiety that many people with eating disorders also suffer. Anxiety is an overestimation of danger. An anxious person could regard overeating food as significantly more dangerous than someone without anxiety. Anorexics and bulimics have very different definitions of 'overeating' thanks to their out-of-whack dopamine-reward set point (see page 23). An anorexic who eats one slice of dry white toast may feel like they have binged and want to purge, but a bulimic might not reach that point until they have had four fried chickens and a Coke.

Orthorexia

A popular line put about in the media is that teenage dieting fashion (for example, going vegan or paleo) is in some way a precursor to an eating disorder. They call it orthorexia, a term coined in 1997, ironically, to highlight to patients that they were taking their children's diet too seriously. There's no such diagnosis and there's as yet no evidence that such a disease exists at all. Many mental health professionals believe that what is being described as orthorexia is either a variant of anorexia or a type of anxiety called obsessive-compulsive disorder (OCD). Orthorexia may not exist but the food obsession the term describes can be early indicators of eating disorders or anxiety, and parents should be vigilant for signs of them in their children.

IS A VEGAN DIET A GOOD IDEA FOR AN ADOLESCENT?

Vegan diets have recently become very popular among teens. In the decade between 2006 and 2016 there was a 350 per cent increase in people claiming to eat a vegan diet in the United Kingdom. If foods claiming to be vegan is anything to go by, a similar trend is also underway in Australia. Almost half of the UK survey respondents were aged 15–34, and many cited the influence of social media as their reason for starting. Instagram makes vegan food look exciting and colourful, rather than the stodgy swamp of chickpea or tofu recipes that filled the public imagination a decade ago.

Humans are omnivores, and our developmental biology assumes the presence of certain critical nutrients that can only be sourced from meat. This means that a diet light on meat can be problematic, particularly for an adolescent constructing the skeleton, musculature and brain they plan to use for the rest of their life. If your child plans to go vegan, here are some basic ground rules it would be a good idea to implement:

1. Stay away from processed foods labelled as vegan – they're usually high in sugar and use seed oils as the fat source, and your teen doesn't need more of either.
2. Increase the amount of protein in their diet (from legumes and nuts) by 15 per cent, as protein from plants is poorly absorbed.
3. Increase iron intake by 80 per cent and zinc intake by 50 per cent (usually with supplements), as these are not as bioavailable in plant sources.
4. Increase calcium intake with supplements, as almost no vegan food except cabbages naturally contain calcium.
5. Supplement with omega-3 fats and try to minimise consumption of vegetable oils, except those from fruits (coconut, avocado, olive), to lower exposure to omega-6 fats.
6. Supplement with vitamins A, D and B12, which are essential and completely absent from vegan foods.
7. Monitor calorie intake to ensure your teen is getting enough, as the high fibre content of the diet may make it difficult for them to eat sufficient food.

Teens will pursue certain diets for reasons as diverse as they are. They might be doing it because it is what their peer group values (see below). They might be doing it because they just don't like meat much or prefer a sweet vegan diet to a not so sweet paleo diet. If your child suddenly declares themselves a vegan, you can ignore it and feed them meat anyway or you can accept it and ensure they take vitamin B12 supplements. It's your choice, based on how many different dietary requirements you are prepared to accommodate. Around here, the answer is very definitely that there are no selections on the menu – you eat what's put in front of you or you get it for breakfast. But whatever approach you choose to take, the science says your decision will do nothing to either increase or decrease the probability of your child having an eating disorder. The driver for that is almost certainly hormonal and has nothing to do with food.

Hormonal influences in eating disorders

A normal reaction to food is to find it attractive and starvation unpleasant. This is why most of us can't stick to a diet that requires us to limit our food intake. We find food rewarding, so we eat it until our brain tells us we've taken in enough energy and then, if everything is operating as normal, we're satisfied and stop. Artificially imposing a limit on the number of calories we consume just leaves us unsatisfied and still seeking food. Every day of a diet is a battle against a hormone-driven reward system telling us we need to eat more. Recent brain-imaging studies confirm that far from finding food repulsive, anorexics are hypersensitive to the reward from food. This means that they require much less of it to find it as rewarding as the rest of us do. Bulimics are the opposite. They find food under-rewarding and as a consequence, need to eat much more of it to obtain a reward.

A normal person will find food attractive up until the point their body has sufficient nutrients and energy to survive. At that point, serotonin and GABA are released, happiness ensues and dopamine is suppressed. In an anorexic, that dopamine set point is too low and they will stop eating before the body has sufficient. Their body is still hungry but their brain tells them to stop. In a bulimic, that set point is too high and they will keep eating well beyond that set point. Their body has more than enough but their brain tells them they need more food. Bulimics need to overeat to feel good and anorexics feel better when they are undereating. Because GABA plays an important part in suppressing dopamine and having us feel good, as you might expect studies have shown that, like unaffected people, bulimics eat more during the luteal (ovulating) phase of their menstrual cycles, when GABA levels are at their lowest.

As the diseases appear to be malfunctions of the reward pathway, you would expect anorexics to be less likely to abuse any form of addiction and bulimics to be more likely. And that is exactly what the studies show. Anorexics are much less likely to abuse alcohol and addictive substances, and bulimics are more likely than anorexics and adolescents without an eating disorder.

Anorexia and starvation

The symptoms of anorexia are identical to the symptoms of purposely induced starvation. Human starvation experiments in the 1940s took healthy male volunteers and starved them for six months by using diets with half their normal calorie intake, designed to reduce their weight by a quarter. These diets were still

1600 calories, significantly more than someone on a 'diet shake' diet (1200 calories) would be consuming today. But it was sufficient to do the trick.

Most of the participants experienced anxiety and depression. Some self-harmed. They all developed an obsession with food, some even collecting magazine cuttings with pictures of food and recipes. They also suffered from a drastically reduced sex-drive and lost all interest in social interaction. Their metabolic rates dropped significantly. They became irritable, fatigued, weak and listless, and felt like they could not think clearly.

The researchers then used a five-month program of re-feeding with high calorie foods to return the men to normal weight. When the re-feeding started, things did not go well. The anxiety, depression and irritability worsened significantly. Thankfully, after about three months those symptoms disappeared but the men were not 'back to normal'. Many ate non-stop and some men binged to the point of vomiting, even eight months after re-feeding started. It seemed like hunger (a biological need) and appetite (a mental need) were different, and the trial had disconnected the two in many of the men.

These men had their dopamine set points forcibly lowered. In some men, the cure was re-feeding over an extended period; however, it was not that simple for many others. We don't know what causes an anorexic to have their set point lowered or a bulimic to have it increased, but we do know that, because of the mechanism of Delta FosB, an extended period of starvation would do the trick for an otherwise susceptible person. Something as simple as being ill for a few months would be enough to lower it sufficiently.

What causes eating disorders?

The big question is, of course, why are young women particularly prone to anorexia and bulimia rather than men, and why does it seem to affect them in their late teens? The obvious candidate for an answer is that women have a different hormone build from men once they start puberty. And so researchers have focused intently on whether that could be responsible for the massive differences (between men and women) in incidence of anorexia and bulimia.

At the risk of stating the bleedin' obvious, but bear with me, the differences in puberty relate to whether you happen to be male or female going in. And that was set up well before you were born. Foetuses carrying the Y chromosome (boys) produce a testosterone surge between weeks six and 13 of gestation (see page 86). This prenatal programming is important from birth onwards but becomes really important during puberty, when a second surge of sex hormones is released. Girls are also exposed to their mother's testosterone, but don't produce any themselves.

The 2D:4D ratio

There's a way to tell how much testosterone you were exposed to before week 13 of your development, and you don't need an MRI scanner or sixteen lab assistants to do it. You just need to look at your right hand.

Our fingers develop during the first 13 weeks of pregnancy. The ratio of the length of our index finger (called the second digit or just 2D) to the length of our ring finger (called the fourth digit or just 4D) is consistent from that point onwards. The 2D:4D ratio is set between weeks six and 13 and stays that way for the rest of our lives. The size of the fourth digit is directly related to the foetus's exposure to testosterone during gestation. The higher the exposure to testosterone, the longer the fourth digit and the lower the ratio.

As you'd expect, studies show that the ratio is generally lower in men than in women, meaning that men tend to have relatively longer ring (4D) fingers because they received more testosterone in the womb. The differences in size are not massive, with the average in Caucasian men being around the 0.95:1 mark and women closer to 1:1. The picture below shows how to calculate the ratio, and you can see that, given the ratio, this is likely to be a male hand.

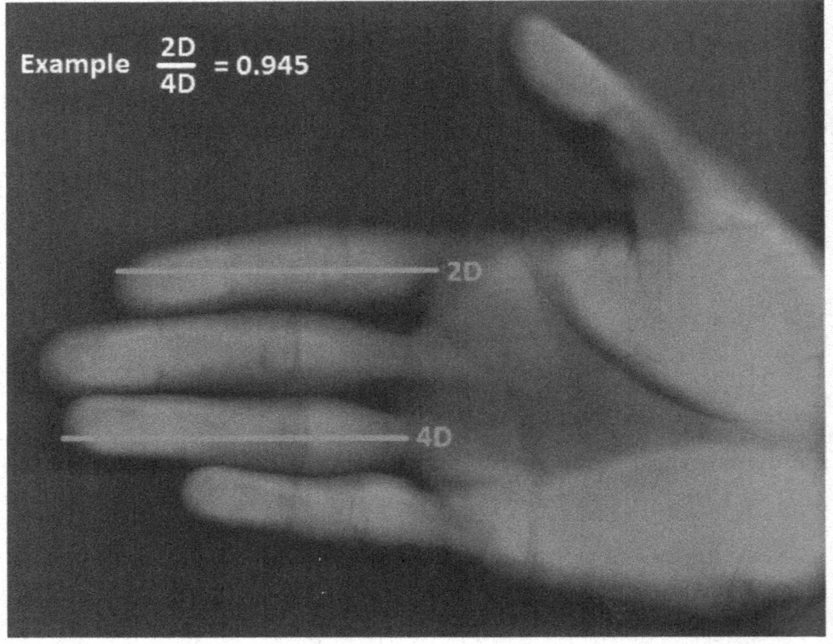

The discovery of the 2D:4D ratio has led to all sorts of studies looking for associations between the ratio and various diseases and traits. These studies have found, for example, that women with lower (more masculine) ratios tend to be more aggressive and assertive and are much more likely to suffer from PCOS than women with more average (for their gender) ratios. These women also earn more than their more feminine counterparts. Men with lower (more masculine) ratios are more likely to suffer from male-pattern baldness, and are less likely to be faithful in a relationship but tend to have longer penises. Men with relatively higher (more feminine) ratios tend to have lower sperm counts, lower risk of prostate cancer, and be more prone to anxiety and depression. Both sexes have higher childhood literacy levels, are less good at sport and more prone to superstitious beliefs if they have higher (more feminine) ratios.

When it comes to anorexia and bulimia, the research shows there are very strong correlations between the 2D:4D ratio and the likelihood of a woman suffering one of these diseases. On average, anorexic women have significantly lower (more masculine) ratios than similar women without the disease. And this matches with the observations in previous studies that, again on average, more athletic women are both more likely to have lower ratios and more likely to be anorexic, although it's perfectly possible, of course, to be non-sporty or have a high ratio and still suffer from anorexia. It and other eating disorders are complex diseases with multiple influences. Consistent with this, a recent study in twins has revealed that girl twins who shared the womb with a sister were at much greater risk of disordered eating than those who had a twin brother, suggesting that the presence of the extra testosterone associated with the male twin was protective for his sister. The opposite is true of bulimic women. They have significantly higher (more feminine) ratios.

INFLUENCES ON A PREGNANT WOMAN'S TESTOSTERONE LEVELS

There are a range of things that we know will change the testosterone levels of a pregnant woman, and this list is growing all the time. Here are the ones where the science appears to be reasonably certain:

Smoking: Smoking significantly increases testosterone levels regardless of gender.

PCOS: Suffering from PCOS (as a result of overconsuming sugar – see page 95) increases testosterone levels in women.

Alcohol: Consuming two drinks per week or more significantly lowers women's testosterone levels.

Seed oils: Fathers who consume seed oils have lower sperm counts. Low sperm counts produce children with low testosterone levels.

Many things can affect a mother's circulating testosterone during pregnancy, and therefore the chances of her child having a higher or lower than normal 2D:4D ratio. If she has higher levels of testosterone herself then the baby is likely to have a lower (more masculine) ratio. Her high ratios could be caused by having PCOS (see page 95), having gestational diabetes or smoking. Alternatively, she could have lower testosterone levels because of drinking alcohol during pregnancy, which we know will produce a higher (more feminine) ratio because alcohol reduces a woman's ability to create testosterone. The quality of the father's sperm can also reduce testosterone in the foetus. Fathers with low sperm counts are more likely to produce children with low testosterone exposure (and hence high – more feminine – 2D:4D ratios).

This is not to suggest some sort of predetermination. Girls will not automatically be anorexic just because they have longer fourth digits. Anorexia isn't caused by being unable to hold a knife because of your gigantic masculine ring finger. And bulimia isn't caused by your ring finger being too short. Rather, it tells us there's a high probability that prenatal testosterone levels, the cause of masculine fourth-digit lengths, can create a susceptibility during puberty that may result in anorexia or bulimia if the appropriate conditions are present. The pre-birth hormonal programming sets up our response to testosterone in puberty. The lower the 2D:4D ratio (the higher the level of testosterone before birth), the greater the sensitivity to testosterone during puberty. Testosterone increases dopamine release in the reward pathway but anorexics are significantly more sensitive to both the testosterone and the dopamine it activates, meaning they are rewarded more quickly than normal. Bulimics are significantly less sensitive to both, and reward takes much longer.

A critical component of adult female development is filling the baby larder. A sexually mature female must be able to store sufficient calories to ensure she can feed herself and grow a brand-new human. This includes building a brain out of a truly vast amount of fat. A normal-weight adult woman has twice the amount of body fat (26 per cent of body weight) of a normal weight male of the same age (13 per cent). Because the fat required for brain-building is the highly heat-sensitive polyunsaturated variety, it needs to be stored as far away as possible from the hot core of the body. Sperm are made of the same type of fat, so the store-as-far-away-as-possible-mode went to even greater extremes with the invention of the scrotum. Puberty ensures the female body is ready to receive those extra calories by creating additional fat stores away from the abdomen (in the breasts, upper arms and upper legs), and creating the desire to fill them (by increasing the reward value of food – moving the dopamine set point up). Anorexics are more 'masculine' in their structural make-up and therefore under-motivated (relative to their actual requirements) by food (compared to the average female). Bulimics are more 'feminine' and therefore relatively over-motivated by food.

The key question is why. What tips them in one direction or another? And is there anything we can do to prevent it or cure it?

Curing eating disorders

When Dr Gull first named anorexia in the 19th century, he quickly realised that nothing he did would change the outcome. Emergency forced feeding would keep alive a patient who was in acute danger of starvation but it wouldn't cure anorexia. Rather like the participants in the starvation experiment, most patients would eventually recover if not normal, then at least sufficient appetite not to die of starvation. But recovery would take the better part of a decade and wasn't influenced by anything he did as far as he could tell. The bad news is that when it comes to eating disorders we haven't progressed an awful long way from there.

Because of the high likelihood that someone with an eating disorder will also suffer from another psychological disorder, all of the drugs used to treat anxiety, depression and psychosis have been trialled as treatments for eating disorders. The results have been disappointing. None of the drug-based treatments has resulted in significant improvement compared to a placebo in controlled trials. Some of them do improve the symptoms of anxiety or depression that are often also present, but they don't seem to improve the underlying eating disorder.

A battery of counselling-based 'treatments' is available, but the evidence on whether any of them is effective is sketchy at best. The popular therapies include cognitive behavioural therapy (CBT), family therapy and educational behavioural therapy (EBT). The CBT approach largely relies on the theory that the disordered eating is caused by the sufferer obsessing about their shape or weight. CBT counselling aims to help them identify and challenge negative thoughts about their body and teach them how to change their behaviour. It's based on the idea that thinking negatively is a habit the sufferer can train themselves out of by working on both their behaviour and those thought patterns. Family therapy is aimed at co-opting members of the family as a 'treatment team'. It involves the therapist helping parents (for example) to encourage the sufferer to eat more (or less) than they might want to, but do so without being critical of the sufferer. Eventually the child is encouraged to take control of the process. EBT involves monitoring food intake with the goal of increasing the amount of food consumed.

At least in adults, none of these therapies is demonstrably effective or superior to any of the others, although some people do recover well with these approaches. Of course, the primary difficulty with all counselling-based treatments is that it's very difficult to tell whether any subsequent improvement is a result of the treatment or just something that was going to happen anyway, given that in the majority of cases improvement eventually occurs.

But family therapy does show signs in controlled trials of being useful in anorexic teenagers. Biochemically, it seems the child's brain is being slowly trained, meal by meal, to eat slightly more (or less) than the dopamine set point says is correct. We know that dopamine set points can be changed by continuous exposure to something that triggers dopamine in addiction or fails to provide it in withdrawal, so the neurochemistry suggests anything that can do that in anorexics and bulimics should work. So far the only mainstream treatment that has been proven to accomplish that for anorexic adolescents is family therapy. One trial of 38 sufferers suggested it can be effective in increasing weight gain for at least a year. In that small trial, the children most likely to maintain weight gain were those whose mother was the least critical of them.

I said 'mainstream treatment' because there's one other increasingly popular treatment that the biochemistry says should work in anorexics. And the limited trials so far, show that it does. The problem is using it will land you in jail in most places. Cannabis contains cannabinoids, the neurotransmitter that motivates food seeking (see page 32), so it seems logical to see if it helps anorexics. The answer so far is a cautious yes, it seems to. A drug containing the appetite-stimulating component of cannabis, THC, has been approved for use in the US since 1986 in the treatment of HIV patients who suffer involuntary weight loss, but its use is heavily restricted. The trouble is that getting ethical approval to use an addictive substance on people already suffering a psychological disorder is pretty hard to come by, so there is just not that much science on the topic. Nevertheless a small but well-conducted recent trial has shown that it's effective in causing small but significant weight gain compared to a placebo in women with severe longstanding anorexia. And according to that august 'scientific journal' *Cosmopolitan* magazine, young anorexic women on the leading edge of the frontiers of science have been conducting their own trials in the dorm rooms at college. They say they feel hungry rather than nauseous at the prospect of food after just a puff or two of marijuana. Weed allows them to eat normally. The same 'journal' also confirms another scientific observation about marijuana to the effect that it reduces anxiety. Young women report feeling less anxious about food after a toke. Experts have no idea what a long-term treatment program using medical marijuana would look like or even if it could lead to long-term recovery, but the early evidence is encouraging.

Self-harm

Self-harm is when kids intentionally hurt themselves. It doesn't mean they intend to kill themselves, but sometimes self-harm can be fatal. The DSM-5 has identified a new disorder called non-suicidal self-injury (NSSI) as one for further study, but the prevailing view among psychiatrists and psychologists is that self-harm is a symptom of an underlying condition rather than a disorder in its own right. The harm is usually some sort of physical injury, such as cutting, burning, hitting, hair-pulling or putting themselves in dangerous situations. It can also be abuse of drugs or alcohol. Eighty per cent of self-harm involves stabbing or cutting the skin with a sharp object.

'Self-harm doesn't mean kids intend to kill themselves, but sometimes it can be fatal.'

Risk factors for self-harm

The Growing Up in Australia study took a thorough look at self-harm in its 2016 release. It used data from when the surveyed kids were turning 14 and 15. They found that 15 per cent of girls and 4 per cent of boys had engaged in self-harm in the previous 12 months. And while many potential factors have been found to increase the risk of self-harm, this study, with its powerful dataset, was able to eliminate many of the traditional explanations, as outlined below. The researchers found that only a very small set of key personal characteristics of the child and one external factor, peer victimisation, remained after eliminating the statistical noise.

'The largest risk factor for self-harm was the presence of symptoms of depression.'

They found that the largest risk factor by far was the presence of symptoms of depression. Depressed teens are more than six times as likely to self-harm. Similarly, girls and teens showing symptoms of anxiety were more than three times as likely to self-harm. Teens who didn't feel generally happy, weren't attracted to the opposite sex, engaged in any risky behaviour (substance abuse, drinking or sexual activity), had a reactive temperament, or felt unfairly treated by their peers or school were all about twice as likely to self-harm.

The list of things that show no statistical association with self-harm (see box opposite) includes pretty much all the things the media generally blames. The usual stalking horses, bullying and the family, aren't statistically significant risk factors. Kids don't self-harm because they're being bullied verbally or physically, or because they're lonely or their family is in financial or other stress. The mother having depression is also not related, and nor is the

THINGS THAT DON'T INCREASE THE RISK OF SELF-HARM

According to the Growing Up in Australia study, the following factors did *not* significantly increase the risk of self-harm:

- physical bullying or victimisation
- verbal bullying or victimisation
- isolation by peers (if anything this significantly reduced the likelihood of self-harm)
- poor belonging to school
- being frequently absent from school
- being poor
- family financial stress
- being part of a single-mum household
- stressful family events
- lack of supervision
- the child being alone often
- their mum being depressed
- parenting style (non-demanding, non-responsive or authoritative)
- conflict between the child and the parents.

level of conflict in the house or even the parenting style. Those knee-jerk explanations might give comfort to a certain crowd but the statistical reality is none of it is true. The data tell us that in reality, kids self-harm for only two primary reasons: because they're depressed or anxious or because they're part of a minority (for example, because of sexual preference) and feel the whole community (including their family and school) is discriminating against them. As you might expect, given the disproportionate prevalence of anxiety and depression in teenage girls, they're four times more likely to self-harm than teenage boys.

Why depressed kids self-harm

Our body is quite the little chemical factory. We can produce all manner of useful stuff on demand, including our own homegrown morphine for pain suppression. Morphine is a powerful opioid drug extracted from opium poppies and one of the oldest known painkillers. It was being used by the Romans as a sedative during surgery from as early as the 2nd century BC. But opium poppies aren't the only source. The human body can manufacture its own morphine. These morphine variants, called endorphins – a contraction of *endogenous* (homemade) and *morphine* – are produced by the human body in response to pain and physical stress. When we put our body under physical stress by doing vigorous aerobic exercise, such as a long-distance run, the body produces morphine and the athlete achieves a 'runner's high'. Long-distance runners sometimes report the effect being as strong as taking a mood-altering drug. More often they say that it simply makes them feel relaxed and at peace.

It seems that any level of exercise that puts the body under stress is sufficient to release some endorphins. I remember feeling exactly that way when I went through a wee bit of an addiction to weightlifting at the university gym. I knew if I went at it hard, it would hurt, a lot. But I also knew I'd feel great afterwards, and that knowledge would drag me back there every day. If I couldn't go for whatever reason, I remember feeling irritable and annoyed that my daily workout high wouldn't be forthcoming. Thankfully, I recovered and am now a happily non-buff example of a middle-aged dad. But that pull of a daily exercise high was very real to me and very hard to resist.

Opioids work by increasing serotonin production and, as a consequence, GABA release. The high we get from opioids like morphine is exactly the same as the one we get from good sex, a good meal, booze or illicit drugs. The increase in serotonin and GABA means, of course, that exercise is an excellent antidepressant. Unfortunately, there's a shortcut to endorphins that doesn't involve hours of effort and sweating. Even more unfortunately, many depressed and anxious teenagers work this out. The shortcut is self-harm.

Self-harm isn't an attempt at suicide. It's an attempt to cure the feelings associated with anxiety and depression. Self-harmers get an endorphin shot that's just as real as for someone who's exercised hard. It takes a lot less physical effort, makes them feel better and can be just as addictive. Self-harm isn't a gen Z phenomenon. It's been with us for as long as humans have experienced anxiety or depression. Two American doctors reported in 1896 that the practice existed in young women all over late-19th-century Europe. It was common enough for there to be a frequently used nickname for the women – 'needle girls' – because they'd intentionally prick them themselves with sewing needles.

'Self-harm has been with us for as long as humans have experienced anxiety or depression.'

If we have a normally operating danger response, pain causes us to head in the other direction. We avoid putting ourselves in situations that will cause pain. But some self-harmers report that pain makes them feel calm and in control. It removes anxiety and makes them feel better. To a cutter, pain is self-help in exactly the way a runner will tell you that going for a run clears their mind and improves their mood. And the opioid rush it produces can be just as addictive as morphine or any other opioid drug.

To reduce the incidence of self-harm, our first step should be to reduce anxiety and depression in teens. As you will soon see, one first step for parents is to introduce limits on screen time and ensure that these (and other parental rules) are enforced consistently and fairly.

Suicide

The link between self-harm and suicide has also been explored in the Growing Up in Australia study. It found that four out of five 14–15-year-old girls who attempted suicide had previously self-harmed. But this was the case with just a third of boys the same age. It also found that a child who has previously self-harmed is more than 20 times more likely to attempt suicide than a child who hasn't harmed themselves before.

Aside from that, the only other independent risk factors to emerge from the Growing Up in Australia study, apart from the depression and anxiety that lead to self-harm, were being homosexual or having engaged in violent crime in the past 12 months. Both doubled the risk of suicide with or without previous self-harm. Once again, all the usual suspects including bullying, family life and economic considerations were eliminated as risks. The science tells us that teenage girls who attempt suicide usually graduate from self-harm, and that the cause of that self-harm is largely anxiety and depression.

'Teenage girls who attempt suicide usually graduate from self-harm.'

Gender differences in suicide rates

The Growing Up in Australia study reported that in the past 12 months, 12 per cent of 14–15-year-old girls said they had thought about suicide, 9 per cent had developed a plan and 6 per cent had attempted suicide. Boys of the same age had much lower rates. Six in every 100 boys had thought about suicide, five had developed a plan and four had attempted suicide. Of those who attempted suicide, 69 per cent of the girls but just 40 per cent of the boys had planned to do so. This finding is consistent with other research that shows boys are much more impulsive when it comes to attempting suicide. Given teenage boys are the ones high on testosterone and low on impulse control (see page 85), this shouldn't come as any particular surprise.

Fewer boys think about and plan suicide but many more manage to end their own lives than girls. Boys aged 15–19 are three times more likely to die by suicide than girls the same age. In Australia in 2016, 101 boys and 36 girls aged 15–19 took their own lives. These are approximately half the numbers for any age group from 20–60. The gender difference is identical to the difference in their respective likelihood of death by injury. Testosterone drives a lack of impulse control, and this may well be the underlying cause of the gender difference in suicide rates, just as it's likely to be the reason for the differences in death by injury.

'Fewer boys think about and plan suicide, but many more manage to end their own lives than girls.'

This theory finds significant support in a strange aberration in male suicide statistics. In general, the rate of both male and female teen suicide has been increasing steadily since the mid-20th century at approximately the same rate as increases in anxiety and

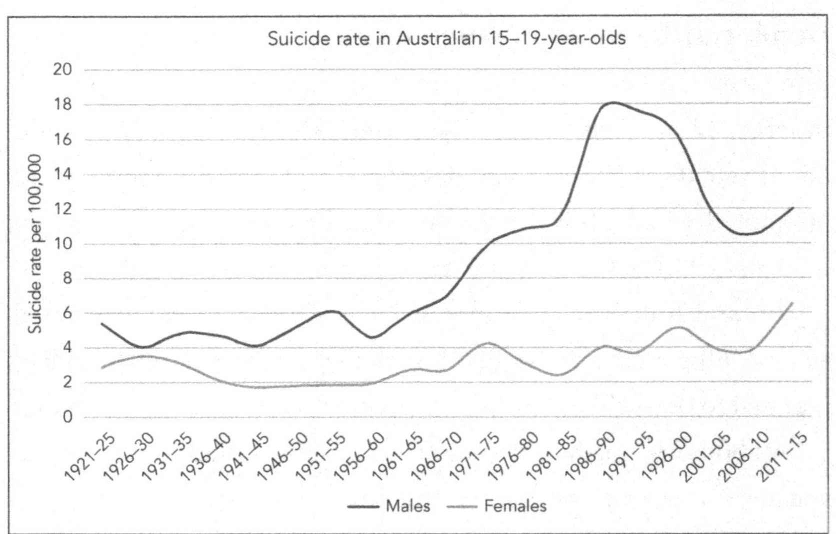

'Both male and female teen suicide rates have increased sharply again in the last five years.'

depression. In 1921, two 15–19-year-old girls and five boys in every 100,000 of the population were likely to commit suicide. Those rates stayed fairly stable until the mid-1960s, when both male and female rates began to climb. By the end of the 1980s, the female rate had doubled to four per 100,000 and the male rate had skyrocketed to 18. They held at those highs in the 1990s, but then dropped suddenly again in the early 21st century. Both male and female rates have increased sharply again in the last five years. US rates and differences between the sexes are almost identical over the same time frame.

This led me to wonder what on earth caused the massive spike in teen suicide, particularly among boys, in the 1990s, and it occurred to me that the other thing teenagers did over the same time frame, and that shows an identical pattern, is use steroids (anabolic–androgenic steroids).

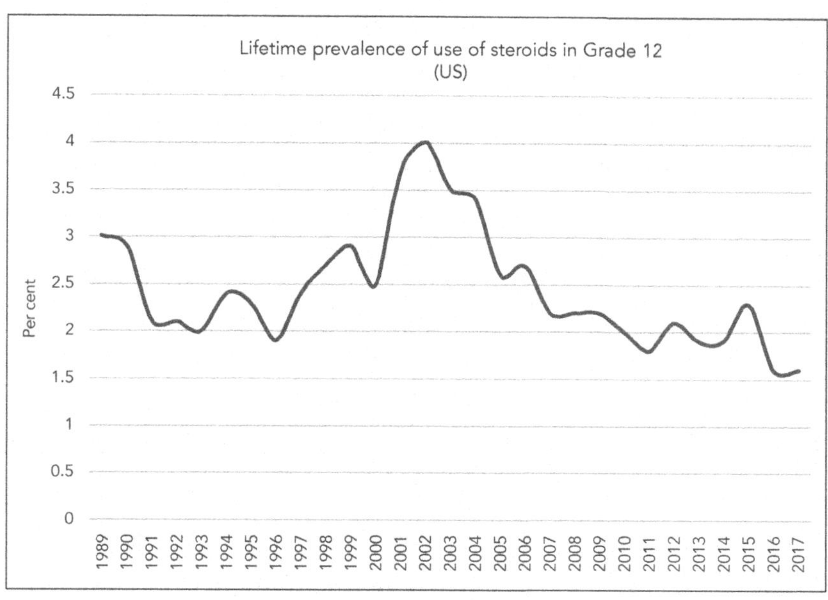

A brief history of steroid use

I'm not sure I want to know how ancient shepherds discovered that removing a ram's testicles made it easier to domesticate, but humans have known the effects of testosterone and its source for at least the last six millennia. Even so, it wasn't until 1929, when a chemistry student from the University of Marburg in Germany was able to isolate it from 25,000 litres (!) of policemen's urine, that testosterone was chemically identified and named. By 1935, a Swiss team of scientists had managed to synthesise it from cholesterol (just as your body does every day) in a lab, and there was no looking back from there.

Testosterone significantly improves bone density, muscle mass and endurance, so it's very tempting to use it in places where those things make a big difference to the result. By the 1950s, Russian weightlifters were being dosed with anabolic steroids based on testosterone to improve performance. By the mid-1960s, steroid use had spread way beyond Olympic athletes into a large subculture of body builders, professional sportspeople and some amateur athletes. The drugs first became widely, albeit illegally, available to the average teenager in the mid-1970s, and had reached mass-market proportions by the late 1980s.

The release of the *Rambo* and *Conan* movies in the early 1980s both encouraged and reflected what was by then becoming a culture of widespread steroid use among young men. By 1988, the use of steroids was becoming so problematic that the US Government upgraded the crime of distribution of anabolic steroids from a misdemeanour to a felony, and in 1989, the Monitoring the Future study (see page 95 and graph on page 145) of US teens added questions about steroid use to its annual questionnaire. In 1991 the US Government added steroids to the list of dangerous regulated substances.

Meanwhile, popular culture kept up the pressure on young men. Boys were told in no uncertain terms they were supposed to look like Arnold Schwarzenegger, and many of them heard the message loud and clear. Steroids provided a handy shortcut to muscled glory. Anabolic steroid use exploded in the 1990s but then pulled back in the early 21st century as significantly greater penalties for distribution were legislated and US drug enforcement agencies had more and more success shutting down illegal factories. But it was only a temporary decline. Offshore manufacturing and new testosterone-like drugs have stepped in to fill the hole left by domestic supply in both the United States and Australia, and their popularity has recently taken off again among gen Z teens. This is perhaps not surprising given those teens are likely to be addicted to social approval by their social media apps. Having a sixpack is just as Instagram-worthy as having a sick new outfit. Steroids are to body image as credit cards are to shopping – a shortcut to approval.

The association between steroid use and completed suicides is just a theory. It may have nothing to do with it, but what little work has been done in the area so far appears to confirm that there is cause for concern. One larger study of 800 gay men attending gyms in London suggested that suicidal thoughts are twice as common in steroid users as in non-users. The evidence is circumstantial, but if there weren't already many excellent reasons, it's good enough for me to make sure my kids don't remotely contemplate the possibility of steroid-fuelled shortcuts to an Instagram-worthy body. Adolescent boys are hyped enough on testosterone already. They certainly don't need to add extra in the form of steroids.

What can a parent do?

While it will definitely help to cut back on your child's screen use, when they've entered the domain of eating disorders, self-harm and suicidal thoughts, it's *vitally important to seek professional help* for your child.

Summary

- As with most things in the human body, pushing a system out of balance will cascade through to other disease states. With addiction, the cascade of consequences can include eating disorders, self-harm and suicide.

- A normal person will find food attractive up until the point their body has sufficient nutrients and energy to survive. At that point, serotonin and GABA are released, happiness ensues, and dopamine is suppressed.
- In an anorexic, that dopamine set point is too low and they will stop eating before the body has sufficient food. In a bulimic, that set point is too high and they will keep eating well beyond that set point.
- So far there are few effective treatments for eating disorders but family therapy is showing signs of being effective for adolescents.
- Kids self-harm for two primary reasons. They do it because they're depressed or anxious, or because they're part of a minority and feel the whole community is discriminating against them. Given the disproportionate prevalence of anxiety and depression in teenage girls, they're four times more likely to self-harm than teenage boys.
- Most girls who attempt suicide have previously self-harmed. But most boys have not. Boys are significantly more impulsive, and it may be that testosterone is to blame. This will not be helped by a boy adding artificial testosterone, steroids, to his system.

PART II

Caring for and Feeding a Garden-Variety Teenager

Being the Parent of an Adolescent

Adolescence is a unique time in human development. Once a child enters puberty, they're an adult under construction, and that building work isn't complete until they hit their mid-20s. During that time they're setting up their brains for the rest of their life. They're working out how to interact with other humans appropriately. They're learning what they find rewarding. And they're finding out what they fear. To allow all this experimentation to happen, the brain takes the brakes off the reward and punishment pathways. Puberty turns your darling little dodgem car into a Formula 1 racing car with dodgy brakes. If it's a boy, it also installs a nitro-booster and a hair-trigger accelerator. The controls will get less tricky throughout puberty, but it's critical that they learn how to drive their powerful new car well, because it's the one they'll be driving for the rest of their lives.

At the risk of straining the analogy to breaking point, think of the decade of adolescence as 100 laps of a very difficult racetrack with lots of sharp bends. A parent's job during that race is to be the adult supervision to the L-plater in the driver's seat. Their task is to show their teen where the road is, remind them how they handled the hairpin bend last time and stop them crashing into the barriers in flames. If you've done a reasonable job with parenting them as a child, your about-to-be-teenager knows how to drive a dodgem at 5 kilometres per hour with rubber bumpers in a 20 by 20 metre arena. They know exactly how their body works and how to get it to do just about anything they want with minimal risk of harm. But when they enter puberty, you're taking them out onto the racetrack in a very tricky racing car that can do 370 kilometres per hour. Get ready to have lots of animated conversations about how fast they're going and where the edge of the road is and shouldn't they be braking now – *now* – NOW!

Just to make things extra fun, the owner of the racetrack has installed massively distracting and addictive flashing billboards all around the track, and you'll need to be extra vigilant to ensure your teen driver is watching the road and not the billboards, or you'll both be having a high-speed conversation with a crash barrier. Oh, and yours isn't the only kid on this racetrack. There are hundreds of others, and they're all driving cars that are just as powerful, just as unpredictable, and with equally lousy braking systems and poorly installed nitro-boosters. So a critical part of what your child must learn is how to account for the behaviour of those other cars while learning to drive their own. And to avoid looking too long at the flashing billboards. Don't let anyone tell you this is easy. To make things just a little bit harder, there's no shortage of experts telling you how to do it, and almost all of them are wrong.

Bear with me for a minute while we look at how attitudes to parenting have changed over time and how we ended up here, with our kids ruling the roost.

A history of parenting theories

Before the Industrial Revolution, nobody thought much about children or adolescence. Agricultural subsistence living meant that every able body was needed to keep the family alive. There was no time for navel-gazing about the psyche of adults, much less kids, or for worries about addiction to anything. Pleasure was hard enough to come by once, let alone enough times to become addicted. There was no porn, there was just sex. There was no danger porn, there was just danger. And there was no approval porn, there was just social acceptance. There were only a few short-cuts to pleasure – alcohol, and eventually nicotine and sugar – but they were hard to obtain in any serious quantity for most of the population. Testosterone was a very good thing because it meant the boys could work harder and longer, and oxytocin was a good thing too, because it bound groups together, normalised helpful group behaviour and meant people looked after those they knew, whether they were related to them or not.

The only rules for parenting were that you raised your kids the way you were raised. No one else had any insight into what you did or any business telling you how to do it. The Industrial Revolution changed all that. Factories needed labour, and that drove a clumping together of humanity around those factories, which in turn produced the technology to make it possible for large numbers of people to live very close together. As factories and technological demands grew, it became necessary for the labour to have skills, so towards the end of the 19th century we invented schools. For the first time ever, large numbers of children were herded together under the control of someone other than their parents. The welfare of the child and how it was raised increasingly became a community concern rather than the exclusive domain of the parent. Children were becoming an important and large component of industrial society, and so the 'science' of child psychology was invented to tell us more about them. After its beginnings in Germany, psychology soon spread throughout the industrialised world.

'The only rules for parenting were that you raised your kids the way you were raised.'

G. Stanley Hall's adolescent psychology, 1904

In 1876, William James, a philosophy lecturer, taught the first US class in psychology at Harvard University. One of the people in the class was G. Stanley Hall, a doctoral student who went on to be the first person to be awarded a doctorate in psychology in America. In 1887, Hall founded *the American Journal of Psychology*, and five years later was the first president of the American Psychological Association, which he remained for the next three decades. Hall helped found the child study movement of the late 19th century, and supervised the 1896 study 'Of peculiar and exceptional children', a collection of case studies of unusual children. The movement was a loose collaboration of parents interested in new ways of parenting, educators interested in possibilities for better education, and psychologists interested in the way children think. In 1904, Hall published the collected results and theories that came out of the child-study movement in the first ever book on adolescent psychology, a 1300-page two-volume page-turner called *Adolescence: Its Psychology and Its Relations to Physiology, Anthropology, Sociology, Sex, Crime, Religion and Education.* Yep, that's right, he didn't want to leave any stone unturned.

Many of Hall's observations about 14–24-year-olds – what he called adolescents – still ring true more than a century after they were published. He noted that it's a time of 'storm and stress' that gives way to stable equilibrium in adulthood. Hall reported that depressed mood occurred more often in adolescence than in other ages, quoting a study that concluded 'The curve of despondency starts at eleven, rises steadily and rapidly till fifteen, culminates at seventeen, then falls steadily till twenty-three.' He said that the causes of this despondency were the teenagers' new reasoning skills creating an oversensitivity to potentially negative events at home, with friends and at school; an over-absorption with self-criticism; a suspicion of being disliked by others; and 'hopeless love'. After noting that there's a significant increase in criminal activity, particularly among boys between the ages of 12 and 20, he says that 'a period of semicriminality is normal for all healthy boys'. He put this down to the adolescent's need for excitement, saying, 'At no time of life is the love of excitement so strong as during the season of the accelerated development of adolescence.' He said that it's a time when both pleasure and pain are intensely felt, and it drives a new sense of enjoyment of the sensation itself for its own sake.

Hall even nailed the link to addiction, saying, '[Y]outh must have excitement, and if this be not at hand in the form of moral and intellectual enthusiasms, it is more prone . . . to be sought for in sex or in drink.' The kids of 1904 might not have had social media and computer games, but Hall slammed their equivalents, saying 'penny dreadfuls' (trashy adventure stories published in weekly parts, sold for a penny and aimed at young working-class boys) inflamed the mind to portray crime as glamorous. He didn't let teenage girls off the hook either, accusing them of what he called 'relational aggression' – gossip, spreading rumours and excluding others from the group. He said a teenage girl will use her 'tongue in place of her fists'.

Adolescence was a Victorian-era book and so had some pretty weird views on sex, masturbation and menstruation, and a tendency to stray into Christian moralising, but putting that aside, much of what it says could be applied today with almost no modification. All Hall's theories were driven by an understanding that biology calls the shots and a parent's job is to understand that and respond appropriately, knowing it's a phase that will pass. Hall knew that adolescence is a period of intense development of the social brain, which makes us prone to anxiety, depression, risk-taking and addiction, and the cure is to acknowledge that and set hard boundaries. If the field of adolescent psychology had stopped where it started in 1904, we'd probably all be a lot better off today. Unfortunately, it didn't.

'All Hall's theories were driven by an understanding that biology calls the shots.'

The hardline approach of John B. Watson, 1928

The mass upheavals of the First World War changed a lot about how modern Western society operated. Middle-class women started working outside the home, and in most developed countries women gained the right to vote. The massive inequities in income and wealth that had dominated the half-millennium until then were blown away by the reset of the Great War, and political movements sprang up with the aim of increasing the wealth and income of all the people rather than a privileged few. In Russia this resulted in a bloody revolution that saw the birth of Soviet communism, but it was no less revolutionary in the rest of the developed world. In the West, the middle class, income taxes, public education and subsidised healthcare became notions whose time had come. As technology improved, so too did medical science. The reasons behind childhood death were gradually understood and addressed. Suddenly a lot more kids were making it to school and staying there a lot longer when they did. The mass state-funded secular education of children that had started a few decades earlier became a widespread phenomenon.

In 1928, the first bestselling parenting advice book came out – *Psychological Care of Infant and Child*, written by American psychologist and advertising executive John B. Watson. Watson was famous for founding the behaviourist view of psychology and ultimately infamous for his Little Albert experiments (see my book *Toxic People*), which involved making a nine-month-old baby terrified of things that aren't inherently dangerous (such as fluffy toys). Behaviourism is focused on the prediction and control of human behaviour, and CBT, one of the most popular psychological treatments (see page 135), is based on it.

Watson's parenting book was written with the help of his lab assistant in the Little Albert experiments, his mistress and, eventually, second wife, Rosalie Rayner. Watson's alcoholic father and a bible-thumping fundamentalist Christian mother raised him with a Christian rod of steel. She desperately wanted him to become a preacher, but he became an atheist instead. The book's central theme is that children should be treated as small adults. It took the boundary-setting advice developed by Hall and went ballistic with it. Watson felt there were dangers in allowing too much motherly love, and advocated for a more transactional and casual relationship between parent and child.

Watson felt that every aspect of a child was imprinted by their parents and that biology played no part. His advice to parents was, 'Let your behavior always be objective and kindly firm . . . Never hug and kiss them, never let them sit in your lap . . . Shake hands with them in the morning. Give them a pat on the head if they have made an extraordinarily good job of a difficult task.' He felt children were modelling clay to be moulded into adult shape by discipline and obedience. He demanded that parents never show affection lest it spoil the child.

'Watson demanded that parents never show affection lest it spoil the child.'

This book paid no regard to the work done by Hall on the biological drivers of adolescence, and advocated a very hardline approach to parenting, of exactly the same sort that had spectacularly failed to ensure he became a priest. The book seemed to be telling parents what they wanted to hear, because it was wildly popular and flew off the shelves between the wars. A child of the generation before the baby boomers, raised in the 1930s and 1940s, was likely parented according to this 'spare the rod and spoil the child' model.

This, of course, inspired a backlash against strictness when these people became parents themselves.

Dr Benjamin Spock's child-centred approach, 1946

By the end of the Second World War, the children raised using the authoritarian Watson methods were becoming parents themselves. They were ready to hear a more modern, more scientific message about how to parent their children, and Dr Benjamin Spock delivered in spades. Spock was a medical doctor specialising in children (i.e. a paediatrician) and a lecturer in paediatrics at Cornell University in the United States. He was the first ever paediatrician to study psychoanalysis, a branch of psychology founded by Austrian neurologist Sigmund Freud and based on treating psychological disorders using a dialogue between the patient and the 'analyst'.

Spock's 1946 book *Common Sense Book of Baby and Child Care* was written as a counterargument to the rigid child rearing methods of the preceding decades, which he felt were cruel and ignored the emotional needs of the child. It was an instant bestseller. Half a million copies were sold in its first six months, and it went on to become one of the bestselling books of all time, with more than 50 million sold at the time of Spock's death in 1998. During the 20th century, one copy of Spock's book was sold for every first-born child in the United States.

Spock encouraged parents to treat their children as individuals and listen to what the children wanted. He focused on telling parents the psychological reasons behind why a child was behaving the way it was and allowing them to make their own decisions about how to deal with the behaviour. For example, he explained that one-year-olds like to explore the world around them, and suggested that parents accommodate that psychological need by making sure the house is safe for exploration. Watson no doubt would have suggested leaving the child in the cot.

Spock's was a message postwar mothers had time to apply. In the United States in 1900, it took 60 hours a week to prepare meals, do the laundry and clean the average family home. By 1950 that figure had halved to just 30 hours. Household appliances, disposable nappies, smaller families and the long postwar economic boom meant parents (mostly mothers back then) had much more time to fuss over their children, and Dr Spock's easy-to-read manual was right there telling them how to fuss.

Much of Spock's analysis was based on the work of Freud, and so he felt that frightening a child about things like toilet-training or sex would lead to the development of anxiety, or 'neuroses' as Freud called them. Spock advocated a softer, gentler, more time-consuming, more permissive approach. Rather than punishing disobedience, he suggested talking to the child and understanding the cause of their aberrant behaviour so that the parent could compensate for what might have been the cause.

Having said that, by modern standards, Spock's book wasn't overly permissive. It just felt revolutionary in comparison to Watson. He wasn't, for example, against spanking. He said it could help clear the air for parent and child, and was preferable to a prolonged bout of disapproval. Spock still advocated limits on how much free expression to tolerate. He later said, for example, 'Moderate strictness – in the sense of requiring good manners, prompt obedience, orderliness – is not harmful to children so long as the parents are basically kind and so long as the children are growing up happy and friendly.'

Spock's discussion of adolescence is very thin and essentially amounts to an observation that teens will be self-centred rebels who are anxious about their appearance. He says they'll try to push the boundaries as they figure out how to be adults, and he suggests that parents talk to other parents with children the same age, find out what reasonable rules should look like, set them and stick to them. The important bit of that being that they consistently stick to the rules they set. Spock says teens won't like the rules but will secretly appreciate that they're there.

'Spock suggests that parents set reasonable rules and stick to them.'

I was raised by baby-boomer parents who were very much of the Spock-mindset. I have no idea if they ever even read Spock, but it seemed to be how every child of the late 1960s was brought up. They recalled being raised under a much stricter hand, but were much more permissive when it came to my sister and I. They were not above a spanking when a rule was broken persistently but it was an exception not an everyday occurrence – the rule breaking and the punishment, that is. We were permitted a lot of latitude but it was broadly in line with what most of our peers were allowed. That being said, no usually did mean no. Negotiation and cajoling was not a thing with my parents. Of course, they didn't have to contend with a house full of addictive devices.

A child-centred free-for-all, 1970s to now

Sociologists call societies that favour tight-knit community groups 'collective cultures'. Societies at the other end of the spectrum are 'individualist cultures'. Before the Industrial Revolution, almost every society in the world would have been classified as a collective culture. Individualistic cultures encourage competitiveness, self-reliance, independence, and temporary or short-lived relationships with no allegiance to anyone other than direct and close relatives such as parents and children. Collective cultures foster subservience to the greater good of the group. Individuals are encouraged to work for the betterment of the group and not themselves. Marriages are usually arranged to unite groups, divorces are rare and, in the workplace, promotion is usually based on membership of a group rather than individual qualities.

Between 1967 and 1973, Geert Hofstede from the personnel department of IBM International conducted an extraordinarily detailed survey of cultural differences in the more than 70 countries in which the company operated. He clustered the results along various axes, one of which he called individualism versus collectivism. The study has since been continuously updated by Geert and many other researchers, and now provides a comprehensive database of the relative level of individualism in more than 100 countries. It reveals that the most individualistic culture in the world is, wait for it . . . the United States, with a relative score of 91 out of 100. Second is Australia (90), third is the United Kingdom (89) and tied for fourth are Canada, the Netherlands and Hungary, all with a score of 80.

At the other end of the scale were the most collectivist countries. The least individualistic country is Guatemala (6), followed by El Salvador (8), Panama (11), Venezuela (12) and Colombia (13). In these countries, the community is a much higher priority than the individual. Harmony within the group to which you belong is paramount. The individual's relationship with the group is always a higher priority than the needs of the individual or any other group.

Even a glance at those lists suggests a very strong correlation between these individualism scores and the wealth of the nation.

Wealthy nations tend to be more individualistic and poor nations tend to be more collective. It's probably no coincidence that as Australia progressed through one of the greatest economic booms it has ever experienced since the end of the Second World War, we became increasingly focused on the needs and right of the individual. Spock's theories were emblematic of the rise of individualism in Western society after the end of the Second World War. The rights and needs of the individual were becoming more important, and the needs of the community secondary. The basic unit of society was changing from the family – a cluster that kept itself to itself and controlled its kids – to the individual, where each person, no matter their age, had rights that must be indulged.

Spock was often accused of being the father of the permissive flower-power culture that arose during the 1960s and 1970s. But it seems more likely that the popularity of his book was just a symptom of a shift towards individuality that was occurring anyway. He didn't start the fire and, if anything, his book just crystallised parents' desire for a different life for their kids from the hardships they endured. He was merely suggesting a more child-centred approach as a desperately needed antidote to Watson's regimented prison-camp ideals. Spock later said of his work, 'I didn't want to encourage permissiveness, but rather to relax rigidity.' It may not have been his intention, but his massively popular book did set theories of parenting on a path towards higher levels of permissiveness. Compared to their parents, gen X were raised as spoilt brats. Compared to gen Z, they were raised in high-security lockdown.

Spock's books continue to be sold to this day, but after the 1970s he was just part of the increasingly crowded field of parenting advice books. The inevitable consequence of the trend towards individualism is that we can't even agree on who our gurus are. We're all so special we need our own guru. From the 1980s onward there hasn't been a dominant 'expert' in parenting like Spock. Instead, the number of parenting authors has grown exponentially, and the types of advice offered look as varied as the 'experts' offering them. Penelope Leach's 2 million–copy 1977 bestseller *Your Baby and Child: From Birth to Age Five* expands Spock's theme of child-centred parenting and asks the gen X parent to 'listen to your child and your own feelings . . . to make things right'. But the wildly popular *Supernanny* TV show, which ran from 2004 to 2012, harked back to more Watsonian times, with the use of the 'naughty step' and much finger-wagging at permissive parents. Still, there has been a prevailing theme of indulgence of the needs and wants of the child.

'We can't even agree anymore on who our parenting gurus are. We're all so special we need our own guru.'

The modern parent

This is all set against a background of rapidly increasing female participation in the workforce. The 30 hours a week required to run a house in 1950 is now down to 14, and the percentage of women working full-time has risen from 33 in 1964 to almost 60 now. The increase has been even more dramatic for married women, leaping from 24.5 per cent in 1964 to 62.3 per cent in 2013. Either as a cause or a consequence of that increased workforce participation (enabled to no small extent by the pill), Australian families are likely to have about half as many children as a family in the 1960s. A woman living in Australia in 1921 could expect to have 3.1 children in her lifetime. During the Depression that dropped to 2.2, but climbed steadily again after the Second World War to peak at 3.5 in 1961. In June 1961, the contraceptive pill was released (see below) and immediately began to affect the birthrate. It has plummeted since then and now sits around 1.78 and heading south. These trends are approximately the same in all Western nations, with the only real variations being due to differences in immigration levels.

Supernanny may be great entertainment, with its weekly trick of turning the tantrum-chucker into the helpful bed-maker, but it's not representative of most of the advice dished out in parenting self-help books. The modern parent is required not only to respond to, but to anticipate, their child's every need or want. They must also ensure their children are academically and athletically successful while attaining peak popularity. They need to provide their child with access to all the most desirable experiences and activities, especially ones the parents are told will give their child a competitive advantage down the road. They must protect their child from every possible negative outcome. If the child forgets their homework, they must take time off work and drive it to school for them. If the child gets in an argument at school, they must publicly declare war on the school and the other child's parents. And most importantly of all, they must be hypervigilant to threats to their child's self-esteem. They must fly to the defence of the child if any errant coach, other child, other parent or teacher suggests their child is anything less than perfect. And they need to accomplish all of this without ever exposing their child to conflict or disharmony inside or outside the home.

Lizzie and I had our first child in 1995. He was not a sleeper. The paediatrician had given us a book that was extremely child-centred. A paediatrician was, after all, the baby's doctor, not ours. It said that the baby should be allowed to go to sleep on us and then transferred to his cot. If he woke, then we should do it again. So, that is what we did. It meant that we would be up every two hours, pacing the halls trying to coerce him back to sleep. By five months, it had almost killed us both. Luckily, Lizzie encountered an old-school Maternal and Child Health Nurse during a baby health check-up. Despite all the literature telling her and us that it was almost a capital crime to let a child cry, she encouraged Lizzie to try controlled crying. This amounted to methodically ignoring the crying child, after checking there was no physical reason for them to be upset. Lizzie and I tried it and – glory of glories – on the very first night it worked! He slept and, even better, so did we. We have never looked back and the five kids that followed him owe their existence to that chance meeting with a clued-up nurse. But time and time again I encounter parents who cannot let their child cry and they are paying dearly for it.

The modern parent can't point to a parenting bible like Spock or Watson and know the correct answer to every parenting problem. They hear different advice every time they turn on the TV or check their Facebook feed. But whether it's an Asian 'tiger mother' advising they push their children to achieve so their self-esteem is founded in tangible skills, or other experts saying self-esteem must be developed first so accomplishments can follow, they all focus on self-esteem – how a child feels about themselves.

The brands and the gurus all have different tweaks, but the undeniable trend is to more child-centred parenting, in line with the societal trend towards higher individualism. In a society where every individual is unique, every child must by definition be 'special'. The child has made the transition from workhorse toiling for the greater good of its family in the 19th century to a special and fragile gift that must be protected and promoted. Children are no longer a robust and critical part of the economy of the household, but rather the expression of everything the parents would want for themselves and a badge of honour in Western societies, which are finding it increasingly difficult to produce children.

CLAYTON'S STRICTNESS

Most modern parents, when asked, regard themselves as being strict. A recent nationally representative survey of US parents asked them to rate their levels of strictness. Almost half (45 per cent) rated themselves as strict, 36 per cent said they were moderately strict and just 19 per cent said they were permissive. But it's a very benign type of strictness. The favourite methods for shaping behaviour were praise and setting a good example (both 86 per cent), instructing children in appropriate behaviour (77 per cent), and discussing bad behaviour at length (61 per cent). The second least favoured method was spanking, with just 22 per cent of parents saying they'd spanked more than rarely. Even less favoured than spanking was 'being emotionally distant', with almost no parents prepared to use it regularly. Modern parenting is the kind of 'strict' you'd select if you were a two-year-old choosing your own punishment.

Parental confidence

The child-centred approach starts well before you're telling little Timmy or Tammy they can have the sweets because it's the only way to stop them chucking a fit in the supermarket. A recent study of UK parenting methods found that 70 per cent of UK mothers feed their babies when they want to be fed (demand feeding), a further 23 per cent tried to feed to a schedule but couldn't, and just 7 per cent actually managed to feed to a schedule. Parents raised in a child-centred culture find it almost impossible to say no to a baby wanting to be fed, and this can have disastrous effects on their personal well-being and confidence as a parent. Mothers who feed to a schedule are 55 per cent more likely to be getting enough sleep at eight weeks and 62 per cent more likely at eight months. At eight months a mother who fed to a schedule will be 18 times (!) more confident in her parenting abilities than a mother who fed on demand, and will be 17 times more likely to be enjoying motherhood. And those significant differences in confidence and skill appear to be permanent, with the comparative rates remaining the same when the researchers checked in again at three years nine months.

Studies like this will sometimes produce results that suggest something a parent does doubles the chance of some favourable outcome. And that might be reported as the best thing since sliced bread. But this study says a parent is *18 times* more confident in their ability as a parent. I can't emphasise enough how monumental that result is. The degree of confidence a parent has in their ability to do their job (of parenting their child) is massively and unequivocally related to their ability to say no to a child demanding to be fed. Setting boundaries and expectations is important from the very start, and the earlier a parent starts the easier it will be every time after that. Don't worry if you didn't schedule feed: it's never too late to make up for lost time. But every minute you delay teaching your kids who's the rule-maker and who's the rule-follower will make it that little bit harder.

Babies are learning machines, and one of the most important skills they learn first is how to manipulate their parents and siblings into providing what they want more quickly. That makes them sound like they're truly evil but that's not quite accurate. It's more that they're not even evil. They have no sense of right and wrong, they just have needs and no concern for your welfare. If you think that makes them sound psychopathic, you wouldn't be far from the truth. The science tells us that we don't develop empathy, the ability to feel what others feel and adjust our behaviour accordingly, until we're well into our fourth year.

'One of the most important skills babies learn first is how to manipulate their parents.'

To a baby's brain, you're a lever to be pushed for them to obtain a rewarding surge of dopamine. If screaming at you in the middle of the night gets them fed (which in turn produces a satisfying surge of serotonin) then that's what they'll do. If screaming at you when they're left alone gets them picked up and hugged (and a lovely surge of oxytocin) then that's what they'll do. If screaming at you in the supermarket gets them a sugar hit, then that's what they'll do. If screaming at you gets them access to your phone so they can play games, then that's what they'll do. Every time we respond to demands for reward, we reinforce the child's learning about how to obtain that reward again.

Demand feeding is just the first in a long line of tests of a parent's abilities to set reasonable boundaries and stick to them. Modern parents have convinced themselves that praising good behaviour is the same as stopping bad behaviour, and that saying no to a child is something to be avoided at all costs. It's Spock without the boundaries and it's a recipe for addicted, depressed and anxious teenagers. Scheduled feeding – or a later equivalent – might not stop you having a fight with your teen about whether they get to use their phone in bed at 11 pm, but it will probably mean the fight is less brutal – and you will win.

GET GOOD AT SAYING NO

Ben Caunt is a Sydney clinical psychologist who specialises in treating teens affected by anxiety, depression, self-harm and suicidal ideation. He says most of his patients are heavy users of screens and a small percentage could be diagnosed as suffering an addictive dependency: the clear majority spend most of their free time on tablets, phones or computers. He believes that many of the applications being used by his patients are purposely designed to create addictive behaviours. The girls seem to mostly use social apps and the boys mostly play games and use the social apps.

He thinks it would be a big call to say the screens cause anxiety and depression but he believes they can definitely make it worse. He says a child's dependency on screens can develop as a product of parents failing to set screen usage limits from a young age. A lot of his work with families is aimed at helping parents take back control but he says that if a teenager already has the reins and has never experienced a parent enforcing boundaries, it can be an almost impossible task. An older teen will fight back and fight back hard. He believes parents have to get good setting limits early and the earlier the better.

What the science tells us

Back to my racing car analogy. Modern parenting advice amounts to telling you to let your young children drive their dodgem cars on the freeway (and anywhere else that takes their fancy) while you run ahead stopping traffic and then mildly pointing out to them that things might be easier if they drive on the legal side of the road. Then, when they get their Formula 1 racing car in puberty, you get to keep doing that, only much, much faster. In fact, so fast that often you arrive at the scene of the latest accident far too late to protect them from anything.

The modern ubiquity of the MRI machine has spawned interest in the neurobiology of childhood. It's where the fascination with cognitive improvement comes from. You know the type of thing – playing Mozart to pregnant tummies (it doesn't work, by the way) and other activities aimed at stimulating neural pathways in early childhood. It's popular because it also provides an escape route for parents. It's not your fault your child is lazy or sullen or hyper-active or disobedient, that's just the way their brain is wired, but don't worry there's a drug that'll fix it.

But there's a much more useful application for all that science. Thanks to it, we increasingly know exactly what's going on in the teenage brain and how to change it or at least accommodate it. The suggestions in the sections that follow are based on the research set out in Part I. They're ideas for preventative maintenance of your children's Formula 1 racing car, and tips for showing them how to control it. They're not advice for how to deal with the accident once it's already happened. For that you need professionals in acute care. The advice in the following sections is for the vast majority of kids.

Summary

- Before 1900, the only rules for parenting were that you did it the way you were raised and the purpose was to produce productive humans as fast as possible.
- Around the turn of the 20th century, we invented teenagers and the science of the time precisely nailed the things we should watch out for: depression, risk-taking and a desire for addictive behaviour and substances. Then we completely forgot all of that and got ourselves in a right pickle. Demand feeding is just the first in a long line of tests of a parent's abilities to set reasonable boundaries and stick to them. Modern parents have convinced themselves that praising good behaviour is the same as stopping bad behaviour, and that saying no to a child is something to be avoided at all costs.
- This has primed a generation of parents to simply let addictive behaviours slide, while giving the marketers an audience with no boundaries (and no one to enforce them, even if there were).

Crime and Punishment

Our kids learn to sense their environment and move around in it up to the age of two. That motor-sensory phase of development is a major structural design period for their brain. During it they're learning which things are worth moving towards – food and hugs, for example – and which things should really be avoided, such as bad-tasting or painful things. Parents have no problem setting boundaries that relate to safety during this stage. They go to extraordinary lengths to ensure their house is safe for the toddler to explore. Electrical outlets are plugged up so baby doesn't try to see how exciting shoving a fork in them can be. Stairs are fenced off so baby doesn't try to see if it can fly. Poisonous substances like cleaning fluids aren't left lying around within reach. And sharp corners on furniture are covered so baby doesn't impale itself while learning to stand and walk. When they're out of the house, they ensure baby is safely cocooned in the car, strapped up in the pram in the supermarket, and generally never out of the parent's sight. As the baby grows more able, some of these boundaries and precautions are slowly relaxed, but they're never completely removed. Parents simply don't drop their two-year-old kids off next to a freeway and tell them to entertain themselves until they come back from doing the shopping.

When that child hits puberty, it's entering a much less obvious but no less important phase of exploration, learning and development. In this phase the boundaries are absolutely critical, because the consequences of failing to enforce them can be just as disastrous and just as predictable as the consequences of leaving a two-year-old to play on the freeway. Just like children, teens are wired, biochemically, to seek out new, rewarding experiences. But unlike children, their sensitivity to reward has been massively amplified and their impulse control has been turned off. Adult levels of reward sensitivity and impulse control would stop a 30-year-old from driving a car at 150 kilometres per hour up a suburban street. And it would stop a 30-year-old posting a nude selfie on a social app. In both cases, they'd think through the consequences, weigh the risk versus the potential reward, and decide it wasn't worth it.

But a teenager can't weigh the risk appropriately. To them the reward to be obtained from the risk of driving a fast car or the approval for their steaming bod far outweighs any potential downside, and so they do it. The role of the adult is to be the risk-control module, to temporarily provide impulse control until the adolescent's brain is developed enough to do it on its own. That risk-control module is called 'setting (and enforcing) boundaries'.

A parent can't change the chemical wiring that's making their teenager want to test those boundaries, but they can make sure that when they're tested they hold firm, or stretch only when a teen shows capacity to manage the increased freedom. It's what a parent does when they gradually allow more freedom to their toddler learning to walk, and, at base, the process is no different for teenagers who are learning to be human.

'Teens are wired to seek out new, rewarding experiences, but they can't weigh the risk appropriately.'

Teenagers need rules

'Boundaries' sounds like something we need a psychologist to develop and interpret, so I prefer the term 'rules'. Whether they're the rules of Monopoly, the rules for driving (called laws) or rules for teenagers (called boundaries), they all have the same basic features. They're clear, they state what's *not* allowed, they outline any exceptions, and they indicate the consequences of not observing them. A rule about speed limits, for example, tells us that if our speed is greater than the limit we may be fined. The only way that won't happen is if we're not caught or if our circumstances fall within a small set of exceptions, such as driving an emergency vehicle with its siren on. Enforcement is critical. If it became generally known that speed limits weren't enforced, people would ignore them.

The other critical thing about a rule is that the person it affects must know about it before they do something that will involve the rule. This is why retrospective laws, that is those that make something illegal years after the event, are so repugnant. It just feels wrong to make something a crime that wasn't at the time you did it. A law that allowed someone to be fined for doing 80 in a 60 zone that was an 80 zone at the time they did it would be irrational and unfair. Rules that are unreasonable are more likely to be broken, even if they're known in advance. If there was a law that all cars must drive at walking speed at all times, drivers would likely regard that as manifestly unreasonable and would very often break the rule. Law-breaking would be so frequent that punishment could never keep up with the crime, and the rule or the punishment would have almost no deterrent effect.

The same basic principles apply to setting rules for teenagers. The rule must be clear, reasonable and unambiguous as to the consequences of breaking it. Exactly what's being prohibited must be crystal clear *before* it happens, as must any permitted exceptions. The reasonableness of a rule must take into account demonstrated ability to comply. A teenager is a moving target. The things they'll want to do will change over time, and the rules will need to take into account how well they've complied with previous versions of the rules. A 17-year-old will expect different rules from a 12-year-old, and if you've done your job right, they should get them.

'Rules for teens must be clear, reasonable and unambiguous as to the consequences of breaking them.'

There's no rule book for teenagers, but remember that the teenage brain is an adult brain under construction, and the rules you set will have a significant part to play not only in keeping them safe but how that adult interacts with the world. A two-year-old learns important lessons about how their body works, what's dangerous and what's rewarding because of the rules you set for them. If you had left them on the freeway at the age of two and they had survived, they'd still have learned without your rules, but you might not like the kid who learned their parents can't be trusted. Similarly, there's a big spectrum of rules you could apply in teenage years. You could insist that your teenager work 12 hours a day cleaning your house then, like Cinderella, go to bed without supper if they missed a spot. Or you could let them do whatever they want while you just provide free room and board. Each system will design a very specific type of adult, and you might not like either of them. The first method might create a repressed, resentful, angry adult who's just as likely to knife you in your sleep as shake your hand. The second might create a severely addicted, anxious and depressed adult to whom you provide free room and board for the rest of their life.

Setting and enforcing rules

I'll cover some specific rules in the sections that follow, but in general rules should cover these seven key areas:

1. access to addictive devices
2. access to addictive substances and behaviours
3. access to dangerous activities, such as driving
4. contribution to the household
5. sleep, including rules about bedtime and curfews
6. friendships
7. relationships and sex.

Every family will have different ideas about where to set their limits in each of these categories and what the consequences will be for breaching those limits, but an absolutely vital component of any of these rules is that there be *consequences*. No consequences means no rule.

The consequence will vary according to the nature of the breach. If it's too harsh, it will encourage the child to believe you're irrational and will increase their incentive to be more devious, to avoid being caught next time. If they're too light, they'll have no deterrent effect. The consequence for a breach must be known ahead of time, must be proportionate and must *always* be applied. It's also good to have some upside for compliance that the teen is

SOME WORKED EXAMPLES OF RULES AND CONSEQUENCES

Two-year-old

Rule: You must eat your peas.

Consequence: If you don't eat your peas, they'll be served to you at every meal until you do.

Upside: If you do eat your peas every night this week, you'll receive pudding on Friday.

16-year-old

Rule: You must be home by 9 pm on a school night.

Consequence: If you're late, your curfew will be 7 pm and will remain so until you've proved that you can abide by a curfew for one month. If you breach the new curfew, you won't be permitted out on a school night.

Upside: If you abide by this rule for a year, we'll make it 10 pm next year.

likely to value, such as loosening the restriction. None of this is rocket surgery. It's the same motivational science that works on two-year-olds – and you.

Be consistent

It's important that you stick to your guns. Everybody will try to bend the rules or have them not apply to them. A baby will do this by screaming at you. A teenager will chuck a tantrum or freeze you out, or try to manipulate you into submission. But this will be less likely if you've trained them from the start to recognise that your rules are non-negotiable.

It's never too late to harden up. Your teen's negotiations should be about as successful as you trying to convince a cop not to give you a speeding ticket. If you cave in to pressure – and there will be pressure – to change the rules or the consequences, you'll be telling your teen that you don't really mean it. Once they believe that, the call of their hyperactive reward system and barely functioning impulse control will loom very large in relation to your puny and highly negotiable rules.

'You must select consequences that you can actually implement and are prepared to enforce.'

Consistency in enforcement is also vitally important. You must select consequences that you can actually implement and are prepared to enforce. To me, this is one of the hardest bits of parenting. You love your kids and you spend most of your waking minutes working your bottom off to make them happy, so the last thing you want to do is intentionally make them unhappy. Luckily, my wife, Lizzie, is much stronger with this than I am, and I usually just have to back her up when she cracks the whip (no, we don't own a whip). If you want your kids to stick to the rules you set, you'll occasionally have to enforce them. To do this, you must select some consequences they don't like and that you're actually prepared to stick to.

BRER RABBIT AND THE BRIARS

One of the stories I remember well from my younger days is the story of Brer (brother) Rabbit and the Tar Baby. It's from a collection of African-American folk tales published in the later 19th century. It's probably not fashionable to tell it now, but it contains an important message about punishment.

In the story, Brer Fox makes a doll from a lump of tar, dresses it and puts it by the side of the road. When Brer Rabbit comes along he greets the Tar Baby amiably but repeatedly receives no response. He's annoyed by this lack of manners and hits the Tar Baby, getting his hand stuck in the tar. The more he fights the Tar Baby to become free, the more stuck Brer Rabbit becomes.

Brer Fox reveals himself as Brer Rabbit's captor, and plans to 'bobby-cue' (barbecue) him but the tricky bunny pleads, 'I don't keer w'at you do wid me, Brer Fox, so you don't fling me in dat brier-patch. Roas' me, Brer Fox . . . but don't fling me in dat brier-patch!' (I don't care what you do with me, Brer Fox, as long you don't fling me in that briar patch. Roast me, Brer Fox, but don't fling me in the briar patch!)

The temptation to inflict the bunny's worst fear before roasting him prompts Brer Fox to do exactly that, not realising that rabbits are at home in thickets of briars. Brer Rabbit then uses the thorns to scrape off the tar and escape, crying as he does, 'Bred en bawn in a brier-patch, Brer Fox – bred en bawn in a brier-patch!'

Choose a real punishment

We fell into a Brer Rabbit trap with our eldest daughter. We'd punish her by sending her to her room without a device. Isolation had worked well on her older brothers, and so it seemed like a good punishment. It wasn't. To her, being sent to her room was like a briar patch to Brer Rabbit. As far as she was concerned, it was a nice bit of peace and quiet where she could lie on her bed and read a trashy book without being annoyed by her siblings or parents.

Don't say they'll be banned from watching telly for a week if they'd rather be on their iPad anyway, and don't say you'll spank them if the last thing you could ever do is spank your child. Choose consequences you can live with and that are actual deterrents. You'll never enjoy handing out a punishment – in fact, you'll probably hate it more than they do – but if you do it, and do it consistently, then you'll need to do it less and less.

PRIMARY CATEGORIES OF TEENAGE PUNISHMENT

Teen punishment follows the same basic rules as criminal punishment. The options are loss of privileges (prison), additional responsibilities (community service) and restitution (compensation to victims). And sometimes the best of all is natural consequences – letting the crime create its own punishment.

- **Loss of privileges**: This is the all-time favourite for most parents. It involves cutting off access to something the teen wants. Devices, telly, going out with friends. It's easy to implement, but best not to do for lengthy periods – days are better than weeks. It requires nonstop discipline from you to enforce it, and the longer it runs the less likely you'll hold to it.

- **Additional responsibilities**: Loss of privilege is a low-commitment consequence. The teen doesn't need to do anything. They're just denied something they like. Additional responsibilities steps the consequence up a notch and requires them to do something. An example might be additional duties around the house: 'For the next two weeks you'll be responsible for cleaning the bathroom.'
- **Restitution**: If the rule-breaking has a victim – for example, the culprit damaged someone else's property – then restitution should form part of the punishment. They should have to face up to what they've done, compensate the victim for their loss, and apologise to their face.
- **Natural consequences**: Some types of rule-breaking have natural consequences, and sometimes they're the best way for a child to learn. If Timmy touches the cooling stove after you've told him not to, he'll learn very quickly not to do it again. If Tammy forgets to take her homework to school after you told her to pack her bag, she'll learn that's not a good thing to do. Don't be too quick to save children from natural consequences – they're rapid learning experiences.

If there are two or more parents involved in rule enforcement, make sure you're on the same page. You must agree with all rules and consequences. If the child gets any sense you can be divided on this, they'll work you mercilessly to create doubt (and a lesser, or no, punishment). If you disagree with the other parent/s, do so in private, never within earshot of the child. Consistency is critical for effective enforcement. My policy, when a juvenile request for permission is received, is to respond with the same line my father did: 'What did your mother say?' It can save a lot of upsetting discussions down the track.

With boys, wherever possible it's good to have any punishment administered by an adult male they respect. The testosterone flooding their brain makes them fearless and completely lacking in impulse control. Testosterone doesn't care about political correctness; it's a bit of biology we share with all mammals and it determines male dominance hierarchies. Testosterone only understands one thing: brute force. Studies in apes tell us that adolescent males will obey their mothers while their mothers are bigger than them, but after that, an adult male is required for enforcement. And there's nothing in the science to suggest human primates operate any differently. An adolescent male is hyped on testosterone and feels invincible. The only thing that will make him feel any different is someone who's clearly stronger and more assertive than he is.

'Testosterone only understands one thing: brute force.'

SCREEN TIME

Cherie and Michael separated when their son Connor was just three. Connor is now 12 and has been shuttling between his parents regularly for most of his life. Cherie and Michael were both relaxed about his screen time when all he did was use one of their computers to play *Minecraft*, but since he discovered action games, things have changed dramatically for the worse. Cherie initially bought the Xbox as a solution to the increasing problem of Connor sneaking off with her phone. She figured he'd have to use it on the household TV in the lounge room and that way she'd know exactly what he was doing and could set limits. To an extent that has worked, but it is getting harder and harder to enforce her rules about access and it isn't helped by Michael having a significantly more lax approach when Connor is with him. Michael even used to play *Call of Duty* with him until Cherie found out and stated her objections to all the blood and gore. Connor switched to *Fortnite* and there is certainly less wet-work, but she thinks it is even more addictive. She finds that when she enforces bans – usually as a punishment – after two or three days his desire to play is much less intense but if he has time with his father when a ban is not enforced, he comes back impossible to deal with. Michael is not on the same page and will let him use it, even going so far as to buy him a new subscription when Cherie cancelled it. This always gets Connor hooked again and sends the family back to square one in dealing with his gaming addiction.

Stay calm

Finally, don't react in the heat of the moment. If there's been a breach of your rules, deal with it when both you and the teenager are calm and in control. Flying off the handle when your teen walks in an hour late will make things worse. Remember, they have impaired impulse control and, if they're a boy, are juiced to the eyeballs on testosterone. They know they've broken a rule and will be anxious about your response. Dopamine will have them irritable, edgy and reactive. And you, hyped on worry and anxiety about their safety, are probably not in your most balanced and cogent state either. Best to go with 'We'll talk about it in the morning' and then, in the calm light of day, have a rational discussion about rules and consequences. But make sure you do it. Don't let it slide because everything seems okay the next day.

In the sections that follow I won't tell you what the detailed parameters of the rules should be or what the consequences for breaking them should be. That will be a matter for you and your teenager to discuss. I will, however, tell you where the science suggests there really should be rules and why.

Summary

- A teenager can't weigh risks appropriately. To them the reward to be obtained from the risk of driving a fast car or the approval for their steaming bod far outweighs any potential downside.
- A parent can't change the chemical wiring that's making their teenager want to test boundaries, but they can make sure that when they're tested they hold firm, or stretch only when a teen shows capacity to manage the increased freedom.
- Rules must be clear, reasonable and unambiguous as to the consequences of breaking them.
- Rules should cover these seven key areas:
  1 access to addictive devices

2. access to addictive substances and behaviours
3. access to dangerous activities, such as driving
4. contribution to the household
5. sleep, including rules about bedtime and curfews
6. friendships
7. relationships and sex.

Addiction

The science tells us that teenagers are simultaneously ravenously seeking new experiences and uniquely susceptible to addictive substances and behaviours once they hit puberty. It also says that any addictive behaviour they take on during adolescence is likely to stick with them for life. Because addiction significantly increases the likelihood that a child will be anxious and depressed, it's vital to manage access to substances and behaviours that are potentially addictive during this phase. It's important at all points in our lives, but it's critically important during adolescence.

The first rule about dealing with addiction is – wait for it – acknowledging it's an addiction. Your kid isn't gaming or eating sugar or spending every waking minute on Snapchat because they have a character defect or because they're wilful, disobedient

'None of us is born addicted to anything.'

or rebellious. They're doing it because they're an addict. If your plan is to preach them out of addiction, you're wasting your time. That will be as effective as talking a heroin addict out of their next hit. The most you'll accomplish is convincing them that you're the problem and they need to do more to hide their addiction from you. They have no more control over their desire to play *Fortnite*, post on Insta or eat sugar than a smoker, an alcoholic or a heroin addict. Addiction is pure biology, and no amount of willpower, positive thinking or counselling is likely to change that biology on its own. But I'm getting ahead of myself.

None of us is born addicted to anything. Before we're addicted, we need to start using the addictive substance or performing the addictive behaviour. If we don't start, we never need to worry about quitting.

Restrict access

I'm not addicted to nicotine because I never started using it. I was a teenager in the 1980s and there were plenty of kids my age who smoked. This was back in the days before the tobacco companies were even prepared to admit that nicotine was addictive, and there was real debate in the media about whether smoking was a problem at all. It was more good luck than good management that I never started smoking. Neither of my parents smoked, so ciggies weren't present in the home. Smoking wasn't permitted at school, and advertising of smoking on radio and television had been banned since I was 10 years old. In short, I wasn't likely to accidentally come across cigarettes in my everyday life. If I'd really wanted to start smoking, I'm sure I could have obtained some, but it just wasn't an opportunity I could easily fall into.

Sugar, on the other hand, was everywhere, and I was being actively encouraged to consume it. And I don't just mean at birthday parties. The 1980s was the start of the low-fat era of dietary advice. Marshmallows were being advertised as 99 per cent fat-free (never mind the sugar). Sugar was in everything and few people thought there was anything wrong with that. Just like every other teen my age, it was easy for me to get addicted to sugar. Two decades later I'd very much regret that (and eventually write several books about what it did to me).

The first rule of addiction management: *Don't start.*

You can't become addicted to something you've never tried. As a teenager I couldn't become addicted to Facebook because it wouldn't be invented for three decades, or gaming because I'd have to wait decades for anything worth playing at a cost I was inclined to afford. The only computer game I ever saw was the newly installed Space Invaders machine at the bakery on the walk home from the bus stop. I tried it and liked it, but I ran out of 20 cent pieces before any real addiction could develop. The only computers in our house were an Apple II set up in the living room. It had a green screen, and the most exciting thing I ever saw it do was go 'beep'. Addiction to software was not going to be a problem for me.

Now, I could become addicted to approval porn and danger porn and even real porn if I tried. It's all very easy to access from the computer I'm typing on right now. But addiction would require much more effort from an adult brain. My dopamine is being actively suppressed by GABA and I have mature impulse control. So I'm writing about addiction instead of practising it.

Addiction-proof your house

The other rule of addiction management: *Keep addictive substances and devices out of the reach of children.*

The most effective way to control adolescent addiction is to not have a house full of potentially addictive substances and devices. No one would suggest it was a good idea to stock the cupboards with crack cocaine or leave packets of cigarettes in your kids' sock drawer. But most people will happily do all of that with an array of other addictive substances and devices.

Sugar

This means remove the sugar from your house. Not just the ice cream and the Coke, all the sugar. Remove the apple juice and the flavoured yoghurt and the breakfast cereals and the sauces and condiments. Your kids (and you) are probably accessing about 40 teaspoons of highly addictive sugar a day and not adding a single teaspoon of that themselves. It's a painstaking job to remove it from your food supply, but it's necessary (luckily, I've written *The Sweet Poison Quit Plan* to show you how). We don't have the word chocoholic in our language for fun. Cocoa isn't addictive. Raw cocoa is about as attractive as dirt and tastes roughly the same, but add sugar and the magic happens. And while there are plenty of terrible downstream effects of sugar addiction (such as type 2 diabetes and kidney disease), even worse for adolescents is the gateway effect of making their brains more prone to other addictions.

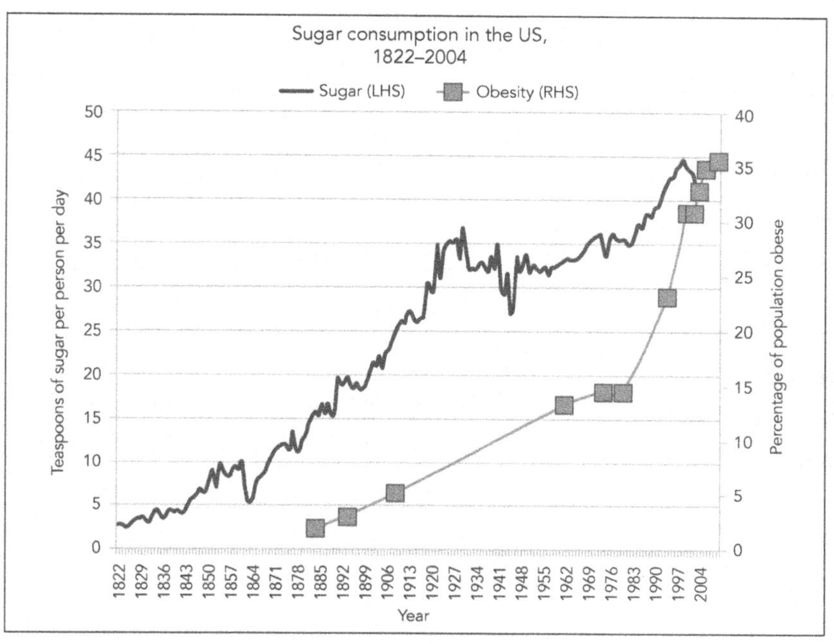

Devices

Next on the list in addiction-proofing your house is to lock up the computers, phones and gaming consoles. If you can deny access to these devices, you've eliminated a vast array of potential addictions. You will have transported your kids back to the pre-digital age. The only porn they'll see will be the copy of *Playboy* swiped from Freddy's dad's stash. The only danger porn they'll experience will be running away from the nasty doberman from two doors down, and the only approval porn they'll experience will be from actually meeting people face to face.

This won't be easy. Your children are probably already addicted to their devices. They've been playing with electronic pacifiers since they were old enough to hold an iPad. Worse than that, their school probably requires them to have one about their person at all times. And just for good measure, you probably gave them a phone as soon as they were old enough to catch a bus to school. Every one of these devices is a dopamine button that can be hit hundreds of times an hour. And none of them existed just over a decade ago.

Like most Australian kids their age, our three youngest attend a high school that all but mandates possession of a tablet device. They are connected to the internet at school, on the train and when they get home. There is barely a second of their lives when the cornucopia of addictive apps is not at their fingertips. We try to limit access by demanding that the devices be placed in a rack by the door, but that is often as effective as pushing water uphill with a rake. Any time I check the rack, there is always at least one missing. It is a constant battle to ensure these highly portable addiction machines are not in a child's hands and it requires a level of vigilance that would make the CIA proud.

'Your children are probably already addicted to their devices.'

It won't be easy

This is an entirely new parenting challenge. You can't ask your mum how she dealt with it any more than you can ask most mums how they dealt with their kids' heroin addiction. But the answer isn't really that different: *deny access*.

Warning! This won't be pretty. Expect a lot of teenage sneakiness, tantruming and outright deception. They'll try every addict trick in the book to get their hit. But you must stand firm. And every time you successfully deny access, you'll allow their Delta FosB (see page 34) to ratchet down one more level and for them to be one step further away from addiction. Every time you fail, the opposite will happen. You'll lose the popular vote for parent of the year, but eventually they'll thank you for it.

One of the side benefits to success will be the invention of time. Dopamine buttons are massive time sinks. A teen without access to one will suddenly find they have acres of spare time. At first they'll be bored, but that boredom will quickly translate into finding something interesting to do with their new-found wealth of minutes. They might – *gasp!* – go outside, or even just discover there is such a thing as 'outside'. They might read a book. They might practise a musical instrument. They might play a sport. They might even walk the dog. And if they get really bored, they might even do some chores around the house (without quite so much resistance).

They'll also be suddenly desperate to do their homework. No, I didn't fall off the back of a turnip truck yesterday. They know that means they need access to their device, and they think you're silly enough to fall for 'I need it for homework'. Unfortunately, they probably do really need it for homework. Our education system has allowed itself to be taken hostage by the device-marketers, and most schools insist on all children having them. This is despite there being a total lack of evidence of improvement in educational outcomes because of them – indeed, quite the opposite is the case.

RESISTANCE IS FUTILE

When our youngest kids, the twins, were in their last year of primary school in 2015, their small public school decided it would ask all senior (Year 5 and 6) students to have a Microsoft tablet device after piloting it in one class the previous year. The school wasn't without computers already. Every classroom had at least four, a shared community asset owned and serviced by the Education Department.

Microsoft was, via the department, offering a spectacular initial deal. The devices would cost parents around $300 each (reduced from $600). Parents would also need to pay an annual IT levy of $100, so the network could be serviced and repaired. The school also needed to spend tens of thousands to install the necessary wi-fi upgrades, but the school and the parents were all convinced it was vitally necessary. So, this 280-student school in an area with middle- to low-income households set out to 'lamington-drive' and 'Bunnings-barbecue' the money for the upgrade. And the parents happily agreed to effectively quadruple their personal annual school-supplies expenditure.

At the time we were living the hell of keeping the twins' older siblings away from high-school-mandated devices, and so, hoping to delay the inevitable, Lizzie and I opted out of the program and refused to buy the tablets, as was our right in a public school. Before the start of Year 6, the principal explained to us that we were the only parents who had refused, and while they couldn't insist we purchase the devices, it was pointed out that since both senior classes would be using them, it might be better if our children were placed in a younger class that wasn't.

We thought about standing firm but decided it was better for the girls to stay with their class. We'd just have to be tough on device use at home. And so we caved. Fighting the device-pushers isn't easy.

Managing devices at home

The insane and irrational insistence on school devices will add immeasurably to your duties as a parent of a teenager. The easiest way to prevent access is not to buy the device in the first place, but that's not an option when it's on the school book list. So instead you'll need to set up a regime of monitoring that would make Vladimir Putin proud.

You'll need to ensure that the device being used 'for homework' is only used in a public area of the home where you can see what's on the screen at all times, and that if you need to leave the house the device leaves with you. No matter how angelic your little darling is when they insist algebra is their only desire, as soon as you can't see the screen, the dopamine button will be singing a siren song in their pubescent brains and they'll be one click away from a quick hit. And killing the wi-fi isn't a solution most of the time. Sure, they might prefer online dopamine hits, but all these devices come fully equipped with games that work just as well whether they access the internet or not.

To eliminate the temptation from phones, I suggest ye olde flip phone without internet access. They're non-addictive, do just one useful thing – make and receive phone calls – and are really cheap. Being cheap is very handy because you'll find they get abandoned, dropped and drenched on a regular basis as your teen attempts to convince you to buy them a replacement phone that wasn't used by Fred Flintstone. I'd prefer to tell you not to buy them a phone at all, but we no longer live in a society where (working) public phones are easily accessible, so a flip phone it must be.

Gaming consoles can go in the bin. There's no good reason to have them in the home. Saying they're there as a 'treat' is like saying

'Any use of an addictive substance or device keeps that addiction alive.'

you'll only let your kids watch porn on the weekends or do crack cocaine after they clean their room. Any use of an addictive substance or device keeps that addiction alive, acts as a gateway to other addictions and makes it that much harder to stop.

Other, more traditional, addictions are easier to deal with because they're to varying degrees regulated by law. Don't give children access to alcohol, cigarettes, marijuana, cocaine or . . . well, you get the gist. Especially don't buy these products for your kids and enable consumption because of some misguided desire to relive your youth vicariously – I'm looking at you, schoolies parents.

It takes time

Time is the only real cure for addiction. Your adolescent needs time to reset that Delta FosB set point. It will start to reset immediately, but it will take months to get back to normal. During that withdrawal phase, cravings will be intense, attempts to get a hit will be very determined, and you'll need to get good at saying no and meaning it. But every time you do, the easier it will become next time. And then, suddenly, your little addict will be out the other side of withdrawal and everything will be much easier – unless you let them at the dopamine buttons again.

This is all well and good for an environment you control, but as your child gets older, they'll be outside the home more and more. You'll be doing them a favour by keeping the addictive stuff under lock and key (or in the bin) at home, but you can't stop them accessing it on the bus, at school and everywhere else. This was much easier for previous generations of parents. They didn't have to worry about software, and just as they do now, they had the law and societal expectations helping them keep teens away from cigarettes, booze and drugs in public. But now there's nothing stopping a teen hitting up Insta in English class, watching porn in the back row of maths, or getting a quick round of *Fortnite* in on the bus. Not only will the school not stop it, it will insist on the child having the necessary equipment at all times.

Your only hope here is talk. Yep, talk. You need to explain carefully exactly what's going on in their brain every time they post a photo to farm likes or play a game or eat sugar. Teens think they're bulletproof, but they're not stupid. They don't want to cause themselves harm any more than you do. Yes, they'll do it anyway, but nothing succeeds like repetition (just ask any advertising executive), so keep repeating the why and eventually they'll listen. Ultimately, many will voluntarily give up under the combined pressure of your Delta FosB–reducing rules at home and your constant nagging. And even if they don't, know that at least for half their time that they're still at home you've removed the dopamine buttons.

'Teens think they're bulletproof, but they're not stupid.'

Needless to say, this is all going to go a lot easier if you schedule-fed your baby, learned to say no to them when they were a toddler, kept them away from sugar and never gave them a device before their school forced you to buy one. But if this isn't you, don't despair – you can still do it. It will, however, take steely determination, and you'll need to develop a highly ingrained habit of saying no first and asking questions later.

Summary

- Teenagers are simultaneously ravenously seeking new experiences and uniquely susceptible to addictive substances and behaviours once they hit puberty.
- Any addictive behaviour a child takes on during adolescence is likely to stick with them for life.
- Because addiction significantly increases the likelihood that a child will be anxious and depressed, it's vital to manage access to substances and behaviours that are potentially addictive during this phase.
- Time is the only real cure for addiction. Your adolescent needs time to reset that Delta FosB set point.

School

Child-centred parenting has created a generation of parents who are fierce advocates for their children. If their child says jump, they say how high. This means that when a school dares suggest their wunderkind is anything other than perfect, the parent will unleash all hell against the school until it cowers under the onslaught. Talk to parents and educators from earlier generations and they'll relate a golden age of parent–teacher relations.

They'll fondly remember a time when parents were part of a team with the school, and if the school said something was wrong with little Johnny, the parent worked with the school to attempt repairs. If the school said little Janice needed detention for her behaviour, then the parents reinforced the message at home. To the extent that it was possible, the school was an extra parent that took over parenting duties between 9 am and 3 pm, and there was barely a seam to be seen. When a teacher made a decision in class, it wasn't open to discussion. It was their way or the highway – to the office. If the child was aggrieved at some perceived injustice, and remembered it by the time they got home, then the parent could take it up with the school in writing. That began a process of arbitration between the adults that would be largely hidden from the children's eyes and ears, and was unlikely to be undertaken lightly. This isn't how it works now.

Now children are in constant communication with their parents during the school day, and they expect their parents to come in swinging because that's exactly how the rest of their life works. The teacher is no longer an authority that any child respects. When the teacher gives Philippa a B+ rather than the A she was expecting, Philippa's mum receives a message within seconds and will likely be at the school office waiting for the offending teacher at the end of the period. And that teacher had better be prepared to negotiate, or a Facebook campaign will start before the parent leaves the premises.

Parents who've never said no to their kids don't think anyone else should be able to either. They perceive their job as being their child's protector. When they get a message from their child with a bruised ego, they feel it's their duty to react immediately. They must be a barrier to anything that could degrade their child's self-esteem, including, of course, the education system. After a generation or two of parents defending their child against the school and blaming the school for just about everything wrong with the world and their child, the

'Now most schools practise what could only be described as defensive teaching.'

education system is in full retreat. Now most schools practise what could only be described as defensive teaching. Awards are given for having a pulse, there are more leaders than followers, and even the followers will be described as vice leaders (or similar nonsensical piffle). Sports teams and bands are named after flowers instead of calling them the A team and the B team. And every decision is subject to negotiation for fear of public retribution from parents.

The school needs to enforce rules

You don't want to do all the rule-setting and -enforcement work I've detailed above only to have it thrown out the window as soon as your kid gets to school. A school that permits unfettered access to devices might as well be handing out cigarettes in every class and requiring the children to smoke them. Those kids will be loaded to the eyeballs with dopamine. This makes them anxious, overreactive and, if they're boys, aggressive. It's hardly the best environment for education, even without the temptations of the internet at their fingertips when maths gets a little boring.

All teens have a reactive temperament and terrible impulse control. It's a very bad idea to give them a tool that simultaneously makes that worse and gives them a way to circumvent authority on the spur of the moment, because that's exactly what they'll do. Apart from the academically and socially disastrous effects of attempting to educate addicted teens high on dopamine, a school like that will have little ability to enforce rules. The helicopter parents will be running the place. Every second kid will be an award-'winner' of some description, behaviour management will be patchy and inconsistently applied, and the children most likely to be selected for more important leadership roles will be the ones with the most vocal parents.

AT LEAST THEY'RE QUIET

Emily is a parent of three teenaged daughters and is a high school maths and science teacher who has been teaching for 20 years in a variety of public secondary schools. She has experienced teaching before pervasive devices and after. She now teaches mainly 13 to 15 year olds. Her current school requests that each child purchase their own Apple iPad and have it with them at all times in class and even though it is a public school almost all children do have them. On balance, she feels the devices deliver marginally more benefit than harm but it is a close call. She feels that having them makes it easier for the children to collaborate and to apply things they learn. She also says that behaviour management is significantly easier in a class full of iPads. Now kids who don't engage with the lesson sit quietly, whereas in the olden days they would have been throwing things across the class and yelling out to their friends.

Emily says most of the kids would stay glued to their devices if she didn't stop them and this significantly increases her workload because she needs to constantly check what they are doing. She does this by frequently walking around the class when they are doing a task that uses the device and by requiring that it be face-down on the desk when it is not needed. Some of her colleagues have experimented with apps that allow them to see what's on the student screens but the pushback from the students has been very vocal with complaints that the Bluetooth required for them to work flattens the batteries and means they cannot get through to the end of a school day. She doesn't think any of her colleagues are using those apps now.

Emily says that some kids cannot manage the self-discipline required to leave the device alone. She estimates that in any class anywhere up to a third of the kids fall into this category. She says it's like putting sweets on a plate in front of them and expecting them not to eat them. Her solution for them is remove the devices and put them in a pile on her desk until the end of the lesson. She prints out any material they need but she is finding this increasingly more difficult to do as the school is clamping down on printing costs. But she says if she didn't do this those kids would learn very little.

Emily says that there is a very strong correlation between results and the inability to control screen time. All the students are drawn to the screens but the higher achieving ones can exercise self-control and leave them to focus on a task. The kids who can't leave the devices alone are invariably the ones who achieve the worst and who need to engage with the lesson the most. Emily says she gets very little pushback from students when she takes the device and she thinks they are actually relieved not to have the option.

At home Emily doesn't enforce device access rules, but she is often frustrated that her daughters cannot seem to put them down. At the moment they are all doing well academically and she thinks they are exercising sufficient self-control. But she is watching closely and at the first sign of trouble she plans to toughen up, exactly the way she does in her classroom.

Emily says one of the trickiest aspects of devices at school and at home is the issue of trust. It's important that her students and her kids know she trusts them, so she doesn't want to accuse them of doing the wrong thing when they aren't but at the same time she knows they often aren't and it is, at the very least, distracting them. Knowing when to intervene is a hard call that she has to make every day, and this is a layer of pressure she never used to experience before devices.

A good school

A good school will look a lot like a good parent. It definitely won't require the purchase of a portable computing device, and it won't permit them or phones in the classroom. And it won't permit mobile phones to be used on the premises – not even ye olde flip phone.

Don't fall for the iPad seller's patter. Children don't need constant access to computers to be 'ready for tomorrow' (or whatever the sales message is today). In the software business, apps are upgraded monthly. Anything they learn today will be obsolete a month from Tuesday. They certainly need to be taught how to use a computer properly, but that can be accomplished in a lab dedicated to the purpose, full of machines attached to the wall, just as they are in most real workplaces.

The research on the use of computers in education clearly shows they're most effective when used by pairs of students rather than as personal devices, and, even then, only for certain highly repetitive rote-learning tasks (such as times tables). A school without personal devices also has no need to provide hideously expensive wi-fi infrastructure or face the constant problems and significant

HOW COMPUTERS SHOULD BE USED IN SCHOOLS

I'm not a luddite. The science tells us computers do improve outcomes in schools, but the best way to achieve those outcomes without all the potential downside is to:

1. Ban personal computing devices (including phones).
2. Do not have a student accessible wi-fi network that can connect to the internet.
3. Set up well-resourced computer labs for intense whole-class work.
4. Have computers that can be used in teams in classrooms, say five in the average class.

expense of policing what's accessed using that infrastructure. It would have vastly more money at its disposal for, well, teaching stuff. And aside from all of those tangible benefits, it will also reap the rewards of an enforceable means of behaviour management that can't be circumvented at the tap of a key.

Rules, rewards and punishment

A good school will have clear rules and consistent enforcement of those rules. It will have transparent systems of reward and punishment, and clearly documented methods for appealing its decisions in writing. The kind of punishment a school dishes out will make a difference to its effectiveness. I undertook an extensive review of school punishment for my book *Free Schools*, but the upshot is that the kind of behaviour management that works at school is the same as what works at home. Discover something they love and threaten to remove it, but make sure there's an upside for compliance.

Public disclosure of crimes and rewards is also a powerful tool in a good school's arsenal. Shame and pride are powerful motivators, but obviously the old tell-the-parents trick will only work if the parents agree that a crime (or something praiseworthy) has occurred. If the result of a note home about breaking a rule is a high-five from Dad, the deterrent effect will be somewhat diminished. Nevertheless, the clearest message from the research is that the most powerful deterrent and the most powerful incentive is communication with the home from the school. If kids do something wrong, it really matters to them that their parents not find out. If they do something right, they want to break the internet with the news.

BEHAVIOUR-MANAGEMENT PLANS

The best way to find out how a school deals with behaviour is to ask to see their behaviour-management plan. It will be an impenetrable nest of edu-speak, but you're looking for just a few things:

1. They have a written behaviour-management plan.
2. It doesn't rely on reasoning with disruptive children.
3. It does include an element of punishment and an element of positive feedback.
4. It escalates quickly to involving you when necessary (but doesn't have you being rung every time your son is pulled up for failing to tuck in his shirt).

Back up the school

Speaking from personal experience, kids have to believe that you agree with the teacher or they'll divide and conquer. Even if you think your child has suffered a terrible injustice when the inevitable note comes home, the last thing you should do is communicate that to the child. Find a time to have a quiet private chat with the teacher, get the full story and ask what you can do to reinforce the desired behaviour at home. If after a little chat like that you still think your kid has been wronged, then take it further up the school's (well-documented and published) chain of command, but once again quietly and away from your kid's ears. If the child gets a sniff that you'll side with them against the teacher, then that teacher's ability to control them will be significantly diminished. Even worse, every other set of eyes and ears in that class will be on you and your child, and that may well make them all much harder to control. Then how much learning will your kid (or anyone else) get done?

Bullying

Children bullying other children is probably one of the most extensively researched areas of child rearing and education, but the studies are often poorly executed. Results are all over the map (technical term), mostly because every researcher has a different definition of what constitutes bullying. Are you part of the bullying statistics because you were called fatso once in your life or because someone posted an ugly photo of you on Snapchat? Or does it require more frequent and harsher abuse, and if so, how often and what?

WHAT IS BULLYING?

The US Centers for Disease Control, the agency responsible for collecting statistics on school bullying, uses the following definition of bullying: 'Bullying is *any unwanted aggressive behavior(s)* by another youth or group of youths who are not siblings or current dating partners that involves an observed or perceived *power imbalance* and is *repeated multiple times* or is highly likely to be repeated. Bullying may *inflict harm* or *distress* on the targeted youth including physical, psychological, social, or educational harm.'

That definition is based on one developed by Dan Olweus, an 87-year-old Swedish professor of psychology and one of the clear leaders in bullying research. More simply put, he lists the three key criteria for bullying as:

1. intentional harm
2. repetition
3. a power imbalance.

Olweus isn't a fan of bullying research that focuses on specific behaviours such as physical abuse, verbal abuse or electronic device use. Rather, he maintains that bullying is defined by the abusive relationship between the bully and the victim, and shouldn't be used as a blanket term for any kind of negative or aggressive action. He does, however, believe that all bullying has the common characteristic of direct verbal abuse. Something else may be layered on top of that, such as physical abuse or cyberbullying, but verbal abuse is at the core of all bullying.

How common is bullying?

A recent US survey of 150,000 students using the definition above found that, on average, 17 per cent of all students were involved in bullying. Of those, 12 per cent were only bullied by others, 3 per cent only bullied other students, and 2 per cent were both bullied and bullied others.

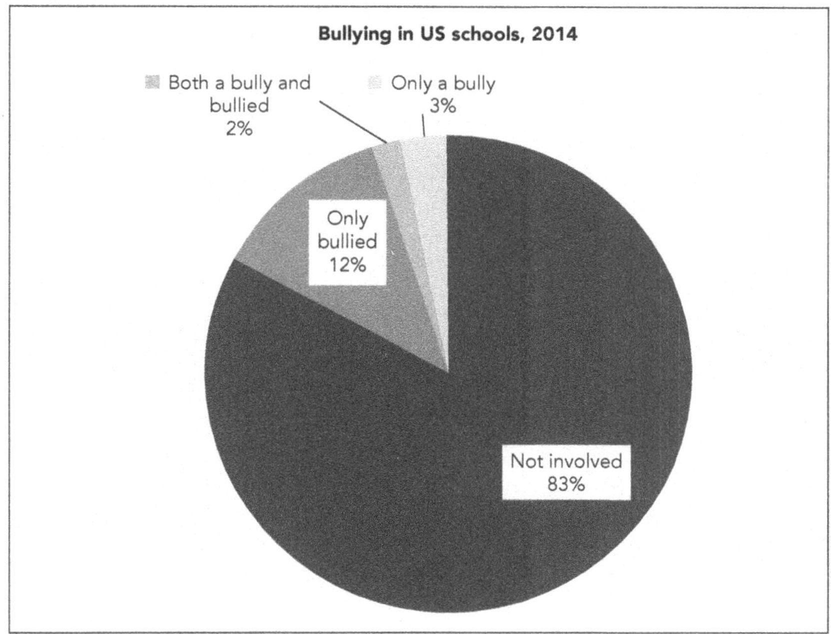

Bullying in the United States is most intense in the 3rd grade, with about 23 per cent of girls and 21 per cent of boys being bullied. The rate drops steadily throughout school, so that by the 12th grade, just 7 per cent of boys and girls will be victims of bullying. The percentage of kids who are bullies stays pretty much the same throughout school, although it drops off for girls once they hit high school. About 7 per cent of boys are bullies at any age. In the 3rd grade about 5 per cent of girls are bullies, but this drops to

3 per cent in the 10th to 12th grades. Recent research that tracked the same children all the way through school has discovered that the group of kids who are being bullied changes constantly and narrows over time. Just 11 per cent of the group of victims will be frequently bullied (one kid in every 3rd-grade class of 35 kids, dropping to one in 200 by the 12th grade). For the others, it happens occasionally (39 per cent) or infrequently (50 per cent). Only 5 per cent of the bullies (one in 400 kids) bully other children frequently.

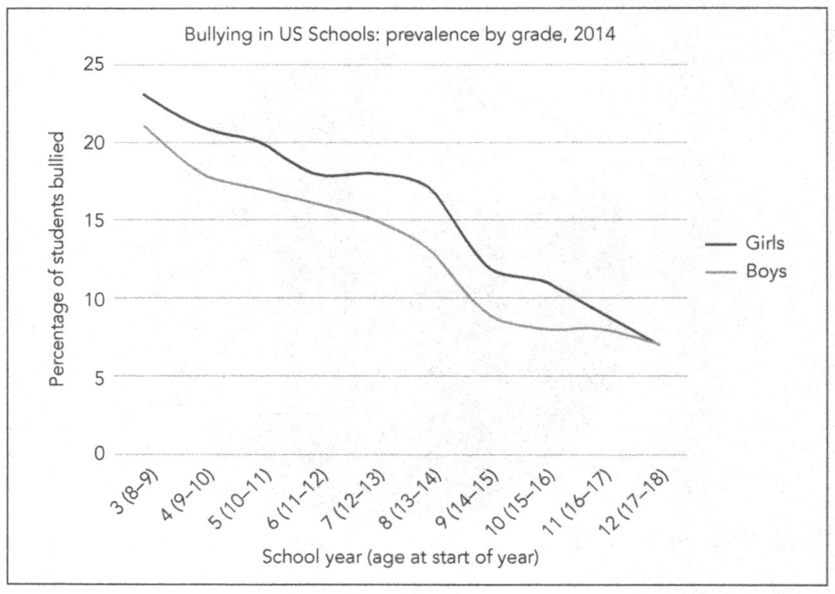

Bullying frequency appears to relate to change in the social order. When all the social cards are thrown up in the air, bullying increases. Kids entering the schooling system are encountering a brand-new form of social organisation, a large group of their peers where they, not their parents or carers, are in charge of relationships. In this fluid social soup, some children seek dominance. It happens again in the United States when children transition from primary to high school at the end of the 6th grade, and again when they transition from junior high to senior high at the end of the 9th grade.

WHO BULLIES AND WHO IS BULLIED?

In his 1993 book, *Bullying at School: What We Know and What We Can Do*, Dan Olweus says that bullies tend to:

- have a strong need to dominate and subdue other students and to get their own way
- are impulsive and easily angered
- show little empathy towards students who are victimised
- are often defiant and aggressive towards adults, including parents and teachers
- are often involved in other antisocial or rule-breaking activity, such as vandalism, petty crime or drug use.

If they're boys, they're physically stronger than other boys in general and their victims in particular. Contrary to many popular theories of bullying, Olweus's research and subsequent studies have revealed that bullies don't have problems with their self-esteem and are usually among the most popular and socially connected students in the school.

Olweus says a victim will tend to be:

- cautious, sensitive, quiet, withdrawn and shy
- anxious, insecure, unhappy and have low self-esteem
- depressed and engage in suicidal ideation much more often than their peers.

They'll also often not have a single good friend and may relate better to adults than to their peers. If they're boys, they're often physically weaker than their peers.

Anti-bullying programs

Olweus's program is one of the only school anti-bullying programs proven to actually reduce bullying. His program has been implemented in thousands of schools in the United States and Europe over the past four decades, and the results have been thoroughly studied and confirmed in academic research. In a recent 210-school evaluation involving 71,000 students, the Olweus anti-bullying program consistently reduced bullying by about a quarter over two years. Longer-term measurements show the rates continue to drop but less dramatically.

Anyone who has read my book on psychopaths (*Taming Toxic People*, 2017) will find the characteristics of a bully listed above eerily similar to those used to classify workplace psychopaths. They'll also be struck by the similarity in prevalence numbers. About one in 20 kids are bullies and about one in 20 people in workplaces are psychopaths. So you won't be surprised that Olweus's program for managing school bullying sounds a lot like what I recommended for containment of psychopathy in the workplace.

His program is based on just four simple principles:

1 Establish a social environment characterised by positive involvement from adults.
2 Set firm limits on unacceptable behaviour.
3 Consistently and visibly enforce those limits.
4 Ensure adults are both authoritative and positive role models.

Key elements of implementing the program are:

1 clearly established rules against bullying
2 clear communication of the rules and the consequences of breaking them to both students and parents
3 effective supervision outside the classroom (where most bullying occurs)
4 development of individual intervention plans
5 parental commitment to the program.

In short, Olweus says, set rules, stick to them, monitor compliance vigilantly and punish any violation consistently. Importantly, the entire community must cooperate in reducing the behaviour. A common feature of effective anti-bullying programs is ensuring that the community reacts against bullying. If the bully thinks bullying will make them an outcast, they'll be much less likely to bully. If the bully's peers react by reporting the behaviour or intervening on behalf of the victim, the bullying will decrease.

'The entire community must cooperate in reducing bullying behaviour.'

Like psychopaths, bullies thrive in environments where supervision is minimal and rules are loosely enforced or non-existent. And just as with psychopaths, cooperation and community values are the most powerful weapons of containment. None of this will stop a bully from wanting to bully, but it will severely curtail their opportunities to do so. As I pointed out in *Taming Toxic People*, psychopaths and bullies are very real and very much in our lives. Their behaviour is biologically hardwired. We can't change them, but we can contain them and severely limit the damage they do.

Kids do it all by themselves as they age. The US figures show that rates of victimisation drop from a quarter of all kids in the 3rd grade to just 6 per cent by the 12th grade, but that can be reduced even further by implementing containment strategies like those in the Olweus program.

Dan Olweus's program is designed to curtail any behaviour that results from the power imbalance rather than focusing on any given expression of it. He's particularly dismissive of research that focuses on cyberbullying, pointing out that large-scale studies show it isn't increasing (after the initial large jump in 2007 when the iPhone hit the market); it represents a small part (about 25 per cent) of the overall spectrum of bullying; and, in any event, 90 per cent of students who are cyberbullied are bullied by traditional means as well.

He backs these assertions with a massive study of bullying in US schools involving almost 440,000 students between 2007 and 2010. In that study, Olweus found that the numbers move around from year to year but that on average 18 per cent of US students had been victims of bullying. This is higher than the 2014 data I mentioned above, but in the same ballpark. The latest US national data confirm that these numbers remained approximately the same through to 2017. Olweus's comparison in the study was a group of Norwegian schools (covering 9000 students) that had all been running the Olweus program for several years. The rates of bullying in those schools were about 12 per cent but, after the initial drop in response to the program, bullying hadn't changed over that time, and cyberbullying remained a minor component, overlapping almost completely with verbal bullying.

CYBERBULLYING IS EXAGGERATED

Emily, the secondary school teacher (page 202), also works part-time as a guidance officer in another school. She says she thinks the threat of cyberbullying is significantly exaggerated. She doesn't see it occurring much, if at all. She observes kids being mean to each other but it is done face to face, just the way it always has been. And just like it always has been, it seems to largely revolve around friendship groups. She thinks peer-mentoring programs (pairing older students with younger students) and better teacher training in classroom management are the solutions to most bullying. She has seen this work to great effect in the school where she teaches. She feels this would be the same whether the devices were present or not.

Bullying and self-esteem

It's not that cyberbullying is irrelevant, just that it's a new delivery mechanism. Importantly, it can significantly increase the frequency of bullying. In the olden days (when I was at school), bullying generally stopped when you got home. The bully probably wasn't going to come around to your house for a little light after-dinner name-calling. Home was a bully-free oasis and a place where a child could rebuild self-esteem and confidence. Now the bullying can continue 24/7 because the school-mandated bullying-delivery mechanism (otherwise known as a tablet device) is on hand at all times. And when it comes to consequences of bullying, frequency matters. The effect isn't massive but research shows that frequency has a direct linear effect on self-esteem. The more frequently a person is bullied, the lower their self-esteem, the higher their anxiety and the more likely they are to become depressed.

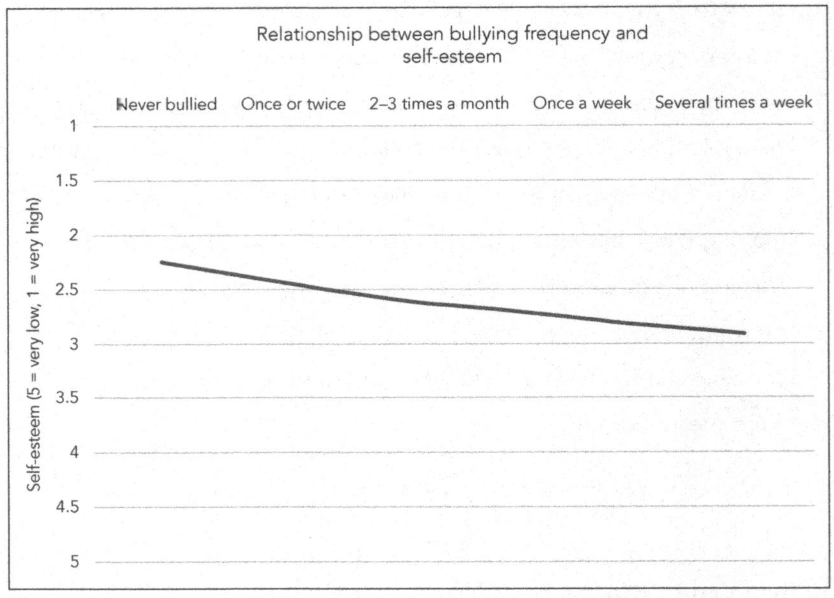

Consistent with this is the research saying that those children more likely to self-harm – kids who are part of a minority group, particularly those who are intellectually or physically impaired or who are openly homosexual – are more likely to be victimised. The human brain is wired to work on a 'them and us' basis. Oxytocin makes us fight for social acceptance and approval. Being like everybody else makes us part of the in-group, and this in turn increases oxytocin and serotonin levels and makes us happy. The downside is that oxytocin also makes us act aggressively against those who are not part of the in-group (see page 53).

'The human brain is wired to work on a "them and us" basis.'

This effect is massively amplified in the no-brakes state of the teenage brain. It should come as no surprise, then, that being different makes a child a candidate for bullying. Any differences count as long as you're in the minority. Fat kids like me were bullied a lot in my school days because back then, there weren't many of us. I suspect the tables are beginning to turn now that a quarter of Australian children are overweight or obese. The new fatties are the homosexual kids.

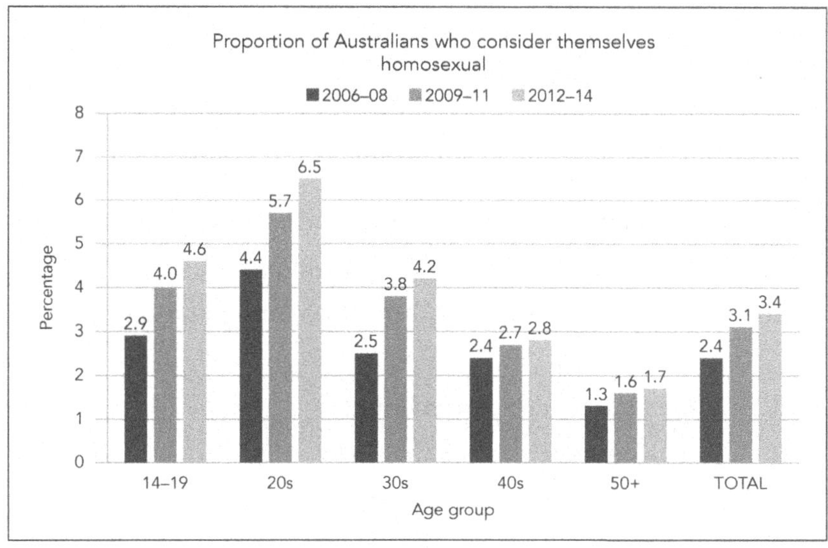

Teenagers with a non-heterosexual orientation are in the minority in Australian schools. In the most recent national polling, just 4.6 per cent consider themselves homosexual. If that orientation is made public, there's little doubt it will increase the likelihood that they'll be bullied. In Australia this has led to the development of a controversial government-funded anti-bullying program that attempts to help that group of potential victims. The Safe Schools program attempts to 'foster a safe environment that is supportive and inclusive of LGBTI students', by providing materials aimed at promoting acceptance of those students. The program is controversial because some fundamentalist Christian groups object to some of the suggested material, describing it as sexually explicit and inappropriate. A 2016 government review found that this wasn't the case. Even so, implementation of the program has been significantly wound back in most Australian states, and there's no evidence to date showing that it has any effect on rates of bullying of LGBTI students. Safe Schools is a highly politicised bolt-on anti-bullying program that's unlikely ever to achieve its stated aims.

Anti-bullying programs that work

The research is clear: an effective anti-bullying program is not an add-on. It's part of the fabric of a well-run school, and it follows exactly the same pattern as all other school and parental rules:

1 Define unacceptable behaviour.
2 Define consequences for that behaviour.
3 Publicly and consistently enforce those consequences.
(4 Make all of this much easier by not requiring the use of personal computing devices or allowing phones that can access the internet.)

Anti-bullying programs shouldn't focus on the reason for bullying, which almost invariably amounts to the victim being part of a minority, or to the delivery mechanism. Rather, they should focus on uniting the community against all bullying. They should provide clear statements of what won't be tolerated, and ensure that the community is empowered to act against any breaches. Remember, four out of every five kids are neither a bully nor a victim. United, they're a powerful suppressing force.

Summary

- Child-centred parenting has created a generation of parents who are fierce advocates for their children and this means most schools practise defensive teaching rather than enforcing boundaries.
- A good school will look a lot like a good parent. It definitely won't require the purchase of a portable computing device, and it won't permit them or phones in the classroom.
- A good school will also have an effective anti-bullying program that is not an add-on. It will be part of the fabric of a well-run school, and it will follow exactly the same pattern as all other school and parental rules:
    1 Define unacceptable behaviour.
    2 Define consequences for that behaviour.
    3 Publicly and consistently enforce those consequences.
    (4 Make all of this much easier by not requiring the use of personal computing devices or allowing phones that can access the internet.)

APPROVAL

Humans like being liked by other humans. This is as hardwired as our desire for food and sex. Being in a group keeps relatively poorly protected humans alive in nature. Approval porn like Instagram, Snapchat, YouTube and Facebook manipulates that wiring to make us addicted, but even without that, adolescence can be tricky when it comes to socialisation – the technical term for getting on with our peers.

Oxytocin is our homegrown approval-motivating drug, and its ability to deliver rewards is controlled by GABA. In a child or an adult, the desire for approval is quickly and easily rewarded and they move on. Addiction to approval is not generally a problem (in the absence of approval porn). But the adolescent is in a GABA-suppressed state and so is chasing the oxytocin hits in the same way they chase other potential addictions. Because oxytocin is an important component of mother–baby bonding, nature has spiced up this whole equation a lot for women. They're much more sensitive to oxytocin than men in general, but this is massively magnified during adolescence by the dialling down of GABA.

A child entering adolescence goes from liking to be liked to obsessing about it. And if that child is a girl, then that obsession is as important to them as breathing – maybe even a little bit more. This need for 'likes' is responsible for the teen obsession with their own appearance, and this in turn drives the demand for steroids, new clothes, new cars, the latest phone, teenage cosmetic surgery, selfies and hanging with the right crowd.

Friends

In young children, friendship is driven by common backgrounds, tastes and values. As a rule, children find other children with similar interests and attitudes likeable. For the same reasons, the person they find likeable is likely to find them likeable too, and so a friendship develops. Childhood friendships are usually relatively permanent, as long as both children continue to see each other on a regular basis (such as at school) and their interests remain similar. The same thing applies to adults and so, for many parents, the development of enduring friendships is a comforting sign of good social adjustment in their kids. And then they hit puberty.

Friendships in adolescence

At around the same time as most kids enter puberty, they're transitioning to a new, usually larger school. Sometimes their childhood friends are there with them and sometimes they're not. Either way, the potential pool of friends just got a lot larger. They're also moving from a classroom-based system where almost everything was the same every day to one where there's constant flux. They spent six to seven years with the same 22 kids sitting in the same class, with the teacher changing once a year and their parents dropping them off and picking them up from school. Their parents also controlled almost all of their out-of-school interactions with friends, and at least one parent was frequently present the whole time. The opportunities for meeting new people were restricted to a 'new kid' coming to the school (or them being the new kid somewhere else).

'Puberty forces teens' approval-seeking mechanism into overdrive and destroys their impulse control.'

In high school they move to subject-based education and the content of their in-class peer group changes on an hour-by-hour basis. Their peer group is suddenly their whole year group or even the whole school, and they're likely to interact with many of them in breaks between class. They're also often getting themselves to and from school with yet another group of kids, and beginning to have less adult-supervised playtime with friends and more after-hours peer-to-peer interaction.

At the same moment puberty happens. This forces their approval-seeking mechanism into overdrive and destroys their impulse control. And just to make it all a little bit more fun, the potential for a new type of friendship, the romantic relationship, gets thrown into the mix by the same hormonal changes driving the need for approval.

Suddenly the criteria for friendship change. Teenagers think everybody is constantly looking at and thinking about them.

Nothing could be further from the truth, because all teens are equally obsessed with themselves, but that's irrelevant to their oxytocin-junkie brains. Now friends and romantic partners become accessories that can score them more 'likes' or detract from their 'likes'. This doesn't mean that kids stop preferring friends who have similar interests, just that the approval gets superimposed and becomes more important, especially for girls.

The quest for popularity

When you're a teen, hanging out with the wrong people can seriously impair your approval rating, while hanging out with the right people can give it a big boost. Yes, you still want to be around people who like you, but not if being around them means a large group of people will think less of you. And you'll associate with people you don't particularly like if being near them gives you a popularity jump. Because this assessment of the flow of approval is a constantly shifting soup, teen friendships become very fluid. It's extremely unlikely that a Year 8 girl's best friend today will still be her best friend in a year's time. The same goes for her 'boyfriend'. If she has one, he'll be on high rotation, just like her friends. Her group of acquaintances (I hesitate to call them friends), her crowd, will also probably be different six months down the track. Some members will be the same and their interests will be similar, but there will be significant changes.

This can be very distressing for parents. Their cherub with the nice little bestie all through primary school is suddenly hanging out with god knows who – and they don't even know their parents! Helicopter parents frequently try to engineer more permanent relationships with 'nice' kids at this stage, but this is likely to be about as successful as nailing jelly to a wall. Hormones are running the show, and what Mum or Dad thinks about your friends is less and less relevant with every passing day.

The exceptions to this friend-go-round are kids at the top and bottom of the pecking order. Teens at the top will be mindful of keeping their status and so will aggressively manipulate their crew of acolytes to ensure they continue only to be seen with the most desirable companions. But they'll often retain a best friend who's perceived as being as popular as they are and who they genuinely like. Teens at the bottom don't have to worry about people wanting to be their friends for the cred, and will likewise find a friend whose values they share and who they genuinely like.

Teens migrate to the top of the pecking order if they naturally possess a quality valued by the majority of their peers, such as good looks, intelligence, money or sporting prowess. The desirable quality will depend a lot on the values of the community the kids are part of, but for middle-class Western kids that's a pretty standard list, although 'number of Instagram followers' could probably now be added. Obviously, context is important. If everyone you mix with is beautiful, rich and an Olympic athlete with a million followers, then you have to be spectacular to get to the top.

Kids end up at the bottom of the social order if they possess none of these things. If the community is large enough, subgroups with a common desirable feature will emerge. The brainiacs will clump around a particularly smart leader because intelligence is a quality they value and they think others like them will approve of them being in that group. The same will happen for the sporty types, the potheads and the rich kids, of course.

Rejection

Kids who don't meet the in-group's criteria for popularity enter what researchers call the 'rejected' group. Kids in this group are unable to get the approval hits all adolescents crave, and are more susceptible to anxiety and depression as a result. This is significantly more devastating for girls, who, due to their hypersensitivity to social cues (i.e. oxytocin), feel rejection much more powerfully than boys do. Making matters worse, bullies target low-status kids because there's less likely to be a social cost for doing so. If the bully is part of a group that awards approval credits for victimising people, there'll also be a tangible reward for doing it.

All this adolescent relationship turmoil is fuelled by the desire for oxytocin, a hormone that makes us feel good and binds groups together. It makes us more aggressive to those outside the group, more jealous of our in-group relationships, and more likely to feel pleasure at the pain of outsiders. It's powerful group-glue, and it's significantly more powerful for girls than for boys. That's just biological fact, so if you want to change that dynamic, you need to work with the hardwired reality rather than against it. What matters is what their peers think about them and the people they're seen with. And the markers for what they value are largely set by the school in particular, and adolescent society in general.

'Girls, due to their hypersensitivity to social cues, feel rejection much more powerfully than boys do.'

A CURE FOR REJECTION

This might sound childishly simple but the research says that an extraordinarily effective way to raise a child's battered self-esteem is to replace it with self-respect. Have them find something they're good at and have them do it regularly. Kids who do extracurricular activities do better in school and feel better about themselves than kids who don't.

There's no agreed psychological theory on why that is, but given what we know about how self-esteem works from a biological perspective, I'd hazard a guess that it's because they've found something where they're not at the bottom of the pecking order. It's probably a 'something' where they're reasonably competent or at least not the worst on ground, and it allows them to recharge their serotonin and therefore self-respect levels. The 'something' doesn't have to be sport – the research clearly shows it can be anything from having an after-school job, or learning a musical instrument or another language, to working on the school newspaper. Anything the kid is good at, or at least not terrible at, works.

Bear in mind that if you don't supply the self-respect booster there are plenty of people standing ready to make them feel better with an addictive substance or product. A rejected kid may well get their self-esteem recharge from being a drug dealer, nude-selfie-poster, or gamer who never leaves their bedroom.

Peer pressure

Oxytocin makes teens model the behaviour of the people they believe have high status in the groups they interact with most frequently. They might not like these de facto leaders or even admire them, but if they think everyone else thinks these kids are high status, they'll follow their lead. In one interesting study, researchers demonstrated exactly this by using previously collected information on students in a school to set up electronic profiles in a chatroom. The true identities weren't disclosed, but any student in the group could infer who a given character was in real life. The researchers used their fake identities to promote aggressive and risky behaviours, then sat back to measure the degree to which others followed. The kids mimicked the behaviour when it seemed to come from high-status peers but rejected the same behaviour when it came from characters they thought to be low-status peers.

There's a lesson about popularity in this for schools. Many schools now choose high-status positions based on a popular vote. If a school picks a popular girl as school captain, they'd better be sure they know all the things she's into, because the kids will for damn sure. They'll already want to follow her lead, but the school's official endorsement and grant of real power and status will be carte blanche to follow her everywhere she goes. A more sensible approach would be to select kids who embody the values the school wants to encourage in its student population. If the school community values academic achievement, for example, it should choose kids who are high achievers, to ensure that's what the other teens will be driving towards.

If the school community values drunken partying, then that's what teens will want on their Facebook page. You might be thinking you're not sure you've ever seen a school telling kids that drunken partying is their primary goal, but you'd be wrong. Teens are hopped up on oxytocin which makes them ultrasensitive to social signals. If the school rewards kids who are known party animals by making them school captain or prefect or handing them a good-citizen award, then that sends a message loud and clear as to what is valued in their community. The adults may say, 'No, we gave that award because Bobby wrote a great application for the position and had all his ducks in a row,' but the oxytocin-fuelled teens just see a party animal being given an elevation in official status.

Anyone who thinks teens can't be manipulated so easily just needs to fire up an online peer-to-peer game (like *Fortnite*) sometime. These games are purposefully designed to addict teens by holding a status reward just out of reach and ensuring everyone is watching them perform. You're only 10,000 points from super-master 3-star level, a reward only 35 other people in your location have the right to display. Most online games allow a player to stay in-game and comment after they're 'killed', and all other players know their performance is on display. Visible (to the peer-based community) status is a reward to all humans, but it's especially powerful for teenagers. A well-constructed status-based reward system can have powerful motivational effects on teenage behaviour, especially if the status rewards are delivered publicly. As teen-driven, pro-social movements like the Ice Bucket Challenge (which had enormous success with gens Y and Z) show, teens can be motivated by good as well as evil.

TEENS TAKE MORE RISKS WHEN THEY THINK THEIR PEERS ARE WATCHING

Teenagers aren't fools. They understand the risks of taking drugs or smoking or teenage sex or riding with an intoxicated driver just as much as you do. But rational consideration of risks goes out the window in the presence of their peers. Oxytocin and lack of GABA-based impulse control makes rewards loom much larger in real life for them. This is bad news for all teens, but especially bad for boys who, thanks to testosterone, already think they're bulletproof.

In a recent series of studies, US researchers have shown that teenagers take more risks and are more sensitive to potential rewards when they think their peers are watching them. And this is true even when they firmly believe they're not influenced by their peers. The participants were asked to play risk-and-reward-based card games when they were in an fMRI machine, so the researchers could monitor how much they were responding to rewards.

Adults and teens were equally excited by the potential for reward, but when subjects were told someone was watching, teenagers showed a significantly higher response. The knowledge that there was an audience barely affected the adults. Similarly, an earlier study by the same researchers found that 14–16-year-olds took twice as many risks on a timed driving simulation when with a peer than when tested alone.

Without exception, kids take more risks to obtain a reward when they think their peers are watching. We all chase rewards, but teens chase them extra hard and take bigger risks when they think others can see. Self-evidently, this effect is significantly magnified for gen Z, because they know their peers are observing their behaviour 24/7 via their school-mandated addiction-delivery devices.

Using peer pressure for good

If schools want groups of teens to value certain behaviours, they need to adopt game theory and construct in-school reward systems that mimic in-game reward systems. And don't think for a minute that school-awarded status has no power. Status is status. If the school doesn't build a status system, the kids will make their own, and you might not like the things they choose that accord status.

Schools should:

1. clearly articulate which behaviours and qualities will be rewarded with additional status
2. ensure that students are consistently rewarded in accordance with those principles
3. bestow these rewards publicly and transparently (meaning everyone will know why Bobby got the award).

Parents should ensure that any school they choose does all of the above, and that the behaviours and qualities being espoused match those they encourage at home.

Relationships

Like friendships during the GABA-impaired teenage years, relationships will be on high rotation. This isn't because your child's taste in what makes a good partner is likely to change much, but because both they and their partner will be neck-deep in the approval-rating soup that is teen society. Being seen with Terrence the Tech Geek might be a high-status move this week but social death by next Tuesday. Oxytocin-fuelled social cues will be driving partner selection more strongly than likeability for most teens most of the time. As with friends, the only real exceptions will be those at the top and bottom of the pile. The Queen Bee will probably stick with a high-status partner like the footy captain for ages, and the rejected kids will partner with low-status kids they actually like because nobody cares what they do.

A parent attempting to intervene in partner selection is likely to meet with all the success they might expect in the friend-selection stakes. The partner a teen chooses this week is driven by their peer group, so attempting to reason with that child based on the partner's personal qualities is a barren exercise. Saying, 'I don't like Bobby because he posts pictures of himself partying every weekend,' may simply serve to emphasise the reason the peer group thinks Bobby is terrific, and that will be much more important than whether your teen actually likes Bobby (or partying) or not. Once again, the guidance for parents is pretty simple:

'During the teenage years, relationships will be on high rotation.'

1 Know what's going on.
2 Have clear rules in place about how and where the relationship will be indulged.
3 Don't inspire oppositional behaviour by attacking the personal qualities of the person your kid's peer group has chosen for your child.
4 Breathe – it will probably be different in six months anyway.

Sex

As with all forms of hormonally rewarding behaviour that require a teenager to be physically present, rates of teen sex have been dropping like a stone since smartphones and tablet devices became widely available in the past decade.

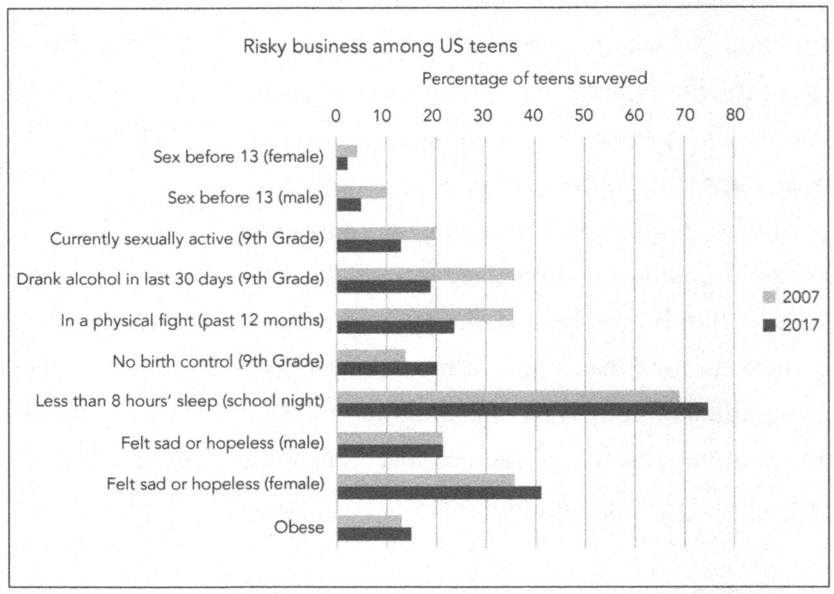

In the United States, the numbers of children first having sex have halved since 2007, and the numbers of children who claim to be currently sexually active have dropped by a similar amount. Even so, it's still the case that more than twice as many boys as girls are having sex. So either some pork pies are being told or there are some very busy young ladies out there. The numbers of children claiming to have experienced oral sex has remained static since 1995 (when it was first surveyed in the United States), at around 15 per cent of boys and girls aged 15–19 who weren't also having sex. We don't have stats for Australia, but data on other teen risky business, such as changes in alcohol and drug use, are similar to the States.

After puberty commences, we're hardwired to enjoy sex and so, as for all rewarding behaviours, teens are much more prone to chase it than adults. But like all potentially addicting behaviours, the opportunity and the motivation must be there. Gen Z children became teenagers after the first iPhone was released in 2007 (and the first iPad in 2010). They've had access to sugar and highly addictive sexual porn, danger porn (games and gambling) and approval porn (social media) from the comfort of their own bedroom for as long as they can remember. A teen in 2007 needed to go out and be physically present to chase addictive behaviour, but now they can get all the thrills they want without breaking a sweat.

Modern parents might take some comfort from the fact that their precious is safely tucked up in bed. Alone. But the massively increasing rates of depressive symptoms among girls (boys are protected by testosterone to an extent; see page 85), mean the dangers of not leaving your room are even more insidious. Rates of obesity, insufficient sleep, anxiety, depression, cutting and suicide are accelerating because addiction is now on tap. No, I'm not advocating for more teenage sex, alcoholism or violence, I'm saying that parents shouldn't be lulled into a false sense of security by these plummeting numbers. Addiction is still driving teen behaviour, it's just much less obvious, much more dangerous and much harder to stop.

Teen motivations for sex

Testosterone is the hormone that motivates sexual behaviour. A teenage boy has testosterone levels that would kill a mallee bull, so don't be surprised that they're significantly motivated by sex. Teenage girls also suddenly have adult-female levels of testosterone, and while these provide nowhere near the male levels of motivation, it's still sex drive.

If your teen is one of the few still having real sex, the research tells us they're doing it for one or all of three reasons:

1. intimacy – 'to feel loved' or 'to have someone really committed to you'
2. social status – 'to be respected by others' or 'to fit in'
3. sexual pleasure – 'to feel physically turned on'.

Unsurprisingly, both genders expect intimacy from having sex, but boys have significantly higher expectations for sexual pleasure and social status than girls. Teen girls want sex partially because the testosterone is amping up their sex drive, but mostly because they think it will bring greater intimacy to their relationship. They feel it will bind their partner more closely to them. Teenage boys want sex for intimacy too, but also because the testosterone is doing the thinking for them. They also think there's the side benefit that it should enhance their social status – so don't expect them to keep it a secret.

Sex makes us feel good, so, like self-harm or jogging, it can act as relief from depression, and that may be motivating the behaviour. But it's more likely that addiction to approval of either the sexual partner or your child's peer group (or both) is the primary motivator.

The dangers of teen sex

Sex is a hardcore way to prove that someone likes you. It's also one with a lot of potentially devastating outcomes. Because the number of teens having sex has been falling, teen pregnancies have also been falling and that's generally regarded as a good thing. Tablet devices have accomplished what no information program about teen sex could ever achieve – no Apple, Microsoft and Samsung, that's not a marketing suggestion – but, perversely, the incidence of sexually transmitted infections (STIs) has been climbing steadily. This is because, while use of the pill has been increasing slowly (in the United States from about 15 per cent in 2007 to around 20 per cent in 2017), condom use has dropped massively, particularly among younger teens. In US 9th-graders, for example, condom use has dropped from 70 per cent in 2007 to 54 per cent in 2017, and this presents a significant danger for disease transmission, particularly for young girls (and their next partner).

A special sexual risk for teenage girls

In the United States, one in four sexually active adolescent girls has an STI and more than half of all STIs are acquired by people aged 15–24. The rates of bacterial (such as chlamydia and gonorrhoea) and viral (herpes and HPV) infections are highest in 15–24-year-old females, and the incidences are accelerating rapidly in line with declines in condom use. This is likely to be because a quirk in the way the cervix matures during puberty makes girls more prone to infection when having sex. This is particularly the case when that sex is without a condom.

The cervical canal is the narrow neck-like passage joining the vagina to the uterus. Before puberty, the cervical cells at both the 'outside' (the vagina end) and the 'inside' (the uterus end) are soft, easily damaged and best suited to being inside the body rather than exposed to the external environment.

As oestrogen levels rise during puberty, the cells at the vaginal end slowly transform into much more heavy-duty cells called squamous epithelial cells. But this process of hardening-up can take a decade. In the meantime, young girls have large areas of fragile cervical cells exposed to the vagina. This is called cervical ectopy. Every teenage girl will have a slowly decreasing area of exposed internal cells. At 18, a woman will have around 40 per cent ectopy and by 21 this will be down to 8 per cent. By the time most women reach full maturity, they'll have none. That area of exposed internal cells is thin, has a high blood-vessel density, and is very easily damaged during normal sexual intercourse. Any damage creates easy access to the blood and lymphatic systems, and significantly increases the risks of infection with STIs.

Chlamydia and gonorrhoea are the first and second most common STIs in adolescents. Between them they affect around 4 million people a year in the United States and at least 50,000 people in Australia, and those rates are rising rapidly. In the first decade of the 21st century, chlamydia diagnosis rates tripled in Australia and gonorrhoea rates doubled. And the rate of increase doesn't seem to be slowing. In the United States the rate of diagnosed chlamydia increased by 14 per cent between 2012 and 2016 alone.

Diagnosis and treatment are simple and quick, but because these infections are asymptomatic, they're often left untreated, and this can lead to infertility. These two diseases combined are one of the main causes of infertility in women. Untreated, around 10–15 per cent of women with chlamydia and 40 per cent of those with gonorrhoea will develop pelvic inflammatory disease, which can cause permanent damage to the female reproductive organs.

All of the primary STIs can be transmitted during unprotected oral sex, so the 15 per cent of teens who think they're playing it safe by avoiding intercourse but still engaging in oral sex aren't really reducing their risks of anything except pregnancy.

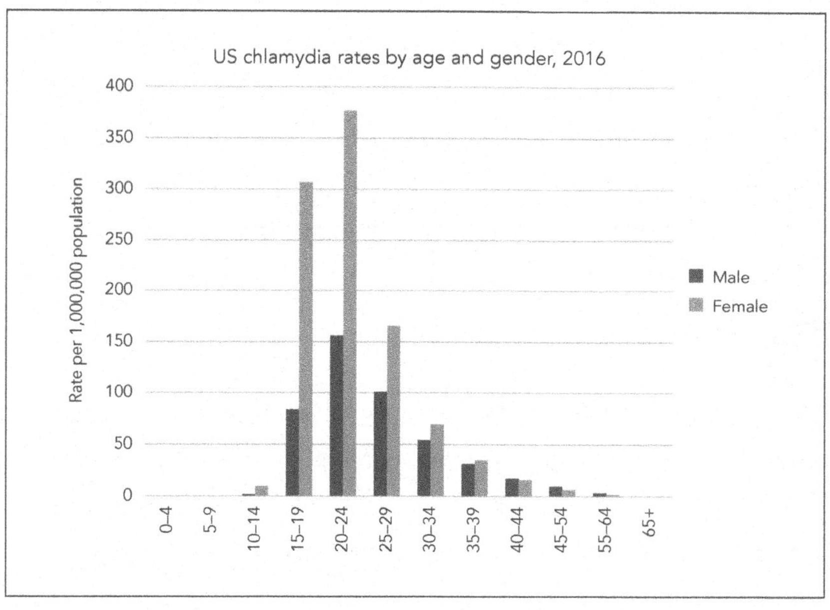

Your teens need you

Teens make bad decisions about having sex for the same reason they make bad decisions about everything risky. They have a hardwired inability to see the downside. To them, taking a risk is like betting in a casino that says you'll always win. Every teen player wins a prize is how they think. They can't make a rational decision about risk because they simply don't have a brain capable of doing so. This is where the adult supervision in the room must step up. No matter how much they fight you on it, you should curtail teen sexual desire. No, that does not mean giving them

'No matter how much they fight you on it, you should curtail teen sexual desire.'

anti-testosterone (whatever that may be), it means realising they have a sex drive much more powerful than yours and ensuring you don't provide opportunities for them to act on it. Unlike you, they'll be largely incapable of doing a proper risk assessment. No matter what line in 'I'm a sweet little innocent' they're running, remember that under the angelic surface lurks a hormone-fuelled craving for risky business and zero impulse control. In short, close supervision and opportunity removal are the orders of the day.

The pill

The pill was initially created because it promised to give women control of their reproductive capacity and their lives. But it's a strong hormonal steroid that, as we'll see, can have devastating effects on a woman's emotional wellbeing, particularly if that woman is an adolescent. It's now dispensed like cough drops for anything that might perturb the average teenage girl. If she's experiencing period pain, acne or an irregular cycle, she'll be handed a script for the pill. It's cheap, and the drug companies say its harmless – and probably for the best anyway, nudge, nudge, wink, wink. No one would criticise a doctor who prescribed the pill for a 15-year-old experiencing period pain or acne. Parents who've spent their lives keeping their precious progeny from all danger (or even every slightly negative experience) are terrified at the new (to them) travails of puberty and eager to take the proffered easy way out.

The pill is designed to be taken daily over a 28-day cycle. For the first three weeks, it usually contains synthetic forms of

A BRIEF HISTORY OF THE PILL

In 1916, Margaret Sanger, a 37-year-old nurse, published the first book on birth control in the United States. She'd spent her career treating working-class women who underwent frequent unwanted pregnancy and suffered (if they survived) through miscarriage and self-induced abortions. She passionately believed there was desperate need for women to be able to control whether and when they became pregnant.

Sanger was prosecuted for her trouble under an 1873 anti-obscenity law that prohibited any person from distributing information on 'any drug, medicinal article or instrument for the purpose of preventing conception'. The law was only finally overturned (for married women) by the US Supreme Court in 1965, one year before Margaret's death at the age of 86. It wasn't until 1972 that it was found to be unconstitutional for unmarried women to be prevented from using contraception.

In 1951, Sanger was responsible for introducing Dr Gregory Pincus to a significant source of funding for the invention of the drug we now know as the pill. Pincus based his work on experiments from the 1930s that showed ovulation could be prevented in rabbits by injecting progesterone. Within six years of meeting Sanger, Pincus had completed human trials and obtained US FDA approval for the pill to be used in women with menstrual disorders. Three years after that, in June 1960, it was approved for use as a contraceptive. In January 1961, Australian woman became the first women outside the United States to have access to the pill.

oestrogen and progesterone, and in the last week the pills are placebos. They're not necessary, but they're usually included to keep women in the habit of taking the pill daily. A woman can still become pregnant on the pill, but the rate is reduced to about nine pregnancies per 100 women per year. That's about half the rate of condom use but still 18 times the rate for female sterilisation and 60 times the rate for male sterilisation – although of course no one is recommending sterilisation of teens! The drug-company literature claims much higher effectiveness but that depends on the medication being taken at exactly the same time every day and never missing a day. Long-acting hormonal contraceptives such as injections, the IUD/IUS/coil, the patch and the ring have recently increased in popularity because women don't have to remember to take them. In Australia, use of this type of long-acting contraception doubled between 2008 and 2015 among 18–24-year-olds.

Teenage girls and the pill

Fewer teens are having sex, but prescription rates for the pill and its long-acting variants are climbing dramatically. Even though the number of US teens having sex halved between 2007 and 2017, usage of the pill increased by 25 per cent. The growth rates are similar in the United Kingdom, where the number of 12–18-year-olds on the pill increased by almost 40 per cent between 2002 and 2011. But those statistics also show that fewer teenage girls are on the pill for contraceptive reasons. In 2002, more than 76 per cent of pill prescriptions were for contraceptive use. By 2011 it was less than 66 per cent.

In the United States, one in three adolescent girls is on the pill only for non-contraceptive reasons, and four out of five are taking

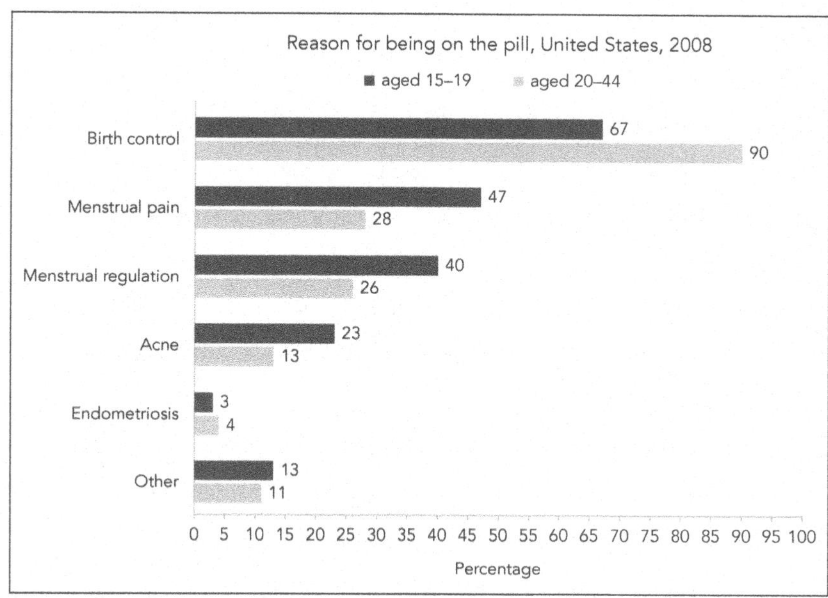

it for those reasons as well as a desire for contraception. The pill is perceived by most doctors as a harmless and cheap ($10–$30 a month) way to treat common conditions associated with puberty, such as acne, menstrual cramps, menstrual irregularity and sometimes PCOS and eating disorders.

The pill as an acne treatment

A quarter of US teenage girls on the pill are taking it for acne. About 85 per cent of adolescents experience acne, but you wouldn't know it by looking at the average schoolyard or Instagram feed. To a teen obsessed with their appearance, acne can be a devastating social impediment that's highlighted by the constant flow of photos on social media. There's no evidence that more frequent washing or scrubbing improves acne. So after they try that to no avail, most teens will demand that their parents do

EFFECTIVENESS OF ACNE TREATMENTS

Skin care: There's no evidence that acne is associated with lack of washing or that increased scrubbing will have any impact.

Salicylic acid creams: There's no evidence these creams reduce acne.

Benzoyl peroxide creams: High-quality human trials show these creams yield moderate or better improvement after 18 weeks of use in 60 per cent of cases.

Retinoid (vitamin A) creams: Available on prescription only, these creams are about as effective as benzoyl peroxide creams and can reduce the severity of acne by 40–80 per cent. They shouldn't be used by pregnant women or girls.

Oral antibiotics: These are about as effective as benzoyl peroxide and retinoid creams, but concerns about antibiotic resistance mean they're now being prescribed much less frequently.

The pill: This will reduce female acne by 75–90 per cent.

Roaccutane (isotretinoin): This is an extremely effective treatment. A single six-month course will clear most cases of severe acne and 80 per cent won't need a further course. It does, however, have potentially serious side effects. In Australia, it can only be prescribed by a specialist dermatologist, and a liver test and a pregnancy test (for girls) are required before commencement. Women and girls must not become pregnant or breastfeed while on the course or within one month of completing it.

Time: About 80 per cent of acne cases will clear up without intervention by the age of 25.

something about it, and most child-centred parents will try their hardest to protect their child from the ills of the world and head for the doctor with their teen in tow.

The influence of sugar

Acne is caused by the increase in testosterone for both boys and girls during puberty. In countries exposed to high-sugar diets, the rate and severity of acne has been increasing steadily in the past three decades. This is to be expected, as the fructose half of sugar increases circulating testosterone (see PCOS, page 95).

The most effective treatment for acne, Roaccutane, is expensive, can only be prescribed by a specialist and needs to be carefully managed because of the potential for liver damage and birth defects (see box). For these reasons, it's considered a last resort by most doctors. But one of the few easily available, effective, treatments

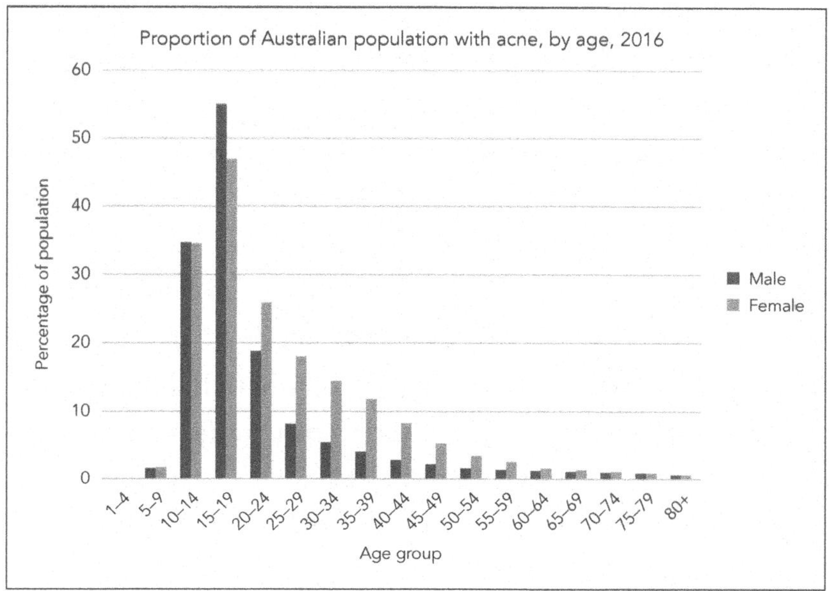

for acne in women is the pill, and so it's often prescribed to teenage girls anxious about their appearance. It works because the oestrogen removes circulating testosterone from the bloodstream. This can also cause the dampening of sex drive some women report as a side effect of being on the pill.

Endometriosis and infertility

Almost half of all teenage girls are on the pill because of menstrual pain or irregular periods. But there's a risk that much of the treatment in this area is medicalising normality. Periods aren't regular for the first three years of puberty, and cramps and heavy bleeds can be a normal part of the body adjusting to menstruation during puberty. Even so, the pill is frequently prescribed as a first response to regularise the period. And it works. It often eliminates period pain, puts the girl firmly on an artificial 28-day cycle, clears up her acne and pregnancy-proofs her (just in case). Magic. Except it's not.

Sometimes period pain and heavy bleeds are the first signs of endometriosis, a disease in which excessive oestrogen causes uterine lining to build up and grow on the ovaries and fallopian tubes rather than being expelled as part of the period. Endometriosis is responsible for about one-third of female infertility and is often not diagnosed until a woman in her 30s is undergoing investigation for infertility. Unfortunately, it requires surgery to diagnose and the pill will mask most of the symptoms. Many women with the disease don't discover they have it until a decade or two after being put on the pill, and by then much of the damage to their fertility has been done. A 2011 French study found that women with severe endometriosis were four and a half times more likely to have been prescribed the pill before they were 18.

The pill and depression

All hormonal contraceptives work by providing a significant boost of oestrogen and progesterone in the same way the body does naturally when ovulating. And so the brain thinks the body is ovulating when it isn't. This suppresses production of the LH and GnRH that would normally trigger actual ovulation. Another way of saying this is that the pill puts women permanently in the luteal phase (see page 84), the phase of the menstrual cycle when GABA is suppressed and impulse control is at its weakest. You'd therefore predict that women on the pill would be more likely to be addicted, depressed and anxious, and that this would especially be so when they're teenagers and their GABA is at its lowest level of their lives. And you'd be right.

'The pill is associated with increased rates of depression.'

A huge long-term study of more than 1 million Danish women over the age of 13 has recently confirmed that the pill is associated with increased rates of depression, particularly among teenagers. The researchers found that 15–19-year-old girls on the pill are twice as likely as girls not on the pill to be prescribed antidepressants or first diagnosed with depression within six months of starting the pill. The rates of depression were increased by about a quarter in older women. As you'd expect, given their GABA-suppressed state, the rates of depression were highest in the youngest hormonal contraceptive users and declined as they aged. The study also found long-acting implants were even worse. They tripled the risk of depression in the 15–19 age group and merely doubled it in older women.

Is the pill worth it?

The best way for a teenager to not get pregnant or acquire an STI is for them to not have sex – warning, parental rules and supervision will be required. If they must have sex (must?) then condom use must be mandatory – even for oral sex. The pill isn't a good option. It takes the sector of the population most likely to experience anxiety, depression, suicidal thoughts and self-harm – adolescent girls – and massively increases the risk of all those things. Yes, that means they'll have to use creams to treat their acne and potentially need to cope with heavy, irregular and/or painful periods, but those are the realities of puberty, no matter what all their friends tell them. Puberty is real, normal, and happens to the best of us. And at least that will mean that if these are symptoms of endometriosis, it will be properly investigated. As far as I'm concerned, the risks associated with giving teenage girls steroid hormones are just too high to justify any other approach.

Gender orientation

This may come as a shock but there only two biological genders, male and female. For more than 95 per cent of the population, after the start of puberty, males are interested in sexual relationships with females and vice versa. In Australia, for one in 25 men and one in 36 women, this orientation is reversed and they're sexually attracted to their own gender. In addition to this, US data suggest that about one in 250 adults are transgender. This means that their conception of their gender doesn't match their biological gender. They are women in men's bodies and vice versa. And sometimes they feel neither male nor female or are not sure. Just like people whose perception of their gender matches their biological gender, a transgender person may also be homosexual or heterosexual. We don't know what leads to non-heterosexual gender orientation, but the scientific consensus is that sexual orientation isn't a choice. If it's not a choice, that pretty much leaves biology as the primary candidate, which makes testosterone, given the central role it plays in sexual motivation, the primary biological candidate.

What science tells us

We know from large numbers of studies in many species of mammal, including non-human primates, that masculine characteristics can be manipulated by introducing additional testosterone at critical phases of development. The exact timing depends on the species, but if testosterone is increased at exactly the right moment, female offspring will behave as if they're male – including mate preferences. They'll still have all the physical female bits you might expect, but they'll act like someone dropped a male brain into their body. Similarly, removing testosterone from developing males will reduce male behaviour and increase female behaviour and mate preferences. Not surprisingly, ethicists get all picky about doing similar experiments on humans, but some medical conditions that produce similar increases or decreases in normal testosterone levels at critical moments in gestation have confirmed, at least partially, that humans aren't exempt from the effects of prenatal testosterone.

One in 14,500 girls are born with congenital adrenal hyperplasia (CAH), an inherited genetic disorder that results in a female foetus receiving too much testosterone. Studies of these women reveal that they're less likely to be heterosexual when matched for age and demographic background. In a group of 100 unaffected women we'd expect two or three to be homosexual. But if those 100 women had CAH we could expect about 20 to be homosexual and 10 to be homosexual about half the time. About one in 20 women with CAH express a desire to live as males. Males can be affected by another rare hereditary disorder called androgen insensitivity syndrome (AIS), which partially or totally blocks the ability of testosterone to activate masculine characteristics. These men act like women, are attracted to men, believe themselves to be women and, depending on the degree of AIS, will also look female, notwithstanding the presence of a Y chromosome.

While studies in people with those rare hereditary conditions at least partially confirm what has been documented in other mammals, they're not perfect because they are by nature very small and therefore potentially unreliable. To study the effect of prenatal testosterone release properly, we need large samples of well-measured pregnancies, and that isn't likely to happen any time soon. But because average 2D:4D ratio (see page 129) appears to give a good approximation of the level of testosterone received by the foetus in the critical six to 13 weeks period of gestation, gender orientation has been a big focus of recent 2D:4D research. A long line of studies has confirmed that homosexual women tend to have lower (more 'masculine') ratios. And some, but not all, recent studies have suggested that higher (more 'feminine') ratios are associated with male homosexuality. One study found that higher (more feminine) ratios in women correlate with a desire for more masculine partners, and other studies have found the same was true of gay and bisexual men.

Hardwired is hardwired

This doesn't mean, of course, that if you're a man with a high 2D:4D ratio you'll be homosexual, nor that if you're a woman and have a low ratio you'll prefer the sexual company of women. It simply means that it's more likely than not that prenatal testosterone programming may play a significant role in something some people regard as either a choice or a state of mind. Similarly with gender dysphoria, the science is far from certain, but it looks reasonable to suggest that the testosterone release between weeks six and 13 of gestation permanently programs the brain of a foetus with a Y chromosome to be masculine. If a male foetus isn't exposed to sufficient testosterone during that phase, then masculine mental characteristics might not fully develop when the second surge comes in puberty. They're still male in the sense that they have all the physical bits you'd expect, but if for some reason the testosterone surge isn't effective, they'll identify as female after puberty and display female behaviours including sexual preference. Equally in girls, overexposure to testosterone before birth may lead to the girl identifying as male after puberty even though she'll look female.

Your child's gender and sexuality are set

This science suggests that our gender orientation is as hardwired as our eye colour or the number of legs we have. That has important implications for the way the more than 95 per cent of our community who aren't affected should respond to the one in 30 who are. First, it means that people can't be talked out of being homosexual or feeling like they're inhabiting a body of the wrong gender any more than they can be talked out of having blue eyes. And it doesn't matter whether it's a priest or a counsellor doing the talking.

Secondly, a person's gender identification isn't caused by their parents, their home life or their love of Barbra Streisand, so there is no point blaming Barbra.

I would suggest, however, that it's important to think carefully about whether the teenage years are the best time for your child to reveal their sexual orientation to their peer group. Teenagers are swimming in a frothing sea of hormones that severely affect their ability to make rational decisions. Critically, they're high on oxytocin, which makes them automatically seek out reasons to reject people who aren't like them and to viciously attack anyone they perceive to be an outsider.

It isn't fair and it isn't politically correct, but it's a biological reality that teenagers are the one group of humans least likely to accept a person with a different gender or sexual orientation, no matter how many rainbows they have on their Instagram account. The statistics are unequivocal: the primary thing, besides depression, likely to increase the chances of self-harm and suicide in teenagers is having a non-heterosexual orientation (see page 137). So a cautionary approach would suggest it's better for these kids to keep it to themselves until their peer group has matured enough to accept the news.

'Our gender orientation is as hardwired as our eye colour.'

Yes, it would be nice if the world wasn't so, but wishing and hoping has less than no effect on the hardwired groupthink biology of the teenage brain. This doesn't mean the school shouldn't know. They should, if the child wants them to. And they should work with you to maintain your child's privacy when it comes to protecting them from their peers (see bullying, page 207).

Summary

- A child entering adolescence goes from liking to be liked to obsessing about it. And if that child is a girl, then that obsession is as important to them as breathing – maybe even a little bit more.
- Adolescent relationship turmoil is fuelled by the desire for oxytocin, a hormone that makes us feel good and binds groups together. It makes us more aggressive to those outside the group, more jealous of our in-group relationships, and more likely to feel pleasure at the pain of outsiders. It's powerful group-glue, and it's significantly more powerful for girls than for boys. That's just biological fact, so if you want to change that dynamic, you need to work with the hardwired reality rather than against it.
- Guidance for parents is pretty simple:
  1. Know what's going on.
  2. Have clear rules in place about how and where the friendship or relationship will be indulged.
  3. Don't inspire oppositional behaviour by attacking the personal qualities of the person your kid's peer group has chosen for your child.
  4. Breathe – it will probably be different in six months anyway.
- Sex makes us feel good, so, like self-harm or jogging, it can act as relief from depression, and that may be motivating the behaviour. But it's more likely that addiction to approval of either the sexual partner or your child's peer group (or both) is the primary motivator.

- This is where the adult supervision in the room must step up. No matter how much they fight you on it, you should curtail teen sexual desire. This means realising they have a sex drive much more powerful than yours and ensuring you don't provide opportunities for them to act on it.
- The best way for a teenager to not get pregnant or acquire an STI is for them to not have sex. If they must have sex, then condom use must be mandatory. The pill is not a good option. It takes the part sector of the population most likely to experience anxiety, depression, suicidal thoughts and self-harm – adolescent girls – and massively increases the risk of all those things.
- Our gender orientation is as hardwired as our eye colour or the number of legs we have. That has important implications for the way the more than 95 per cent of our community who aren't affected should respond to the one in 30 who are.
- The primary thing, besides depression, likely to increase the chances of self-harm and suicide in teenagers is having a non-heterosexual orientation. So, a cautionary approach would suggest it's better for these kids to keep it to themselves until their peer group has matured enough to accept the news.

SLEEP

All oxygen-breathing life forms sleep. From an evolutionary point of view, sleep looks like a pretty stupid 'improvement'. Being out cold a quarter of the time makes us an easy target for animals with sharp teeth. So the fact that we nevertheless do it suggests it's non-negotiable and vital. It seems its primary function is to clean up the garbage we produce by burning oxygen. If we don't sleep our brain starts to seriously malfunction within days.

Simply put, our brains work progressively worse and worse the longer we go without sleep. Recent studies of shiftworkers have confirmed the results of large numbers of animal studies. The effects of sleep deprivation are similar to drunkenness – without the buzz. Sleep-deprived adults had lower scores on vigilance, intellectual ability, reaction time and inhibition. They were less

'The effects of sleep deprivation are similar to drunkenness.'

alert, dumber, slower and had less impulse control – and it got worse the longer they were sleep deprived. Other research has shown that people who drive after 17–19 hours without sleep perform worse than people with a blood-alcohol reading over the legal limit (.05). Up to 15 per cent of fatal car crashes are a result of fatigue, and it's estimated that 100,000 deaths a year occur in US hospitals due to sleep deprivation (of the staff, not the patients).

But I suspect I'm not telling you anything you don't already know. I know I'm significantly less capable of thinking clearly at midnight than I am at 5 am – which is why these words are being typed at 5 am.

Melatonin

Oxygen is a highly reactive substance, so when an animal like us uses it to burn glucose for energy, a lot of highly reactive bits of garbage are produced. Those reactive oxygen species (aka free radicals or simply radical) can cause significant damage to our cell structure and DNA. This is known as oxidative stress. We have a natural way of getting rid of the rubbish – we produce antioxidants, which react with free radicals and defuse them. One of our most powerful antioxidants is melatonin, the hormone that regulates sleep (and changes the colour of a reptile's skin, but I diverge). From about three months of age, our melatonin levels vary in accordance with our circadian (day–night) rhythm. Melatonin is lowest in the middle of the day and peaks between midnight and 8 am.

Melatonin is an extraordinarily powerful antioxidant because it easily crosses cell membranes and the blood–brain barrier. There's nowhere a free radical can hide from a melatonin molecule on clean-up duty. Even more powerfully, it's the one antioxidant that has a cascading effect. Even after it reacts with a radical to eliminate it, the chemical by-products of the reaction are still powerful antioxidants themselves. This superpower is why melatonin is found in the brains of all oxygen-breathing life forms.

The human brain is a massive consumer of oxygen. At rest it burns one-fifth of our total oxygen intake (but is only 2 per cent of our body weight) and that percentage increases substantially when the brain is active. It's also made of a large amount of easily oxidised polyunsaturated fat. As you might imagine, the combination of easily oxidised fat and huge amounts of oxygen make the brain oxidation central. This, of course, means we need an antioxidant with superpowers, and so the brain is a primary site for melatonin. There are a lot of free radicals to clean up after a day of heavy thinking, and a good night's sleep will do the job thanks to melatonin.

Like all hormones, melatonin has more than one function. It's the clean-up crew, but it's also what signals a circuit to shut down. It has similar effects to GABA on the dopamine circuits, so it has strong anti-addictive, antidepressant, anti-pain and anti-anxiety effects. Because of this, several drugs that mimic melatonin have now been approved for use as antidepressant and anti-anxiety medications.

What happens while we sleep

We don't know why all oxygen-breathers sleep, but it likely has something to do with the fact that our peak production time for melatonin is while we're asleep. If you're going to do a full system clean-up, it's probably easier to do it with as much of the system shut down as possible. And that brings us neatly to one of melatonin's other little tricks. It shuts down our neuronal connections before it goes to work. When we sleep, our brains are getting a full 100,000 kilometre service. And I don't mean the kind of service where the mechanic vacuums the carpets and tells you they've checked the brakes, I mean a stripped-back-to-the-chassis full break-down and rebuild – every night.

There are two distinct phases to sleep, NREM (non-rapid eye movement) and REM (rapid eye movement). About 80 per cent of a night's sleep is NREM, and we cycle between NREM and REM four or five times during the night. During NREM, our brain is effectively shut down bit by bit and cleaned up. Neurotransmitters are turned off in the part being cleaned and then restarted again for testing during the next REM sleep cycle.

'Melatonin is the brain's clean-up crew.'

REM sleep is a high-activity restart of the circuits that were just shut down. We almost wake up during the REM phase, but not quite. During REM sleep we run simulations of the things those circuits do when we're awake, to make sure everything is back up to speed. We call those simulations dreams. We could, of course, just wake up to do this, but that would require waking the whole brain, and the lag time to get us fully operational again (that 'Where's the snooze button?' feeling you have first thing in the morning) is just too inefficient. After each REM phase we shut down again, go back to NREM and close down the next lot of circuits. Once all necessary circuits have been cleaned to operational readiness, the cycle stops and we wake up.

I like to think of melatonin as like the clean-up crews on aeroplanes. When the plane arrives, they empty it out, clean it up and get it ready for flight again. Then, just before take-off, they let the REM pilots and crew back on to make sure everything still works properly.

Sleepy teens

The massive hormonal changes that occur during puberty affect sleep timing. In particular, the huge increases in oestrogen and testosterone cause a 'phase shift', the scientific term for pushing everything back an hour or two. Teenagers still need as much sleep as everybody else, but their body won't let them go to sleep for up to three hours later than they did as a child. A child who would be out cold by 8 pm will, after puberty commences, be unable to get to sleep before 9 pm, and by the time they reach their late teens will struggle to go to sleep before midnight.

The timing of this phase shift matches the onset of puberty, so it happens to girls about one year earlier than boys. Over the course of puberty, the delay becomes gradually larger, peaking at around 19 in girls and 20 in boys. This, of course, is music to the ears of a teenager who wants to stay up later and play *Fortnite* or chat with their friends online. And it means you can't entirely blame devices for the delay. Huge numbers of studies in hundreds of human cultures at various times have confirmed that the delay will occur regardless of access to Netflix. That's not to say devices don't make it worse than it otherwise would be.

A full sleep cycle in a teen still needs to be around eight hours, so this means that if they didn't go to sleep until midnight but have to be up at 6 am, they'll have a brain that's only partly cleaned up and ready for the next day of wear and tear. They will have missed at least one NREM phase, and bits of their brain they probably need will be very dodgy until they can get a decent sleep cycle. As a parent, you can't change puberty and you can't change a puberty sleep-time phase shift, but you can control access to things that will make it harder for them to commence sleep. And it's going to be an awful lot easier if you implement rules about bedtime and device use well before your dear little cherub has turned into a steaming hormonal lump of pubescent teenagerdom.

Our teenage children have always had earlier bedtimes than their friends, or at least what their friends say their bedtimes are. But we don't care. As they age, their bedtimes get gradually later. It started with 7:30 pm on school nights in primary school, moved to around 8:30 pm in Year 9 and was about 10 pm by the end of Year 12. This does not mean they will go to sleep at those times, just that we expect them to be in bed without a device with the lights out by then. It's an almost nightly struggle to make sure it happens and they will exploit every chance to crib a little extra time, but it's worth it the next morning. A teen after a solid eight hours is a very different beast to one who's only had five.

Sleep and screens

Melatonin release is triggered by darkness and suppressed by light. We're particularly sensitive to the blue-wavelength light emitted by computer screens. Lying in bed looking at a light-emitting device is not going to help anyone get to sleep. A teenage child will complain that they can't get to sleep and they'll be telling the truth, but the best antidote (after giving them a slightly later bedtime) is to tell them to lie in a darkened room. It's reasonable to allow them to stay up later, because biology really won't let them go to sleep as early as they did as a child. But it's not reasonable to allow them to indulge in light-emitting addictive behaviour while they're doing it. Both the light and the dopamine generated as part of the addiction will make it even harder for them to get to sleep. This is the equivalent of you expecting to go straight to sleep after knocking back six black coffees just before you hopped into bed. The stimulant effect of caffeine is identical to the stimulant effect of the dopamine-stimulating apps installed on your child's device.

'Lying in bed looking at a light-emitting device is not going to help anyone get to sleep.'

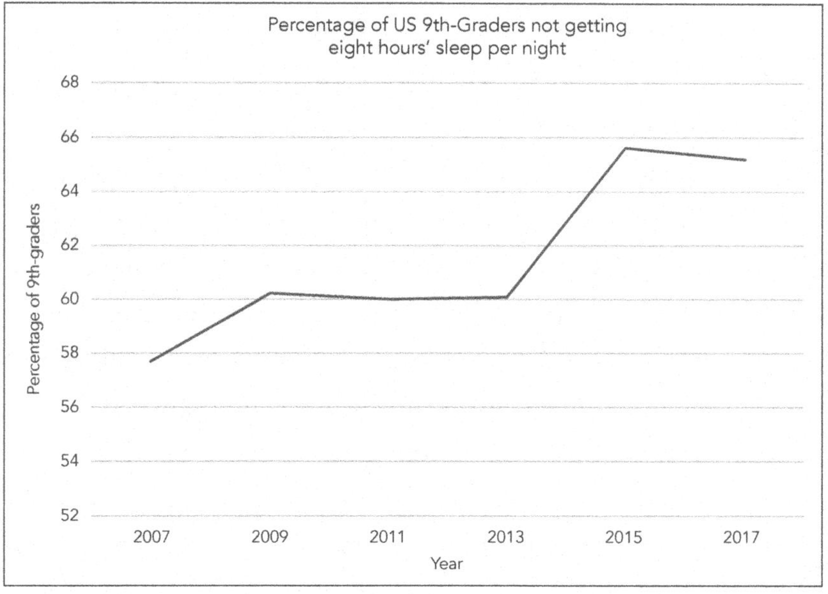

We don't have a lot of good recent data on teenage sleep, but the information we do have (see the graph above) tells us that the numbers of teens not getting sufficient sleep has accelerated wildly since the introduction of tablets and phones. Our ability to cope with anxiety and depression is impaired by lack of sleep. We become irritable and overreactive when we're sleep-deprived. A teen who's already on a hair-trigger and who's already been driven to the edge of anxiety or depression by addiction won't be improved by missing out on a good night's sleep.

Ensuring your teen sleeps

The science suggests that a policy incorporating a one- to three-hour shift in bedtime from the start of puberty until adulthood, along with banning the use of devices within the hour before that bedtime, is reasonable. But I also suggest you build this into your plans from very early on in the child's life, by getting them used to the concept that you'll be expecting them to be in bed, without a device, early. That way, when the biology of puberty requires a phase shift of bedtime, you'll have a time buffer up your sleeve. You'll also have a child who knows no other way to go to sleep than lying in a darkened room until sleep happens. If your eight-year-old is going to bed at 11 pm with an iPad, then you're going to be in serious trouble when puberty demands that be shifted to two in the morning. The child is going to be in even worse trouble trying to operate a brain that's only half-serviced every night.

Our twins are now 15 and very much obsessed by their school iPads. If we let them, they would have them in bed and be on them until dawn (or until they conked out from sheer exhaustion, whichever came first). But even with our strict zero-tolerance policy of devices in rooms, and a 9 pm bedtime, we have to deal with them staying up and chatting (they share a room) later and later. Every now and then one will emerge at 11 pm, bleary-eyed, and claim to be unable to sleep. Our response is always, go back to bed, don't talk, shut your eyes. They are usually asleep within minutes.

If for any reason a child isn't going to get seven to eight hours of sleep, they won't be playing with a full deck until they do. And while getting enough sleep is important for an adult and a child too, for a teenager it's critical. They're very low on the hormones that control addiction, depression and anxiety, so they need all the anti-addictive, antidepressant and anti-anxiety effects they can get from melatonin. Sleep is a powerful counterbalance to the highly addiction-primed state of the teenage brain. Quite apart from that, as we've seen, a brain without sufficient sleep behaves like a brain on too much alcohol. Sending a teenager out into the world without enough sleep is like giving them 10 shots of vodka for breakfast and expecting them to drive to school safely, do well in a maths test and make rational choices about how they interact with others.

'Sleep is a powerful counterbalance to the addiction-primed state of the teenage brain.'

During puberty a teenager's body is telling them they need to stay awake later. As a parent we need to accommodate that but not use it as an excuse to make the problem worse by allowing device use before bed. Most importantly of all, we need to make sure they get enough sleep anyway. This won't be easy. They simply don't feel like going to sleep and most teens will fight long and hard for every extra hour before bed. But like so much else in dealing with adolescents, it's important to set a rule and stick to it. And again, like so much else it will go a lot easier if the rule has been established and enforced throughout their lives to that point.

The very worst thing you can do for a teenager is allow them to set their own bedtime and use addictive devices before attempting to sleep. It's a recipe for addiction, depression and anxiety, and all the horrors that cascade from that.

Summary

- The effects of sleep deprivation are similar to drunkenness.
- We sleep so all the rubbish created from burning oxygen in the brain can be cleaned up. This is only really possible when our brain is largely shut down. When we don't get enough sleep, the rubbish accumulates, and we become progressively less and less able to think.
- The massive hormonal changes that occur during puberty affect sleep timing, but not the amount of sleep we need. The huge increases in oestrogen and testosterone cause a 'phase shift' that pushes everything back an hour or two.
- A full sleep cycle in a teen still needs to be around eight hours, so this means that if they didn't go to sleep until midnight but have to be up at 6 am, they'll have a brain that's only partly cleaned up and ready for the next day of wear and tear.
- A teenage child will complain that they can't get to sleep and they'll be telling the truth, but the best antidote (after giving them a slightly later bedtime) is to tell them to lie in a darkened room. It's reasonable to allow them to stay up later, because biology really won't let them go to sleep as early as they did as a child. But it's not reasonable

to allow them to indulge in light-emitting addictive behaviour while they're doing it.

- Sleep is a powerful counterbalance to the highly addiction-primed state of the teenage brain.

How to manage your teenagers' use of screens: the rules

I went to a lot of trouble to write this book. First, I found a girl, Lizzie, who wanted a large number of children. Then, without revealing my devious plan, I convinced her to produce a representative sample of kids. We had six, three males and three females. I also made sure there were three left-handers and three right-handers – hey, it might matter! And I also threw in a set of twins at the end for controlled trials that minimise genetic effects. I also took the trouble of making sure Lizzie was from a large family herself – she is one of five. This was so I would have a basis for comparison to the way she and her siblings were raised in the 1980s. Then I waited until all six kids, now aged 15–23, became adolescents. While I was waiting I got involved in technology start-up based in the United States, so

I could understand exactly how the next wave of technology might impact teenagers. I did all of this just so you could read this book about parenting teenagers. You're welcome.

Throughout this book I've suggested ground rules that will help keep kids safe from bullying, addiction, anxiety, depression, peer pressure, self-harm and even suicide, but you might have noticed something about them. They all looked very similar and all essentially boiled down to five simple rules.

The rules

1. Parents make rules and kids follow them. So be a parent.
2. Those rules should severely restrict access to personal electronic devices (and all other addictive substances).
3. The rules should be clear and unequivocal.
4. Breaches of rules should be punished – consistently.
5. All teens need eight hours' sleep a night.

In this chapter I want to focus on what I believe to be the crucial element of modern parenting. Device control. No other generation has had this level of exposure to potential addiction. Ever. No other generation has been within an order of magnitude of it. No other generation has had the ability to access highly addictive behaviour, anywhere, at any time. According to recent research, a quarter of all US adults are online almost constantly and among those aged 18–29 that number rises to 39 per cent. Just 1 in 10 said they were online less than daily and only 1 in 20 said they were online less than several times a week. Of those with access to a mobile device, 89 per cent are online daily. That constant ability to press the dopamine button is having disastrous consequences among gen Z, but that is just the start of the disease cascade that awaits them – and the next generation and the one after that. You can't save all the kids. You can't change all the schools. And you can't change the way society treats technology. But you can limit the damage to your children.

We are by no means perfect in our device access limitations, but here are some of the things we do. These rules did not spring fully formed into life. They have accumulated over time through long and hard-won experience, starting with our eldest. He became among the first tablet users in his school when he purchased, using his part-time work savings, one of the first shipment of iPads available in Australia. He was in Year 11 and it was 2011. He already had a serious obsession with *Minecraft* (first released in 2009) well under way, but playing it required him to be in a public space in front of a very non-portable computer. Usage was easy to monitor and limit. The new iPad meant he had the ability to take his device to school, to the bathroom and to bed with him, and that pushed his screen time numbers into the stratosphere. We quickly discovered that while teenage boys are hardly the most electrifying company in the world, adding a screen addiction and the inevitable sleep deprivation to the mix does not improve things one little bit. We were on the first wave of screen-addicted teens and it didn't take us long to be determined to be in front of the problem. We resisted buying school-mandated devices for as long as possible (see page 193) but since they have inevitably invaded we have tried hard to implement the following rules. Ironically, our eldest, now a veteran of screen use, has become one of our greatest allies in enforcing the limitations set out below.

No private screen time

This is much easier said than done. But it is critically important you do the best you can. Without this rule enforced you have very little chance of enforcing the other rules that follow. Our rule is that tablets are not permitted in bedrooms at any time and preferably should be in a charging rack next to the TV, so anyone can see at a glance where they are. If they need to be used 'for homework' then it must be in a public place, preferably at a table or desk where anyone can see what is on the screen. Because these devices are extremely portable and they are actually required for schoolwork, this is a rule that is extraordinarily difficult to enforce. It requires hypervigilance and an iron determination to just say no. I am not good at that, but I am getting better and my resolve has been significantly stiffened by the research I have laid out above. Our only real holiday from the enforcement regime is on school holidays. We lock 'em up or leave them behind for the duration. We reason that they are clearly not needed for school so why have them available at all during holidays? The screeching and moaning of the addicted is loud for the first few minutes. But they quickly get over it, because history has taught them, on this, we are immovable. Holidays are a glorious break from the continual monitoring of devices. At first the kids are bored but it doesn't take long for the boredom to motivate imagination. Without the ubiquitous devices, they are transported back to an earlier age, where the only way something rewarding or even interesting was going to happen was if they got off their bottom and looked for it. The device-holiday transforms screen-obsessed kids into book-reading, beach-going, movie-attending, socialising teenagers like magic. Obviously, it doesn't mean parental control is no longer needed but now it becomes the much more traditional, low-volume addiction control of the 'Is Sally's mum going to be there?' variety.

Restricting screen use to public areas only during term and not at all on holidays should curtail the obvious addictions like gambling and porn (the kind involving sex). But more detailed intervention is needed for a few of the others.

No internet-enabled phones

The easiest way to circumvent any prohibitions you may have is simply for the child to have access to the internet without going through your home network or the school network. Any modern mobile will come with the ability to connect to the internet and most will enable hotspotting so that other devices can connect via it. Kids need phones these days because the community has stopped investing in public phone infrastructure. But they don't need those phones to be internet capable. We purchase flip phones for our teenagers and they are not internet enabled. They can call and be called, but they can't do much else. This means they cannot be used as a back door to addiction.

No social media

The big social media companies require a child to be 13 to have an account. This is loosely enforced and widely disregarded and, in my view, pointless anyway. Kids under 13 are not at any great risk from the addictive properties of social media. The hormone mix is simply not sufficient to motivate them to do much more than glance at the photos with the same level of interest that I might have in Aunt Joan's slide-night from her recent trip to Croatia, plus they generally don't have sufficient motivation to get too adventurous with photos of themselves. Lizzie and I don't permit the kids to have social media accounts that allow them to post photos. They still use Messenger because, apparently, they are physically incapable of talking to a person face to face, but they don't have the ability to post photos of themselves to farm likes. This does not stop them browsing the accounts of their mates, but it does neuter the addictive potential of approval-porn type apps. We have found that simply saying 'no' is remarkably effective as a control on social media posting. By its very nature, it's a public activity and so relatively easy to detect should they decide they don't need to listen to you.

No games

Games are free, installed in seconds and available all the time. It is virtually impossible to stop a determined child from getting access to a game if they really want to. And they always really want to. Every now and then we have a games purge on all the kids' devices. We ask to see all the installed apps. Any that aren't required for school are deleted. Yes, we know they can be reinstalled in seconds, but it reinforces the message that games are not permitted. There is nothing we can do to stop kids playing games on the bus or at school, but rather like limiting sugar consumption in the home, every little bit of abstinence we can impose gives their Delta FosB just a little more of a chance to reset.

No purchasing capability

Many online stores save your credit card details. This is especially true if you are using Apple devices, where your credit card details will be stored as part of your Apple ID. I discovered this the hard way when I entered my credit card details on one of the kids' iPads so they could purchase a school book. A few weeks later I noticed charges coming through for music, books and other apps and discovered that I needed to explicitly delete the payment information to stop it being used. If kids see an app or song they like and the store says they have the ability to download it, they will often automatically go ahead and do it. So be cautious about leaving payment capabilities on children's devices. Remember online shopping is a powerful addiction too.

What about Parental Control Software?

There is of course an automated solution to controlling what is accessed on devices. The category is called Parental Control Software (PCS) and it is well served by a large number of software vendors. Many of them promise to be able to limit which websites and apps are accessed on devices under your control. We don't use them. The primary reason is that even though I am an IT professional (of sorts), I have zero confidence that I could implement the router and client configuration that would allow my kids to use the bits of the internet and the apps that I wanted them to, when I wanted them to, without creating gigantic loopholes and back doors and impairing the ability of the rest of the household to use what they needed or wanted. We feel vigilance and awareness are a better defence than the false sense of security that automation could bring. Hacking this kind of software is trivial for many tech-aware kids. It can be as simple as switching to incognito mode in the browser or using your friend's hotspot, changing the device DNS settings or grabbing some VPN tunnelling code from a more techy mate. Our kids' school control software was subverted within days of being installed even though it was the latest and greatest and they had the resources of a fully staffed IT department overseeing it. It was done by a student seeing what he could do. It turned out he could do an awful lot. Lizzie and I prefer enforced physical control to the police state-emulating, trust-eroding, barely effectual alternative. If you feel that is something you could properly implement, here is a list of popular packages. All of these will competently block named websites and most will monitor social media and even chat activity.

- Qustudio
- Norton Family
- Net Nanny
- Surfie
- SpyAgent
- McAfee Total Protection Family.

Just don't ever assume that because you've installed some software, your kids aren't accessing addictive apps, games and social media anyway. In my view, a more robust solution is to understand that you are dealing with addiction and prohibit access to the device delivering the addictive behaviour as much as possible. Talk to your kids about what you do and don't want them doing online and why, then make sure they do as you say. They don't want to be addicted any more than you want them to be, so give them the chance to understand what is going on and why it matters. You might be surprised at how they respond.

Find something else to do

Screens become a default behaviour when a child is bored and has nothing better to do. Alongside all the prohibitions above, there is something positive you can do. Encourage your kids to try things that don't involve screens. This does not mean you need to buy a pony or have them take up expensive hobbies. But it does mean you should keep an eye out for opportunities to participate in new experiences outside the home. It might be as simple as turning up to the come-and-try day that most sports run before their seasons start or finding out about the local rocketry club or pushing them (gently) towards a new sport or taking up a musical instrument at school. Your kid will be terrified that they will be the noob and everyone else will be an Olympic athlete or just about to join the Australian Youth Orchestra, but the reality is everyone is largely, well, average. Within minutes of their first attempt, most kids will figure out they aren't as crap as they thought. Usually they also discover it's fun to learn something new and even more fun to meet different people. They will resist your initial attempts but don't take no for an answer. Our kids have all tried at least four or five extracurricular activities each. They are not world champions at any of them, but over the years they have whittled them down to the ones they really like. I know they like them because I can take a cranky, nasty teenage girl to a music lesson or netball training and pick up a playful, happy girl after an hour. She will never admit it made her feel good but the evidence is there for everyone to see. The science (see page 140) says the endorphins from activity and the oxytocin from socialisation will have that effect. And I can definitely verify that any time off screens and out in the real world practising something that uses physical skills or solving problems is almost magical in its ability to re-centre a teenage mood.

These rules are the ones we currently use. They are not a complete solution. That is, of course, throwing the iPads in the bin. Unfortunately, that is not an option while they are required for school. This is our band-aid solution. It is a daily struggle to keep these highly addictive and highly portable devices out of our kids' hands while they are at home and it is tiresome. But we have found that the more definite we are, the less frequently we have to prove that we mean it. Good luck!

Summary

Portable screens are the single most dangerously addictive thing in most teens' lives. If you want to minimise your child's contact with them, here are some rules we have found helpful:

- No private screen time.
- No internet-enabled phones.
- No social media.
- No games.
- No purchasing capability.
- Use Parental Control Software only if you know what you're doing and don't rely on it to do your job of supervising screen time.
- Find something else to do with all the time your child now has available because they aren't glued to a screen.

Conclusion

The adults in the room

A mid-20th-century mother didn't have time to scratch herself. She had three or four children and probably a husband to tend to, and most of the food she fed the family was made from raw ingredients by her hands in her kitchen. There were no packaged meals and no microwave ovens to cook them in, appliances were only just starting to enter the home, and even toasters weren't smart enough to know how long to cook your bread. Running the home was a full-time job. The house had one income, there was almost no refrigeration and the shops were only open during working hours. Children were growing up in a busy workplace. A new baby had to fit into the rhythm of an efficient household, and it wouldn't occur to anyone that it might have an opinion about that or, even if it did, that it would change anything. Dr Spock gave the postwar mother permission not to use a stopwatch to feed the new arrival, but the priority was still what worked for the household rather than for the baby.

By the end of the century, that position had completely reversed. The household workload had halved, and so had the number of children in that house. Shops were open 24 hours a day, and a meal could be cooked in less time than it would take to peel a carrot. Those babies of the 1960s and 1970s were now the parents, and they believed firmly that baby knew best. Parents were rendered powerless servants to the needs of the attention-seeking baby. Babies must be demand fed. Controlled crying (or whatever the euphemism was that week) was akin to cruelty. Suddenly there was a huge market for so-called baby-whisperers, people you could hire to do what you couldn't – put your child into a routine and save your sleep and sanity. Anything that produced trepidation in the child should immediately be removed from its life. In general, the parent's job became that of a sherpa for a Mount Everest climber: carry the bags, keep danger at bay and otherwise be invisible.

Children were no longer seen-but-not-heard. Their every utterance, no matter how banal, was given the weight of a Commandment. Every child became 'special'. That's not to say earlier generations were not loved and valued, but they were given limited choices and a greatly reduced set of pathways forward. The role of a parent was to protect and encourage, but not to indulge flights of fantasy. The typical parent of a gen Z is supposed to cater to every whim that credit can buy and to trail along unquestioningly in the wake of their special progeny.

In my youth, the community in general, and parents in particular, provided boundaries to teen impulses. Those boundaries would flex but never allow the teen to go too far off the reservation. Having to call a home phone to speak to the girl of your dreams ensured at least two sets of adults were (vaguely) aware of goings on. Now a 'chat' at midnight from your bed is invisible to the boundary riders. Having to feign an interest in motorcycle magazines just to scope out the cover of Playboy imposed real access limits to porn that are completely foreign to a gen Z.

When I was growing up no one was important. We all went to school to learn. There were neither accelerated courses, nor programs for the 'gifted and talented'. This was not a sign of neglect, quite the opposite: it was a sign we all mattered. If you got a concept faster than others it was your job to sit down and shut up so as to not disturb them while they caught up. The emphasis was on everyone attaining a standard. Everyone mattered. In today's individualistic society, the tables have turned. Each child is important, and yet collectively doesn't matter. Each child is encouraged to believe that their every opinion is valuable. Everyone is 'special'. What no one tells you is that when everyone is special, no one is special.

In spite of this, we are told that a child's every preference counts. And wherever there are preferences you will find marketers ready to 'guide' those choices. We have created a marketer's dream: impulsive, self-important, self-obsessed children as consumers without gatekeepers. Marketers have the perfect play, the ability to appeal directly to the decision-maker's notion of self-worth without having to go through their parents. And if that means using dirty tricks like the psychology of addiction then so be it. By stepping back from the boundaries and promoting our teenagers to 'Kings of the World', we have unwittingly simultaneously removed the parental and community controls on teenage impulsiveness and told marketers to use every trick in the book to sell to our kids. We have flung open the doors and told them whatever choice they make will be the right one. The reality is that for brains buzzing with addiction, testosterone and oxytocin, that is almost never true.

Any number of things could explain this collective decision to bubble-wrap kids. It might be their declining numbers, smaller families in general, or the fact that the decision to have a child is a highly prized and increasingly rare event. It could even be

BIRTH TIMING

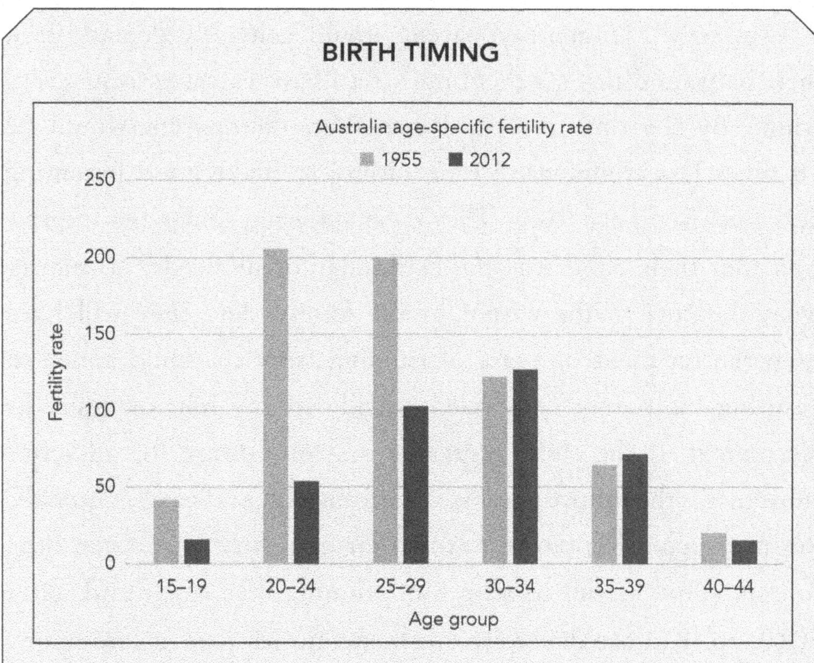

In 1955 most women had their children in their early 20s and they would be having twice as many as a modern woman. In 2012, most women had their children in their early 30s.

that the number of single-parent families has almost tripled from 6 per cent in 1966 to 16 per cent in 2016. No longer are women having children early and easily. Increasingly, people are waiting until almost the last biological minute and, after a lifetime on the pill, women are frequently struggling to conceive with a partner whose fertility has probably been severely compromised by seed oils (see page 83). Or it could be all of that combined with our drive towards individualism. But whatever the reason, it's a very real inversion of the parent–child relationship, and it meant that those parents were spectacularly ill-prepared for the addiction tidal wave heading their way.

An early 21st-century parent would generally demand-feed their baby, and this set them up for a life of catering to its every whim. By the time the child was four, that parent would be 18 times less confident in their ability to make good parenting decisions (see page 168). They'd be suffering under the impression that their child was the best judge of its needs, no matter what the cost to the parent or the family. And they will have been the recipient of years of training from the child aimed at ensuring the parent responded quickly to any hint of desire or discomfort. If the child expressed a strong desire for addictive substances, then most parents would cave in, and cave in quickly. I'm not suggesting parents are so far gone that they fetch little Johnny some heroin to stop him whining, but sugar and, after 2010, an iPad are definitely on the menu. Most of us are happy to disengage our cynicism, accept the marketers' assurances that there's nothing wrong with either of them, welcoming the gift of a pacified child with open arms. The combination of a generation of parents who mustn't say no and the mass availability of dopamine-exciting hot-buttons in every teen's pocket have created the start of a rolling disaster in mental health that will be with us for decades and that can only get much, much worse.

But there is a solution. Discipline. Yours, not theirs.

The change in the teen landscape

Sorry, but I have some bad news. You peaked at 25. That's not to say you're not that good now (assuming you're older than that), just that from our brain's perspective, us at 25 is as good as it gets. We spent the first decade or so of our lives laying a solid foundation and becoming a standard-issue fully functional human prototype. Even so, by the start of puberty, we weren't much more sophisticated than any mammal, except we could talk. We were empty vessels waiting to be filled with what was to come. Then the real growth began.

Between the onset of puberty and the age of 25, we built the adult part of our brains from scratch. We learnt how to assess risk, plan for consequences, control our emotions, manage impulses, take responsibility, lead, follow, focus, persist and finish. We also learnt how to live with other adults, how to like and help them and have them like us and help us, and how to love and be loved. To make all this possible, our brains removed the brakes and made us chase new experiences. And once we were neck-deep in them, our brains opened the data channels so everything we experienced would imprint on the adult human we were building.

After 15 years or so of this hyper-learning, the brain locked everything down, and what we were at 25 is what we are now – until the Alzheimer's sets in. That doesn't mean we can't learn new things, but how hard or easy that is depends on how good the brain hardware was we created in our teens. There are no hardware upgrades in our future.

The downside to this massive brain growth spurt is that it makes adolescents highly susceptible to addiction. The reward pathway is dialled up so high and the controls loosened so much that any dopamine-inducing behaviour has the potential to become addictive if it's experienced on high rotation. When the original specs were laid down for humans, this wasn't much of a risk. Rewarding behaviour was pretty damn hard to come by, and even harder to obtain repeatedly in a short time. There were no ways to repetitively simulate sex, danger or approval, and shortcut substances were also very much rarer than hen's teeth. In short, the body wasn't taking much of a chance disabling the brakes on the reward pathway, because addiction was a possibility so remote that it was worth the risk.

Then, during the last half of the 20th century, we dabbled with giving teens more and more access to addictive substances. We didn't do it on purpose, they were just the collateral damage from an adult society that was doing a bit of experimentation for its own pleasure. As teens obtained more and more access to the substances that were theoretically for adults only, we started to see the downsides of letting that happen. We saw an upswing in teen depression and anxiety, and we watched teen violence, crime and pregnancy spiral out of control, even though relatively few teenagers were actually able to circumvent the modest barriers we put in place. We still ID-checked teens purchasing alcohol, we still prohibited the sale of cigarettes to minors, and we theoretically wouldn't even sell them a scratch ticket. If you wanted to place a bet on the seventh at Randwick, you'd have to convince the bloke behind the cage at the TAB you were over 18, then hang about with some distinctly less than savoury chaps to pick up your winnings. Even *Playboy*, which would be way too tame to make a buck online now, was shrink-wrapped to keep it from prying teen boys' eyes.

And then, almost without thinking, we decided to allow every teen access to all of the world's most addictive dopamine buttons 24 hours a day, seven days a week. Not satisfied with that, we even invented some more – a special version of danger porn for boys called online gaming, and some sweet, sweet, approval porn action for girls in the guise of social media. Then we asked our schools to sell the educational advantages to parents to ensure they had access to all of it during class as well. I remember staying up late as a teen in the 1980s just to catch a glimpse of Jane Fonda's breasts in *Barbarella*, but now nakedness is just one tap away. It's now harder to avoid nudity than it is to see it. And now we're talking about a lot more than a three-second shot of Ms Fonda's exposed mammary glands. It's impossible to find an app (except perhaps an office or accounting program) that hasn't been intentionally designed to addict teenagers. Gaming is available in every bedroom, on every bus and in every classroom, and the local betting shop is now available in every pocket and in every classroom. Thanks to approval porn – Facebook, Snapchat, Instagram, YouTube and [insert name of whatever is the latest hot social app when you are reading this] – our kids are also the first generation to be constantly connected, at all times, to their friends and their enemies. They live and die by the number of likes they got on their latest post, and they've never experienced a time when they weren't accessible during every waking minute – and have no sense of what that would even be like.

But, perversely, they're also the loneliest generation ever. If we wanted to design a high-addiction environment, I'm struggling to think how we could have done it more thoroughly. Even more incredibly, we've accomplished all of this in less than a decade. It's so recent that the statistics that should be ringing alarm bells are scattered and piecemeal. But the early warning signs are clearly there.

Gen Z teens aren't like any generation of humans ever before. No other generation has had their reward pathways so pervasively corrupted. I'm not talking about a few bad eggs who got addicted to weed and wrecked their lives. I'm talking about a generation where every single child has had their reward pathways permanently rewritten with a strong bias towards addiction, depression and anxiety. These are the kids we'll be expecting to take over the reins of our society in a few years. And a few years after that we'll be expecting them to look after the enormous numbers of us growing old before our time because of a processed food diet high in sugar and seed oils. But they'll be spectacularly unsuited to either job. A third of them are anxious or depressed, none of them get enough sleep, which makes them more anxious and depressed, and an accelerating number of them will be infertile.

The good news is that in a single blow the new flood of electronic addiction all but wiped out all the old ones we invented in the 1960s and expanded in the 1980s and 1990s. The iPad killed teen pregnancy, illicit drug use, teen violence and teen alcoholism more thoroughly than any government anti-addiction program could even dream of. But the cost is a tidal wave of the consequences of addicted teens. Academic performance is plummeting. Fertility is sinking even faster. Anxiety and depression are rocketing, and self-harm and suicide are catching up fast. It's not your imagination, gen Z is seriously messed up and they were just the first wave. Wait until those addicted teens hit their 30s and the gateway effect has them seeking out alcohol, opioids and illicit drugs on top of their electronic addiction.

Our biology hasn't changed. Teenagers are still skating on the edge of human experience so they can push it as far and as fast as they can. But now they're doing it in a soup of addiction, where everyone wants a piece of them and their school is helping the marketers push the worried parents out of the way.

How to make a difference

You can't save all the kids or even some of them. But you can help your kids. Unfortunately, it won't be fun and you won't be thanked for your efforts for many years to come, if at all. It will require you to do the one thing parents have been told they shouldn't do since we decided Dr Spock was uncool in the 1980s: say no – a lot. And the earlier we start, the easier it will be.

Teenagers need rules. They don't need a pal to hang out with. They don't need someone else to do Insta with. They don't need someone to play computer games with. They need whatever adults they have in their lives to be placing hard boundaries at the on-ramps to the addiction highway. This doesn't mean you have to stop them trying new things, even assuming you could. But it does mean you need to pay attention and, when they hit a no-go zone, stop them. This of course means you'll also need to put down your own iPad and make them talk to you.

To do this, you'll have to stick to the five simple *rules* I outlined earlier:

1 Parents make rules and kids follow them. So be a parent.
2 Those rules should severely restrict access to personal electronic devices (and all other addictive substances).
3 The rules should be clear and unequivocal.
4 Breaches of rules should be punished – consistently.
5 All teens need eight hours' sleep a night.

Those are the only things you, as an individual parent, can control directly, but it would be enormously helpful if you could also ensure that everyone who has anything to do with your teenager follows the same rules. It means that if you're co-parenting, your other half is signed on to the same concept. I realise that's easier to say than do, but if they care at all about the mental health of their child, they need to understand the critical importance of addiction in that child's life, and why that means they need to join you as a card-carrying member of the 'Dr No' club.

Whether both parents live together or not is really irrelevant. Rules will be significantly more effective if they're agreed upon out of the earshot of the teens, and consistently enforced – always. It means selecting a school that behaves like an extra parent by making it abundantly clear what behaviour is acceptable and what isn't, and by ensuring its role models are actually people that embody those principles. It's harder than it sounds in the age of defensive education, but every now and then you'll strike a school leader with a backbone and a yearning for the old days. A sure sign of being on the right track will be a complete device ban on school premises and a school culture that places values above popularity.

You might be worried that it's a little too late to start schedule-feeding your 14-year-old, and it is, but it's *never too late* to start making and enforcing rules. Sure, the research says this will be easier for you and them if you started straight after their birth. But any day you start is better than waiting until tomorrow.

So now you're armed with why you should bother, how about you start? Now.

ENDNOTES

Page

6 During that phase . . . S.V. Siddiqui et al., 'Neuropsychology of prefrontal cortex', *Indian Journal of Psychiatry*, 2008, vol. 50, no. 3, pp. 202–208, www.ncbi.nlm.nih.gov/pmc/articles/PMC2738354

16 From the sixth week of . . . I. Bystron, 'Development of the human cerebral cortex: Boulder Committee revisited', *Nature Reviews Neuroscience*, 2008, vol. 9, no. 2, pp. 110–22, www.ncbi.nlm.nih.gov/pubmed/18209730

16 An adult brain has more . . . F.A. Azevedo et al., 'Equal numbers of neuronal and nonneuronal cells make the human brain an isometrically scaled-up primate brain', *Journal of Comparative Neurology*, 2009, vol. 513, no. 5, pp. 532–41, www.ncbi.nlm.nih.gov/pubmed/19226510

17 It then grows . . . E. Courchesne et al., 'Normal brain development and aging: quantitative analysis at in vivo MR imaging in healthy volunteers', *Radiology*, 2000, vol. 216, no. 3, pp. 672–82, www.ncbi.nlm.nih.gov/pubmed/10966694

17 Just after birth . . . G.M. Innocenti & D.J. Price, 'Exuberance in the development of cortical networks', *Nature Reviews Neuroscience*, 2005, vol. 6, no. 12, pp. 955–65, www.ncbi.nlm.nih.gov/pubmed/16288299

18 And this is significantly enhanced . . . B. de Boer & P.K. Kuhl, 'Investigating the role of infant-directed speech with a computer model', *ARLO*, 2003, vol. 4, no. 4, pp. 129–34, asa.scitation.org/doi/pdf/10.1121/1.1613311

19 In the last two decades . . . N. Gogtay et al., 'Dynamic mapping of human cortical development during childhood through early adulthood', *PNAS*, 2004, vol. 101, no. 21, pp. 8174–79, www.ncbi.nlm.nih.gov/pmc/articles/PMC4 1 9576

19 Animals raised with their littermates . . . J.A. Markham & W.T. Greenough, 'Experience-driven brain plasticity: beyond the synapse', *Neuron Glia Biology*, vol. 1, no. 4, pp. 351–63, www.cambridge.org/core/journals/neuron-glia-biology/article/experiencedriven-brain-plasticity-beyond-the-synapse/263BF348B6A1981F6F3F658458FC6642

22 In the prefrontal cortex . . . P.R. Huttenlocher & A.S. Dabholkar, 'Regional differences in synaptogenesis in human cerebral cortex', *Journal of Comparative Neurology*, 1997, vol. 387, no. 2, pp. 167–78, www.ncbi.nlm.nih.gov/pubmed/9336221

24 Animals whose dopamine-producing . . . J.D. Salamone et al., 'Nucleus accumbens dopamine and the regulation of effort in food-seeking behavior: implications for studies of natural motivation, psychiatry, and drug abuse', *Journal of Pharmacology and Experimental Therapeutics*, 2003, vol. 305, no. 1, pp. 1–8, jpet.aspetjournals.org/content/305/1/1.long

24 When we encounter danger . . . P. Belujon & A.A. Grace, 'Regulation of dopamine system responsivity and its adaptive and pathological response to stress', *Proceedings of the Royal Society B*, 2015, vol. 282, no. 1805, article no. 20142516, rspb.royalsocietypublishing.org/content/282/1805/20142516

25 The paper described . . . Charles E. Moan & Robert G. Heath, 'Septal stimulation for the initiation of heterosexual behavior in a homosexual male', *Journal of Behavior Therapy and Experimental Psychiatry*, 1972, vol. 3, no. 1, pp. 23–26, www.sciencedirect.com/science/article/pii/0005791672900298

25 A similar experiment . . . P.K. Portenoy et al., 'Compulsive thalamic self-stimulation: a case with metabolic, electrophysiologic and behavioral correlates', *Pain*, 1986, vol. 27, no. 3, pp. 277–90, www.ncbi.nlm.nih.gov/pubmed/3492699

26 Scientists are not yet clear . . . A.G. Fischer & M. Ullsperger, 'An update on the role of serotonin and its interplay with dopamine for reward', *Frontiers in Human Neuroscience*, 2017, vol. 11, article no. 484, www.frontiersin.org/articles/10.3389/fnhum.2017.00484/full

26 It, in turn, increases . . . L. Ciranna, 'Serotonin as a modulator of glutamate- and GABA-mediated neurotransmission: implications in physiological functions and 'n pathology', *Current Neuropharmacology*, 2006, vol. 4, no. 2, pp. 101–14, www.ncbi.nlm.nih.gov/pmc/articles/PMC2430669

27 The object of our desire . . . J.D. Salamone, 'A role for accumbens neurons in exertion of effort and evaluating effort-related costs of instrumental actions (commentary on Day et al.)', *European Journal of Neuroscience*, 2011, vol. 33, no. 2, pp. 306–307, onlinelibrary.wiley.com/doi/full/10.1111/j.1460-9568.2010.07566.x

27 Our brains are constantly . . . Jeff A. Beeler, et al., 'Putting desire on a budget: dopamine and energy expenditure, reconciling reward and resources', *Frontiers in Integrative Neuroscience*, 2012, vol. 6, article no. 49, www.ncbi.nlm.nih.gov/pmc/articles/PMC3400936

32 The Ancient Greeks . . . J.L. Butrica, 'The medical use of cannabis among the Greeks and Romans', *Journal of Cannabis Therapeutics*, 2002, vol. 2, no. 2, pp. 51–70, www.tandfonline.com/doi/abs/10.1300/J175v02n02_04

32 And that's exactly . . . David A. Raichlen et al., 'Wired to run: exercise-induced endocannabinoid signaling in humans and cursorial mammals with implications for the "runner's high" ', *Journal of Experimental Biology*, 2012, vol. 215, pp. 1331–36, jeb.biologists.org/content/215/8/1331.long

32 Endocannabinoids stimulate appetite . . . V. Di Marzo et al., 'Leptin-regulated endocannabinoids are involved in maintaining food intake', *Nature*, 2001, vol. 410, no. 6830, pp. 822–25, www.ncbi.nlm.nih.gov/pubmed/11298451

32 Cannabinoids also directly . . . R.W. Foltin, 'Effects of smoked marijuana on food intake and body weight of humans living in a residential laboratory', *Appetite*, 1988, vol. 11, no. 1, pp. 1–14, www.ncbi.nlm.nih.gov/pubmed/3228283
M.A. De Luca et al., 'Cannabinoid facilitation of behavioral and biochemical hedonic taste responses', *Neuropharmacology*, 2012, vol. 63, no. 1, pp. 161–68, www.ncbi.nlm.nih.gov/pmc/articles/PMC3705914

33 In rat studies . . . N.M. Avena et al., 'Evidence for sugar addiction: behavioral and neurochemical effects of intermittent, excessive sugar intake', *Neuroscience and Biobehavioral Reviews*, 2008, vol. 32, no. 1, pp. 20–39, www.ncbi.nlm.nih.gov/pmc/articles/PMC2235907

34 One of the most powerful . . . M.C. Mithoefer et al., 'Durability of improvement in post-traumatic stress disorder symptoms and absence of harmful effects or drug dependency after 3,4-methylenedioxymethamphetamine-assisted psychotherapy: a prospective long-term follow-up study', *Journal of Psychopharmacology*, 2013, vol. 27, no. 1, pp. 28–39, journals.sagepub.com/doi/abs/10.1177/0269881112456611; 'MDMA-assisted psychotherapy', MAPS (Multidisciplinary Association for Psychedelic Studies), maps.org/research/mdma; Dave Philipps, 'F.D.A. agrees to new trials for ecstasy as relief for PTSD patients', *New York Times*, 29 November 2016, www.nytimes.com/2016/11/29/us/ptsd-mdma-ecstasy.html
https://maps.org/news/media/6786-press-release-fda-grants-breakthrough-therapy-designation-for-mdma-assisted-psychotherapy-for-ptsd,-agrees-on-special-protocol-assessment-for-phase-3-trials.
M.C. Mithoefer et al., 'Novel psychopharmacological therapies for psychiatric disorders: psilocybin and MDMA', *Lancet Psychiatry*, 2016, vol. 3, no. 5, pp. 481–88, www.ncbi.nlm.nih.gov/pubmed/27067625

34 One of the more recent . . . S. Lai, 'The association between cigarette smoking and drug abuse in the United States', *Journal of Addictive Diseases*, 2000, vol. 19, no. 4, pp. 11–24, www.tandfonline.com/doi/abs/10.1300/J069v19n04_02

35 Heat shock factor (HSF) . . . I. Shamovsky & E. Nudler, 'New insights into the mechanism of heat shock response activation', *Cell and Molecular Life Sciences*, 2008, vol. 65, no. 6, pp. 855–61, www.ncbi.nlm.nih.gov/pubmed/18239856
T.G. Smith et al., 'The human side of hypoxia-inducible factor', *British Journal of Haematology*, 2008, vol. 141, no. 3, pp. 325–34, www.ncbi.nlm.nih.gov/pmc/articles/PMC2408651

35 So having sex . . . C.M. Olsen, 'Natural rewards, neuroplasticity, and non-drug addictions', *Neuropharmacology*, 2011, vol. 61, no. 7, pp. 1109–22, www.ncbi.nlm.nih.gov/pmc/articles/PMC3139704

35 All illicit drugs . . . A.J. Robison & E.J. Nestler, 'Transcriptional and epigenetic mechanisms of addiction', *Nature Reviews Neuroscience*, 2011, vol. 12, no. 11, pp. 623–37, www.ncbi.nlm.nih.gov/pmc/articles/PMC3272277

36 Once Delta FosB . . . C.M. Olsen, 'Natural rewards, neuroplasticity, and non-drug addictions', *Neuropharmacology*, 2011, vol. 61, no. 7, pp. 1109–22, www.ncbi.nlm.nih.gov/pmc/articles/PMC3139704

36 We know, for example . . . C.M. Olsen, 'Natural rewards, neuroplasticity, and non-drug addictions', *Neuropharmacology*, 2011, vol. 61, no. 7, pp. 1109–22, www.ncbi.nlm.nih.gov/pmc/articles/PMC3139704/ - S5title

36 Cocaine-addicted rats . . . M. Lenoir et al., 'Intense sweetness surpasses cocaine reward', *PLoS One*, 2007, vol. 2, no. 8, article no. e698, www.ncbi.nlm.nih.gov/pmc/articles/PMC1931610

36 And humans addicted . . . J.J. Prochaska et al., 'Physical activity as a strategy for maintaining tobacco abstinence: a randomized trial', *Preventive Medicine*, 2008, vol. 47, no. 2, pp. 215–20, www.ncbi.nlm.nih.gov/pubmed/18572233

36 This is likely to be . . . J.A. Swanson et al., 'The impact of caffeine use on tobacco cessation and withdrawal', *Addictive Behaviors*, 1997, vol./ 22, no. 1, pp. 55–68, www.ncbi.nlm.nih.gov/pubmed/9022872

38 With its aura of . . . Amos Barshad, 'The Juul is too cool', *New York Times*, 7 April 2018, www.nytimes.com/2018/04/07/style/the-juul-is-too-cool.html

38 Australia has a complex . . . https://www.aph.gov.au/Parliamentary_Business/Committees/House/Health_Aged_Care_and_Sport/ElectronicCigarettes/Report

38 They were initially . . . Mark L. Rubinstein et al., 'Adolescent exposure to toxic volatile organic chemicals from e-cigarettes', *Pediatrics*, 2018, vol. 141, no. 4, article no. e20173557, pediatrics.aappublications.org/content/early/2018/03/01/89

38 In the United States . . . Lloyd D. Johnston et al., *Monitoring the Future: National Survey Results on Drug Use. 2017 Overview: Key Findings on Adolescent Drug Use*, Institute for Social Research, University of Michigan, Ann Arbor, 2018, monitoringthefuture.org//pubs/monographs/mtf-overview2017.pdf

39 Recent detailed studies . . . S. Soneji et al., 'Association between initial use of e-cigarettes and subsequent cigarette smoking among adolescents and young adults: a systematic review and meta-analysis', *JAMA Pediatrics*, 2017, vol. 171, no. 8, pp. 788–97, www.ncbi.nlm.nih.gov/pmc/articles/PMC5656237
N.M. Avena et al., 'Evidence for sugar addiction: Behavioral and neurochemical effects of intermittent, excessive sugar intake', *Neuroscience and Biobehavioral Reviews*, 2008, vol. 32, no. 1, pp. 20–39, www.ncbi.nlm.nih.gov/pmc/articles/PMC2235907

39 Nicotine is the addictive . . . M.S. D'Souza & A. Markou 'The "stop" and "go" of nicotine dependence: role of GABA and glutamate', *Cold Spring Harbor Perspectives in Medicine*, 2013, vol. 3, no. 6, article no. a012146, www.ncbi.nlm.nih.gov/pmc/articles/PMC3662348

39 The studies show . . . J. Hartmann-Boyce et al., 'Nicotine replacement therapy versus control for smoking cessation', *Cochrane Database of Systematic Reviews*, 2018, no. 5, article no. CD000146, cochranelibrary-wiley.com/doi/10.1002/14651858.CD000146.pub4/pdf

39 A major analysis . . . B. Coleman et al., 'Transitions in electronic cigarette use among adults in the Population Assessment of Tobacco and Health (PATH) Study, Waves 1 and 2 (2013–2015)', *Tobacco Control*, published online 25 April 2018, doi: 10.1136/tobaccocontrol-2017-054174, www.ncbi.nlm.nih.gov/pubmed/29695458

39 Some treatments use . . . 'Varenicline (Champix) for smoking cessation', NPS Medicinewise, 1 August 2011, www.nps.org.au/radar/articles/varenicline-champix-for-smoking-cessation

40 To actually break . . . R. Jain et al., 'Pharmacological intervention of nicotine dependence', *Biomed Research International*, 2013, vol. 2013, article no. 278392, www.ncbi.nlm.nih.gov/pmc/articles/PMC3891736

42 But if the reward . . . C.D. Fiorillo et al., 'Discrete coding of reward probability and uncertainty by dopamine neurons', *Science*, 2003, vol. 299, no. 5614, pp. 1898–902, www.ncbi.nlm.nih.gov/pubmed/12649484

43 Delta FosB, and voilà! . . . S.W. Kraus et al., 'Neurobiology of compulsive sexual behavior: emerging science', *Neuropsychopharmacology*, 2016, vol. 41, no. 1, pp. 385–86, www.ncbi.nlm.nih.gov/pmc/articles/PMC4677151

43 Naltrexone . . . N.C. Raymond et al., 'Augmentation with naltrexone to treat compulsive sexual behavior: a case series', *Annals of Clinical Psychiatry*, 2010, vol. 22, no. 1, pp. 56–62, www.ncbi.nlm.nih.gov/pubmed/20196983

44 Pay attention to . . . K. Chapman et al., 'How much food advertising is there on Australian television?', *Health Promotion International*, 2006, vol. 21, no. 3, pp. 172–80, academic.oup.com/heapro/article/21/3/172/561184

44 Cortisol increases dopamine . . . G.S. Wand et al., 'Association of amphetamine-induced striatal dopamine release and cortisol responses to psychological stress', *Neuropsychopharmacology*, 2007, vol. 32, no. 11, pp. 2310–20, www.nature.com/articles/1301373

Note also that higher stress levels enhance the effects of addictive substances – addicts get a better high if they're stressed when they consume an addictive substance.

47 The latest highly . . . 'Worldwide digital games market: July 2018', Superdata, 23 August 2018, www.superdataresearch.com/us-digital-games-market

47 It's been described . . . L. Damour, 'Parenting the *Fortnite* addict', *New York Times*, 30 April 2018, www.nytimes.com/2018/04/30/well/family/parenting-the-fortnite-addict.html; N. Paumgarten, 'How *Fortnite* captured teens' hearts and minds', *New Yorker*, 21 May 2018, www.newyorker.com/magazine/2018/05/21/how-fortnite-captured-teens-hearts-and-minds

47 Launched in September 2017 . . . *Fortnite: Battle Royale* product page, Epic Games, 2018, www.epicgames.com/fortnite/en-US/buy-now/battle-royale

47 By mid-June 2018 . . . https://www.businessinsider.com.au/fortnite-size-statistics-players-worldwide-2018-6?r=US&IR=T

47 In just one recent . . . C. Smith, '45 interesting *Fortnite* stats and facts', 19 September 2018, DMR: Business Statistics, Fun Gadgets blog, expandedramblings.com/index.php/fortnite-facts-and-statistics

47 The biggest Fortnite broadcasting . . . N. Paumgarten, 'How *Fortnite* captured teens' hearts and minds', *New Yorker*, 21 May 2018, www.newyorker.com/magazine/2018/05/21/how-fortnite-captured-teens-hearts-and-minds

47 Sixty-eight per cent of Fortnite players . . . https://newzoo.com/insights/articles/a-profile-of-the-battle-royale-player-and-how-they-compare-to-other-gamers/ https://www.vertoanalytics.com/chart-week-deep-dive-fortnite/

47 The game is free . . . C. Cwik, 'Xander Bogaerts breaks out popular "Fortnite" dance to celebrate his hot start', Yahoo! Sports, 30 March 2018, sports.yahoo.com/xander-bogaerts-breaks-popular-fortnite-dance-celebrate-hot-start-234604286.html 'Fortnite Battle Royale: item shop', Orcz, orcz.com/Fortnite_Battle_Royale:_Item_Shop

49 This is called the 'near-miss' . . . L. Clark et al., 'Gambling near-misses enhance motivation to gamble and recruit win-related brain circuitry', *Neuron*, 2009, vol. 61, no. 3, pp. 481–90, www.sciencedirect.com/science/article/pii/S0896627309000373

51 Gamblers have exactly . . . J.J. Paris, 'Gambling pathology is associated with dampened cortisol response among men and women', *Physiology and Behavior*, 2010, vol. 99, no. 2, pp. 230–33, www.ncbi.nlm.nih.gov/pmc/articles/PMC2813972

51 You no longer . . . Casino Heroes website, www.casinoheroes.com/en; 'Casino Heroes review', Vegas Slots Online, www.vegasslotsonline.com/reviews/casino-heroes

51 Or you can participate . . . 'Epic Games will provide $100,000,000 for *Fortnite* esports tournament prize pools in the first year of competitive play', Epic Games, 22 May 2018, www.epicgames.com/fortnite/en-US/news/epic-games-will-provide-100-000-000-for-fortnite-esports-tournament

52 Naturally with something . . . G.A. Matthews et al., 'Dorsal raphe dopamine neurons represent the experience of social isolation', *Cell*, 2016, vol. 164, no. 4, pp. 617–31, www.cell.com/cell/fulltext/S0092-8674(15)01704-3

52 They also become . . . G. Dölen et al., 'Social reward requires coordinated activity of accumbens oxytocin and 5HT', *Nature*, 2013, vol. 501, no. 7466. pp. 179–84, www.ncbi.nlm.nih.gov/pmc/articles/PMC4091761

52 The same mechanism . . . A. Browne et al., 'Prisons within prisons: the use of segregation in the United States', *Federal Sentencing Reporter*, 2011, vol. 24, no. 1, pp. 46–49, fsr.ucpress.edu/content/24/1/46

53 It stimulates dopamine . . . G. Dölen et al., 'Social reward requires coordinated activity of accumbens oxytocin and 5HT', *Nature*, 2013, vol. 501, no. 7466.

pp. 179–84, www.ncbi.nlm.nih.gov/pmc/articles/PMC4091761; A. Acevedo-Rodriguez et al., 'Oxytocin and estrogen receptor β in the brain: an overview', *Frontiers in Endocrinology*, 2015, vol. 6, article no. 160, www.frontiersin.org/articles/10.3389/fendo.2015.00160/full

53 It's released when . . . L. Heon-Jin et al., 'Oxytocin: the great facilitator of life', *Progress in Neurobiology*, 2009, vol. 88, no. 2, pp. 127–51, www.ncbi.nlm.nih.gov/pmc/articles/PMC2689929

53 Just petting a dog . . . J.S. Odendaal & R.A. Meintjes 'Neurophysiological correlates of affiliative behaviour between humans and dogs', *Veterinary Journal*, 2003, vol. 165, no. 3, pp. 296–301, www.ncbi.nlm.nih.gov/pubmed/12672376

53 The reward pathway . . . S. Uhl-Bronner et al., 'Sexually dimorphic expression of oxytocin binding sites in forebrain and spinal cord of the rat', *Neuroscience*, 2005, vol. 135, no. 1, pp. 147–54, www.ncbi.nlm.nih.gov/pubmed/16084653

53 When we think . . . S.G. Shamay-Tsoory et al., 'Intranasal administration of oxytocin increases envy and schadenfreude (gloating)', Biological Psychiatry, 2009, vol. 66, no. 9, pp. 864–70, www.ncbi.nlm.nih.gov/pubmed/19640508

54 We're much more . . . T.M. Love, 'Oxytocin, motivation and the role of dopamine', *Pharmacology Biochemistry and Behavior*, 2014, vol. 119, pp. 49–60, www.ncbi.nlm.nih.gov/pmc/articles/PMC3877159

54 The oxytocin also . . . G. Domes et al., 'Oxytocin improves "mind-reading" in humans', *Biological Psychiatry*, 2007, vol. 61, no. 6, pp. 731–33, www.biologicalpsychiatryjournal.com/article/S0006-3223(06)00939-5/abstract

58 In one recent study . . . L.E. Sherman et al., 'The power of the like in adolescence: effects of peer influence on neural and behavioral responses to social media', *Psychological Science*, 2016, vol. 27, no. 7, pp. 1027–35, journals.sagepub.com/doi/abs/10.1177/0956797616645673

58 Taking the concept . . . Z. Brousard, '#proposed: lying to friends and family for social media attention', YouTube, 23 July 2015, youtu.be/PBzhJrrz-dk

64 The chance of . . . H. Hartston, 'The case for compulsive shopping as an addiction', *Journal of Psychoactive Drugs*, 2012, vol. 44, no. 1, pp. 64–67, www.ncbi.nlm.nih.gov/pubmed/22641966

64 Around 80 per cent . . . 'Digital dopamine: 2015 global digital marketing report from Razorfish', at Digital Agency Network, 16 November 2014, digitalagencynetwork.com/razorfish-released-2015-global-digital-marketing-report-digital-dopamine
https://www.slideshare.net/realtop466/digital-marketing-report-2015

66 From a biochemical . . . M.-R. Zarrindast & F. Khakpai, 'The modulatory role of dopamine in anxiety-like behavior', *Archives of Iranian Medicine*, 2015, vol. 18, no. 9, pp. 591–603, www.ams.ac.ir/AIM/NEWPUB/15/18/9/009.pdf

68 Anxiety is the most . . . Australian Bureau of Statistics, *4326.0 – National Survey of Mental Health and Wellbeing: Summary of Results*, 2007, ABS, Canberra, 2008, www.ausstats.abs.gov.au/ausstats/subscriber.nsf/0/6AE6DA447F985FC2CA2574EA00122BD6/$File/National Survey of Mental Health and Wellbeing Summary of Results.pdf

69 When bad things . . . P. Dayan & Q.J.M. Huys, 'Serotonin, inhibition, and negative mood', *PLoS Computational Biology*, 2008, vol. 4, no. 2, article no. e4, www.ncbi.nlm.nih.gov/pmc/articles/PMC2222921

70 From a biochemical . . . P.J Cowen & M. Browning, 'What has serotonin to do with depression?', *World Psychiatry*, 2015, vol. 14, no. 2, pp. 158–60, www.ncbi.nlm.nih.gov/pmc/articles/PMC4471964

70 Several recent studies . . . Y. Zhou et al., 'Comorbid generalized anxiety disorder and its association with quality of life in patients with major depressive disorder',

Scientific Reports, 2017, vol. 7, article no. 40511, www.nature.com/articles/srep40511

70 According to the Australian Bureau of Statistics . . . ABS, *4326.0 – National Survey of Mental Health and Wellbeing: Summary of Results*, 2007, ABS, Canberra, 2008, www.ausstats.abs.gov.au/ausstats/subscriber.nsf/0/6AE6DA447F985FC2CA2574EA00122BD6/$File/National Survey of Mental Health and Wellbeing Summary of Results.pdf

73 Anti-anxiety drugs . . . T.A. Furukawa et al., 'Antidepressants plus benzodiazepines for major depression', *Cochrane Database of Systematic Reviews*, 2001, no. 3, article no. CD001026, cochranelibrary-wiley.com/doi/10.1002/14651858.CD001026/full
T. Sharma et al., 'Suicidality and aggression during antidepressant treatment: systematic review and meta-analyses based on clinical study reports', *BMJ*, 2016, vol. 352, article no. i65, www.bmj.com/content/352/bmj.i65

74 Gambling addicts are . . . D. Harrison, 'Gambling linked to depression', *Sydney Morning Herald*, 15 June 2008, www.smh.com.au/national/gambling-linked-to-depression-20080614-2qo2.html

74 Equally, people suffering . . . M. Bussing-Birks, 'Mental illness and substance abuse', US National Bureau of Economic Research, www.nber.org/digest/apr02/w8699.html

78 Until the age . . . E. Terasawa, 'Role of GABA in the mechanism of the onset of puberty in non-human primates', *International Review of Neurobiology*, 2005, vol. 71, pp. 113–29, www.ncbi.nlm.nih.gov/pmc/articles/PMC1478204

80 While a woman . . . 'Laboratory reference ranges', US Endocrine Society Center for Learning, education.endocrine.org/system/files/ESAP 2015 Laboratory Reference Ranges.pdf
https://www.mayomedicallaboratories.com/test-catalog/Clinical+and+Interpretive/83686

80 Testosterone levels vary . . . 'Total, free, and bioavailable testosterone', Foundation Laboratories, Pomona, California, foundationlaboratory.com/docs/Bioavailable testosterone.pdf

81 Then, for timing reasons . . . A. Lomniczi & S.R. Ojeda, 'The emerging role of epigenetics in the regulation of female puberty', *Endocrine Development*, 2016, vol. 29, pp. 1–16, www.karger.com/Article/FullText/438840
M.M. Silveri et al., 'Frontal lobe GABA levels during adolescence: associations with impulsivity and response inhibition', *Biological Psychiatry*, 2013, vol. 74, no. 4, pp. 296–304, www.ncbi.nlm.nih.gov/pmc/articles/PMC3695052

82 The average age . . . https://www.ncbi.nlm.nih.gov/pmc/articles/PMC3613238/

82 And there's some evidence . . . F.M. Biro, 'Onset of breast development in a longitudinal cohort', *Pediatrics*, 2013, vol. 132, no. 6, pp. 1019–27, www.ncbi.nlm.nih.gov/pmc/articles/PMC3838525

82 Oestrogen, a primary driver . . . E.E. Kershaw & J.S. Flier, 'Adipose tissue as an endocrine organ', *JCEM*, 2004, vol. 89, no. 6, pp. 2548–56, academic.oup.com/jcem/article/89/6/2548/2870285

82 Studies in humans . . . M.M. Silveri et al., 'Frontal lobe GABA levels during adolescence: associations with impulsivity and response inhibition', *Biological Psychiatry*, 2013, vol. 74, no. 4, pp. 296–304, www.ncbi.nlm.nih.gov/pmc/articles/PMC3695052

83 And in about half . . . A. Hirsch, 'Male subfertility', *BMJ*, 2003, vol. 327, no. 7416, pp. 669–72, www.ncbi.nlm.nih.gov/pmc/articles/PMC196399

83 We've known for . . . A. Lenzi et al., 'Lipids of the sperm plasma membrane: from polyunsaturated fatty acids considered as markers of sperm function to possible

scavenger therapy', *Human Reproduction Update*, 1996, vol. 2, no. 3, pp. 246–56, humupd.oxfordjournals.org/content/2/3/246.full.pdf+html

83 But a 2009 study . . . M.R. Safarinejad et al., 'Relationship of omega-3 and omega-6 fatty acids with semen characteristics, and anti-oxidant status of seminal plasma: a comparison between fertile and infertile men', *Clinical Nutrition*, 2010, vol. 29, no. 1, pp. 100–105, www.ncbi.nlm.nih.gov/pubmed/19666200

83 This study didn't relate . . . D.R.E. Abayasekara & D.C. Wathes, 'Effects of altering dietary fatty acid composition on prostaglandin synthesis and fertility', *Prostaglandins, Leukotrienes and Essential Fatty Acids*, 1999, vol. 61, no. 5, pp. 275–87, www.ncbi.nlm.nih.gov/pubmed/10670689

84 This decrease in . . . C.N. Epperson, 'Sex, GABA, and nicotine: the impact of smoking on cortical GABA levels across the menstrual cycle as measured with proton magnetic resonance spectroscopy', *Biological Psychiatry*, 2005, vol. 57, no. 1, pp. 44–48, www.ncbi.nlm.nih.gov/pubmed/15607299, particularly Figure 2, www.ncbi.nlm.nih.gov/pmc/articles/PMC4097033/figure/F2

84 https://en.wikipedia.org/wiki/Follicular_phase#/media/File:MenstrualCycle2_en.svg

85 It's little wonder . . . R. Tomelleri & K.K. Grunewald, 'Menstrual cycle and food cravings in young college women', *Journal of the American Dietetic Association*, 1987, vol. 87, no. 3, pp. 311–15, www.ncbi.nlm.nih.gov/pubmed/3819250

85 Men taking testosterone . . . R.I. Wood, 'Anabolic-androgenic steroid dependence? Insights from animals and humans', *Frontiers in Neuroendocrinology*, 2008, vol. 29, no. 4, pp. 490–506, www.ncbi.nlm.nih.gov/pmc/articles/PMC2585375

86 In 1881, a Mauritian neurologist . . . J.M. Hoberman & C.E. Yesalis, 'The history of synthetic testosterone', *Scientific American*, February 1995, pp. 76–81, www.mvla.net/view/20926.pdf

86 In short, it's the perfect human . . . A. Hutchinson, 'The science of why we fall on mountain trails', Sweat Science, 17 May 2018, www.outsideonline.com/2309871/science-why-we-fall-mountain-trails
http://journal.sjdm.org/jdm06016.pdf

87 This is why males . . . 'Overall injury-related death statistics', CDC, 2016, wisqars-viz.cdc.gov:8006

87 In 2015, three out of . . . 'Table 40', 2015 Crime in the United States, Department of Justice, FBI, ucr.fbi.gov/crime-in-the-u.s/2015/crime-in-the-u.s.-2015/tables/table-40
I had to create the data set myself (see the graph below) by combining the data in Table 39 (males by age) and Table 40 (females by age)

91 And that's exactly . . . K.C. Winters & A. Arria, 'Adolescent brain development and drugs', *Prevention Researcher*, 2011, vol. 18, no. 2, pp. 21–24, www.ncbi.nlm.nih.gov/pmc/articles/PMC3399589

92 In one of the largest . . . K.C. Winters & C.-Y.S. Lee, 'Likelihood of developing an alcohol and cannabis use disorder during youth: association with recent use and age', *Drug and Alcohol Dependence*, 2008, vol. 92, nos 1–3, pp. 239–47, www.ncbi.nlm.nih.gov/pmc/articles/PMC2219953

92 If they could get away . . . C.D. May, 'How Coca-Cola obtains its coca', 1 July 1988, www.nytimes.com/1988/07/01/business/how-coca-cola-obtains-its-coca.html

93 Between 1978 and 2004 . . . E.S. Powell et al., 'Added sugars intake across the distribution of US children and adult consumers: 1977–2012', *Journal of the Academy of Nutrition and Dietetics*, 2016, vol. 116, no. 10, pp. 1543–50, www.ncbi.nlm.nih.gov/pmc/articles/PMC5039079

93 'Consumption of added sugars among U.S. adults, 2005–2010', US National Center for Health Statistics, CDC, www.cdc.gov/nchs/data/databriefs/db122.htm - x2013;2010

K.J. Newens & J. Walton, 'A review of sugar consumption from nationally representative dietary surveys across the world', *Journal of Human Nutrition and Dietetics*, 2016, vol. 29, no. 2, pp. 225–40, www.ncbi.nlm.nih.gov/pmc/articles/PMC5057348

93 Sugar makes us fat . . . See *Sweet Poison*

93 It's well established . . . E.L. Ding et al., 'Sex hormone–binding globulin and risk of type 2 diabetes in women and men', *New England Journal of Medicine*, 2009, vol. 361, no. 12, pp. 1152–63, www.nejm.org/doi/full/10.1056/NEJMoa0804381 - t=abstract

94 Having low levels . . . J.S. Brand et al., 'Testosterone, sex hormone-binding globulin and the metabolic syndrome: a systematic review and meta-analysis of observational studies', *International Journal of Epidemiology*, 2011, vol. 40, no. 1, pp. 189–207, academic.oup.com/ije/article/40/1/189/660762

94 A 2012 study . . . https://onlinelibrary.wiley.com/doi/pdf/10.1038/oby.2011.375 Intra-Abdominal Adipose Tissue Is Independently Associated With Sex-Hormone Binding Globulin in Premenopausal Women Maria Azrad1 , Barbara A. Gower1 , Gary R. Hunter2 and Tim R. Nagy1

94 One sure way to . . . See Sweet Poison, 2008

94 In 2007 a group . . . D.M. Selva et al., 'Monosaccharide-induced lipogenesis regulates the human hepatic sex hormone–binding globulin gene', *Journal of Clinical Investigation*, 2007, vol. 117, no. 12, pp. 3979–87, www.ncbi.nlm.nih.gov/pmc/articles/PMC2066187/?tool=pmcentrez

95 Due to the still-massive . . . W.A. March et al., 'The prevalence of polycystic ovary syndrome in a community sample assessed under contrasting diagnostic criteria', *Human Reproduction*, 2010, vol. 25, no. 2, pp. 544–51, www.ncbi.nlm.nih.gov/pubmed/19910321?dopt=Abstract

95 Every year, the US National Institutes of Health . . . 'Monitoring the Future 2017 Survey Results', US National Institute on Drug Abuse, NIH, www.drugabuse.gov/related-topics/trends-statistics/infographics/monitoring-futu re-2017-survey-results

99 Boy and girl teens . . . 'Drug misuse: findings from the 2016 to 2017 CSEW', UK Government, www.gov.uk/government/statistics/drug-misuse-findings-from-the-2016-to-2017-csew

'1.6 Prevalence of smoking – teenagers', Tobacco in Australia: Facts and Issues, Cancer Council, www.tobaccoinaustralia.org.au/chapter-1-prevalence/1-6-prevalence-of-smoking-teenagers

99 With their testosterone-fuelled . . . N. Hing et al., 'A comparative study of men and women gamblers in Victoria', Victorian Responsible Gambling Foundation, November 2014, responsiblegambling.vic.gov.au/documents/76/Research-report-comparative-study-of-men-and-women-gamblers.pdf

99 The US Centers for Disease Control and Prevention (CDC) . . . 'YRBSS results', Adolescent and School Health, CDC, www.cdc.gov/healthyyouth/data/yrbs/results.htm

101 The Growing Up in Australia . . . 'About the study', Growing up in Australia: the Longitudinal Study of Australian Children, data.growingupinaustralia.gov.au/about/index.html

101 Another survey of . . . D. Lawrence et al., *The Mental Health of Children and Adolescents: Report on the Second Australian Child and Adolescent Survey of Mental Health and Wellbeing*, Commonwealth of Australia, Canberra, 2015, www.health.gov.au/internet/main/publishing.nsf/Content/9DA8CA21306FE6EDCA257E2700016945/%24File/child2.pdf

102 The same survey . . . 'Anxiety and depression checklist (K10)', Beyond Blue, www.beyondblue.org.au/the-facts/anxiety-and-depression-checklist-k10

102 Similar US studies . . . R. Mojtabai et al., 'National trends in the prevalence and treatment of depression in adolescents and young adults', *Pediatrics*, 2016, vol. 138, no. 6, article no. e20161878, pediatrics.aappublications.org/content/early/2016/11/10/peds.2016-1878

102 They also found . . . K. Ries Merikangas et al., 'Lifetime prevalence of mental disorders in US adolescents: results from the National Comorbidity Study-Adolescent Supplement (NCS-A)', *Journal of the American Academy of Childhood and Adolescent Psychiatry*, 2010, vol. 49, no. 10, pp. 980–89, www.ncbi.nlm.nih.gov/pmc/articles/PMC2946114

102 The numbers are . . . H.L. Egger & A. Angold, 'Common emotional and behavioral disorders in preschool children: presentation, nosology, and epidemiology', *Journal of Child Psychology and Psychiatry*, 2006, vol. 47, nos 3–4, pp. 313–37, www.ncbi.nlm.nih.gov/pubmed/16492262

102 Anxiety in prepubescent . . . D. Lawrence et al., *The Mental Health of Children and Adolescents: Report on the Second Australian Child and Adolescent Survey of Mental Health and Wellbeing*, Commonwealth of Australia, Canberra, 2015, www.health.gov.au/internet/main/publishing.nsf/Content/9DA8CA21306FE6EDCA257E2700016945/$File/child2.pdf

103 The survey used . . . A. Angold et al., 'The development of a short questionnaire for use in epidemiological studies of depression in children and adolescents', *International Journal of Methods in Psychiatric Research*, 1995, vol. 5, no. 4, pp. 237–49, psycnet.apa.org/record/1996-02633-002

103 Mood and Feelings Questionnaire . . . Should you wish to administer the MFQ to your clients or for your research study, you may download a PDF of any version of the MFQ free of charge. We only ask that you cite the authors in any published work. http://devepi.duhs.duke.edu/mfq.html

104 Anxiety numbers peak . . . 'Any anxiety disorder', US National Institute of Mental Health, NIH, www.nimh.nih.gov/health/statistics/any-anxiety-disorder.shtml

106 Similarly the Australian study . . . D. Lawrence et al., *The Mental Health of Children and Adolescents: Report on the Second Australian Child and Adolescent Survey of Mental Health and Wellbeing*, Commonwealth of Australia, Canberra, 2015, www.health.gov.au/internet/main/publishing.nsf/Content/9DA8CA21306FE6EDCA257E2700016945/$File/child2.pdf
Similar results in UK too
E. Fink et al., 'Mental health difficulties in early adolescence: a comparison of two cross-sectional studies in England from 2009 to 2014', *Journal of Adolescent Health*, 2015, vol. 56, no. 5, pp. 502–507, www.jahonline.org/article/S1054-139X(15)00064-6/abstract

106 Australian research tells us . . . 'Rising unemployment among young Aussies matched by increasing anxiety, depression and stress', Roy Morgan, 25 May 2015, www.roymorgan.com/findings/6244-rising-youth-unemployment-increasing-anxiety-stress-depression-201505220539
A. John et al., 'Recent trends in the incidence of anxiety and prescription of anxiolytics and hypnotics in children and young people: an e-cohort study', *Journal of Affective Disorders*, 2015, vol. 183, pp. 134–41, www.sciencedirect.com/science/article/pii/S0165032715002943

107 There are well north . . . 'Number of apps available in leading app stores as of 1st quarter 2018', Statista, www.statista.com/statistics/276623/number-of-apps-available-in-leading-app-stores

107 Making programs addictive . . . I. Leslie, 'The scientists who make apps addictive', *The Economist 1843*, October–November 2016, www.1843magazine.com/features/the-scientists-who-make-apps-addictive

108 In 2016, more than . . . '2017 sales, demographic, and usage data: essential facts about the computer and video game industry', Entertainment Software Association, Washington DC, 2017, www.theesa.com/wp-content/uploads/2017/04/EF2017_FinalDigital.pdf

109 'Children's well-being measures', UK Office for National Statistics, www.ons.gov.uk/peoplepopulationandcommunity/wellbeing/datasets/childrenswellbeingmeasures

110 In 2016, the Australian . . . J.E. Brand et al., 'Digital Australia report 2018', Interactive Games and Entertainment Association, Sydney, 2018, igea.net/2017/07/digital-australia-2018-da18

111 But there's no limit . . . 'Is there an age limit for kids on social media?', Office of the eSafety Commissioner, Australian Government, www.esafety.gov.au/education-resources/iparent/staying-safe/social-networking/is-there-an-age-limit-for-kids-on-social-media
'Information for parents', Australian Classification, Department of Communication and the Arts, www.classification.gov.au/Public/Resources/Pages/Parents.aspx

112 It's telling indeed . . . N. Bilton, 'Steve Jobs was a low-tech parent', *New York Times*, 20 September 2014, www.nytimes.com/2014/09/11/fashion/steve-jobs-apple-was-a-low-tech-parent.html?_r=0

112 According to a recent report . . . https://www.nytimes.com/2018/10/26/style/silicon-valley-nannies.html?action=click&module=Top%20Stories&pgtype=Homepage

113 The latest statistics . . . 'Census of computers in schools', Department of Education and Training, Victoria State Government, www.education.vic.gov.au/school/teachers/management/infrastructure/Pages/censuscomputers.aspx

116 The three main disorders . . . F.R.E. Smink et al., 'Epidemiology of eating disorders: incidence, prevalence and mortality rates', *Current Psychiatry Reports*, 2012, vol. 14, no. 4, pp. 406–14, www.ncbi.nlm.nih.gov/pmc/articles/PMC3409365

116 While our knowledge . . . W.H. Kaye et al., 'Nothing tastes as good as skinny feels: the neurobiology of anorexia nervosa', *Neural Control of Appetite*, 2013, vol. 36, no. 2, pp. 110–20, www.cell.com/trends/neurosciences/fulltext/S0166-2236(13)00006-4

116 We know from . . . S. Ulfvebrand et al., 'Psychiatric comorbidity in women and men with eating disorders: results from a large clinical database', *Psychiatry Research*, 2015, vol. 230, no. 2, pp. 294–99, www.psy-journal.com/article/S0165-1781(15)30292-4/fulltext

116 A similar study . . . B.J. Blinder et al., 'Psychiatric comorbidities of female inpatients with eating disorders', *Psychosomatic Medicine*, 2006, vol. 68, no. 3, pp. 454–62, www.ncbi.nlm.nih.gov/pubmed/16738079

116 And other US studies . . . W.H. Kaye et al., 'Comorbidity of anxiety disorders with anorexia and bulimia nervosa', *American Journal of Psychiatry*, 2004, vol. 161, no. 12, pp. 2215–21, www.ncbi.nlm.nih.gov/pubmed/15569892
S.A. Swanson et al., 'Prevalence and correlates of eating disorders in adolescents: results from the National Comorbidity Survey Replication Adolescent Supplement', *Archives of General Psychiatry*, 2011, vol. 68, no. 7, pp. 714–23, www.ncbi.nlm.nih.gov/pmc/articles/PMC5546800

117 These studies have . . . M. Salaa & C.A. Levinson, 'The longitudinal relationship between worry and disordered eating: is worry a precursor or consequence of disordered eating?', *Eating Behaviors*, 2016, vol. 23, pp. 28–32, www.ncbi.nlm.nih.gov/pmc/articles/PMC5124505

117 A recent UK study . . . T.J. Raney et al., 'Influence of overanxious disorder of childhood on the expression of anorexia nervosa', *International Journal of Eating Disorders*, 2008, vol. 41, no. 4, pp. 326–32, www.ncbi.nlm.nih.gov/pubmed/18213688

117 The physician first . . . W.W. Gull, 'V. – Anorexia nervosa (apepsia hysterica, anorexia hysterica', *Obesity Research*, 1997, vol. 5, no. 5, pp. 498–502, onlinelibrary.wiley.com/doi/10.1002/j.1550-8528.1997.tb00677.x/epdf

118 Those data tell us . . . A.R. Lucas, '50-year trends in the incidence of anorexia in Rochester, Minn.: a population-based study', *American Journal of Psychiatry*, vol. 148, no. 7, pp. 917–22, citeseerx.ist.psu.edu/viewdoc/download?doi=10.1.1.464.4401&rep=rep1&type=pdf

118 The diagnostic criteria . . . L.R. Godier & R.J. Park, 'Compulsivity in anorexia nervosa: a transdiagnostic concept', Frontiers in Psychology, 2014, vol. 5, article no. 778, Figure 1, www.ncbi.nlm.nih.gov/pmc/articles/PMC4101893/figure/F1

119 Studies in the Netherlands . . . https://pdfs.semanticscholar.org/01f8/fc12cff0d465c7a5343622c8dec1528a6cda.pdf
It is a Dutch study of primary care incidence comparing rates from 1985-1989 to 1995-1999 – overall incidence did not increase but in the 15-19 age group it doubled.

119 More recent studies . . . K.A. Halmi, 'Anorexia nervosa: an increasing problem in children and adolescents', *Dialogues in Clinical Neuroscience*, 2009, vol. 11, no. 1, pp. 100–103, www.ncbi.nlm.nih.gov/pmc/articles/PMC3181903

119 Anorexia results in . . . K.L. Allen, 'Neurocognitive functioning in adolescents with eating disorders: a population-based study', *Cognitive Neuropsychiatry*, 2013, vol. 18, no. 5, pp. 355–75, www.ncbi.nlm.nih.gov/pubmed/22803827

119 The long-term effects . . . M.A. Spaulding-Barclay et al., 'Cardiac changes in anorexia nervosa', *Cardiology in the Young*, 2006, vol. 26, no. 4, pp. 623–628 https://www.cambridge.org/core/journals/cardiology-in-the-young/article/cardiac-changes-in-anorexia-nervosa/7BE512B4F0203019EF6EFC304F82C55B

119 The peak growing . . . N.H. Golden, 'Osteopenia and osteoporosis in anorexia nervosa', *Adolescent Medicine*, 2003, vol. 14, no. 1, pp. 97–108, www.ncbi.nlm.nih.gov/pubmed/12529194

119 The significant malnutrition . . . S. Grinspoon et al., 'Prevalence and predictive factors for regional osteopenia in women with anorexia nervosa', *Annals of Internal Medicine*, 2000, vol. 133, no. 10, pp. 790–94, www.ncbi.nlm.nih.gov/pubmed/11085841

120 Unfortunately, there's no evidence . . . K.K. Miller et al., 'Androgens in women with anorexia nervosa and normal-weight women with hypothalamic amenorrhea', *Journal of Clinical Endocrinology and Metabolism*, 2007, vol. 92, no. 4, pp. 1334–39, www.ncbi.nlm.nih.gov/pmc/articles/PMC3206093

120 Anorexics have about . . . D.B. Herzog et al., 'Recovery and relapse in anorexia and bulimia nervosa: a 7.5-year follow-up study', *Child and Adolescent Psychiatry*, 1999, vol. 38, no. 7, pp. 829–37, www.jaacap.com/article/S0890-8567(09)66531-X/abstract

120 It has the highest mortality rate . . . J. Arcelus et al., 'Mortality rates in patients with anorexia nervosa and other eating disorders: a meta-analysis of 36 studies', *Archives of General Psychiatry*, 2011, vol. 68, no. 7, pp. 724–31, jamanetwork.com/journals/jamapsychiatry/fullarticle/1107207

121 Unlike those with anorexia . . . "In all eating disorders there is an increased genetic heritability and frequency of a family history. A family history of 'leanness' may be associated with anorexia nervosa and a personal or family history of obesity with bulimic eating disorders." https://www.ranzcp.org/Files/Resources/Publications/CPG/Clinician/Eating-Disorders-CPG.aspx

122 For a diagnosis of . . . American Psychiatry Association, Diagnostic and Statistical Manual of Mental Disorders: DSM-5, 5th edn, American Psychiatric Publishing, Washington DC, 2013, p. 350

122 It could be that . . . "The findings suggest that bulimic eating disorders exist on a continuum of clinical severity, from bulimia nervosa purging type (most

severe), through bulimia nervosa nonpurging type (intermediate severity), to binge-eating disorder (least severe)." https://onlinelibrary.wiley.com/doi/abs/10.1002/%28SICI%291098-108X%28199801%2923%3A1%3C7%3A%3AAID-EAT2%3E3.0.CO%3B2-Q

123 But I'm not entirely . . . During treatment, people with the disorder must also accept that, as with all eating disorders, the illness is chronic and recovery can be a lifelong process, said weight-loss and food addiction specialist Molly Carmel, who runs the eating disorder treatment center Beacon House.
Carmel also told Fusion that understanding the addictive nature of some foods, like sugar, is key. "Studies show that long-standing untreated binge eating disorders progress into substance disorders. So for many struggling with B.E.D., if the sensitivity and/or addiction to sugar is not addressed, it is very hard and almost impossible to put the disease into remission," she said. https://splinternews.com/why-are-people-up-in-arms-about-binge-eating-disorder-1793846075

123 Under current diagnosis . . . Under the classification 'Other specified feeding and eating disorder', American Psychiatry Association, *Diagnostic and Statistical Manual of Mental Disorders: DSM-5*, 5th edn, American Psychiatric Publishing, Washington DC, 2013

123 If you think that . . . K.L. Allen et al., Distinguishing between risk factors for bulimia nervosa, binge eating disorder, and purging disorder', *Journal of Youth and Adolescence*, 2015, vol. 44, no. 8, pp 1580–91, link.springer.com/article/10.1007/s10964-014-0186-8

123 The only significant . . . A.E. Field et al., 'Prospective Association of Common Eating Disorders and Adverse Outcomes', *Pediatrics*, 2012, vol. 130, no. 2, pp. e289–e295, www.ncbi.nlm.nih.gov/pmc/articles/PMC3408691

124 They call it . . . S. Bratman, 'Orthorexia essay', Orthorexia, www.orthorexia.com/original-orthorexia-essay
https://www.nytimes.com/2009/02/26/health/nutrition/26food.html

124 There's no such diagnosis . . . A. Korinth et al., 'Eating behaviour and eating disorders in students of nutrition sciences', Public Health Nutrition, 2010, vol. 13, no. 1, pp. 32–37, www.cambridge.org/core/journals/public-health-nutrition/article/eating-behaviour-and-eating-disorders-in-students-of-nutrition-sciences/AAF3BA109472ED95B487E175BF0F9760

124 Many mental health professionals . . . https://www.nytimes.com/2009/02/26/health/nutrition/26food.html and "Bratman didn't originally intend for orthorexia to become a diagnosis." https://www.washingtonpost.com/news/morning-mix/wp/2015/11/05/psychiatry-doesnt-recognize-orthorexia-an-obsession-with-healthy-eating-but-the-internet-does/?noredirect=on&utm_term=.0bd218e5188c

124 In the decade . . . 'Veganism booms by 350%', Vegan Life, www.veganlifemag.com/veganism-booms

124 If foods claiming . . . 'Vegan trend takes hold in Australia', SBS News, 1 May 2018, www.sbs.com.au/news/vegan-trend-takes-hold-in-australia

124 Almost half of the UK . . . S. Marsh, 'The rise of vegan teenagers: "More people are into it because of Instagram"', *The Guardian*, 27 May 2016, www.theguardian.com/lifeandstyle/2016/may/27/the-rise-of-vegan-teenagers-more-people-are-into-it-because-of-instagram

125 If your child plans . . . M. Amit, 'Vegetarian diets in children and adolescents', *Paediatrics and Child Health*, 2010, vol. 15, no. 5, pp. 303–308, www.ncbi.nlm.nih.gov/pmc/articles/PMC2912628

126 But whatever approach . . . https://epublications.marquette.edu/dissertations_mu/76/

126 Recent brain-imaging studies . . . W.H. Kaye et al., 'Does a shared neurobiology for foods and drugs of abuse contribute to extremes of food ingestion in anorexia and

bulimia nervosa?', *Biological Psychiatry*, 2013, vol. 73, no. 9, pp. 836–42, www.ncbi.nlm.nih.gov/pmc/articles/PMC3755487

127 In an anorexic . . . 'Compared to CW, individuals recovered from AN showed a significantly lower neural activation of the insula, including the primary cortical taste region, and ventral and dorsal striatum to both sucrose and water.' https://www.nature.com/articles/1301443 and https://www.ncbi.nlm.nih.gov/pmc/articles/PMC3971875/
Compared to matched control women ($n=14$), women recovered from anorexia ($n=14$) had diminished ($F(1,27)=7.79$, $p=0.01$) and women recovered from bulimia ($n=14$) had exaggerated ($F(1,27)=6.12$, $p=0.02$) right anterior insula hemodynamic response to tastes of sucrose.

127 Because GABA plays . . . K.L. Klump et al., 'Ovarian hormones and binge eating: exploring associations in community samples', *Psychological Medicine*, 2008, vol. 38, no. 12, pp. 1749–57, www.ncbi.nlm.nih.gov/pmc/articles/PMC2885896

127 And that is exactly . . . https://www.ncbi.nlm.nih.gov/pmc/articles/PMC2788663/ "Across ED groups (not relative to the referent), the BN and ANBN groups were more likely to have had alcohol abuse/dependence relative to the AN group."

127 Anorexics are much less likely . . . A.E. Field et al., 'Prospective Association of Common Eating Disorders and Adverse Outcomes', *Pediatrics*, 2012, vol. 130, no. 2, pp. e289–e295, www.ncbi.nlm.nih.gov/pmc/articles/PMC3408691

127 Human starvation experiments . . . Keys, A., Brozek, J., Henshel, A., Mickelson, O., & Taylor, H.L. (1950). The biology of human starvation, (Vols. 1–2). Minneapolis, MN: University of Minnesota Press.]
The 2D:4D . . . S.M. et al., 'Early prenatal attainment of adult metacarpal-phalangeal rankings and proportions', American Journal of *Physical Anthropology*, 1975, vol. 43, no. 3, pp. 327–32, www.ncbi.nlm.nih.gov/pubmed/1211429

129 The size of the fourth . . . J.T. Manning, *Digit Ratio: A Pointer to Fertility, Behavior, and Health*, Rutgers University Press, New Brunswick, New Jersey, 2002.
E. Nelson et al., 'Digit ratios predict polygyny in early apes, *Ardipithecus*, Neanderthals and early modern humans but not in *Australopithecus*', *Proceeding of the Royal Society B*, 2011, vol. 278, no. 1711, pp. 1556–63, rspb.royalsocietypublishing.org/content/278/1711/1556

130 As you'd expect, studies . . . S. Jeevanandam & P.K. Muthu, '2D:4D ratio and its implications in medicine', *Journal of Clinical and Diagnostic Research*, 2016, vol. 10, no. 12, pp. CM01–CM03, www.ncbi.nlm.nih.gov/pmc/articles/PMC5296424

130 https://en.wikipedia.org/wiki/Digit_ratio#/media/File:Hand_zur_Abmessung_2D4D.jpg

130 These studies have found . . . G.D. Wilson, 'Finger-length as an index of assertiveness in women', *Personality and Individual Differences*, 1983, vol. 4, no. 1, pp. 111–12, www.sciencedirect.com/science/article/pii/0191886983900612
https://www.ncbi.nlm.nih.gov/pubmed/16522691/

131 These women also earn . . . https://www.sciencedirect.com/science/article/pii/S1570677X16301903

131 Men with lower . . . https://www.ncbi.nlm.nih.gov/pmc/articles/PMC4861561/
https://www.ncbi.nlm.nih.gov/pubmed/19862809?access_num=19862809&link_type=MED&dopt=Abstract
http://rspb.royalsocietypublishing.org/content/278/1711/1556
https://www.ncbi.nlm.nih.gov/pmc/articles/PMC3739592/

131 Men with relatively higher . . . https://academic.oup.com/humrep/article/13/11/3000/701493
https://www.nature.com/articles/6605986

https://www.ncbi.nlm.nih.gov/pmc/articles/PMC2768336/
https://www.sciencedirect.com/science/article/pii/S0191886905001133

131 Both sexes have higher . . . http://onlinelibrary.wiley.com/doi/10.1348/000712607X197406/abstract
http://www.ehbonline.org/article/S1090-5138(00)00063-5/fulltext
https://www.sciencedirect.com/science/article/pii/S0191886909000804

131 On average, anorexic women . . . S.J. Quinton et al., 'The 2nd to 4th digit ratio (2D:4D) and eating disorder diagnosis in women', *Personality and Individual Differences*, 2011, vol. 51, no. 4, pp. 402–405, www.ncbi.nlm.nih.gov/pmc/articles/PMC3134962

131 And this matches . . . J. Hönekopp et al., 'Digit ratio (2D:4D) and physical fitness in males and females: Evidence for effects of prenatal androgens on sexually selected traits', *Hormones and Behavior*, 2006, vol. 49, no. 4, pp. 545–49, www.ncbi.nlm.nih.gov/pubmed/16403410

'In eating disordered women, 2D:4D was positively and significantly related to current weight, lowest weight and current BMI, with strongest associations for right 2D:4D. Among women, low 2D:4D is related to AN and high 2D:4D to BN, suggesting a differential causal influence of prenatal sex hormones on later eating pathology.' https://www.ncbi.nlm.nih.gov/pmc/articles/PMC3134962/

J. Sundgot-Borgen & M.K. Torstveit, 'Prevalence of eating disorders in elite athletes is higher than in the general population', *Clinical Journal of Sport Medicine*, 2004, vol. 14, no. 1, pp. 25–32, www.ncbi.nlm.nih.gov/pubmed/14712163

131 Consistent with this . . . K.M. Culbert et al., 'Prenatal hormone exposure and risk for eating disorders: a comparison of opposite-sex and same-sex twins', *Archives of General Psychiatry*, 2008, vol. 65, no. 3, pp. 329–36, www.ncbi.nlm.nih.gov/pubmed/18316679

132 Smoking significantly increases . . . D.B. Kandel & J.R. Udry, 'Prenatal effects of maternal smoking on daughters' smoking: nicotine or testosterone exposure?', *American Journal of Public Health*, 1999, vol. 89, no. 9, pp. 1377–83, www.ncbi.nlm.nih.gov/pmc/articles/PMC1508780

W. Wang et al., 'Cigarette smoking has a positive and independent effect on testosterone levels', *Hormones* (Athens), 2013, vol. 12, no. 4, pp. 567–77, www.ncbi.nlm.nih.gov/pubmed/24457405

132 Suffering from PCOS . . . T. Sir-Petermann et al., 'Maternal serum androgens in pregnant women with polycystic ovarian syndrome: possible implications in prenatal androgenization', Human Reproduction, 2002, vol. 17, no. 10, pp. 2573–79, academic.oup.com/humrep/article/17/10/2573/607731

132 Consuming two drinks . . . R.G. Stevens et al., 'Alcohol consumption and serum hormone levels during pregnancy', *Alcohol*, 2005, vol. 36, no. 1, pp. 47–53, www.ncbi.nlm.nih.gov/pubmed/16257353

132 Her high ratios . . . P.S. Uzelac et al., 'Dysregulation of leptin and testosterone production and their receptor expression in the human placenta with gestational diabetes mellitus', *Placenta*, 2010, vol. 31, no. 7, pp. 581–58, www.ncbi.nlm.nih.gov/pubmed/20421132

L.M. Smith, 'Prenatal nicotine increases testosterone levels in the fetus and female offspring', *Nicotine and Tobacco Research*, 2003, vol. 5, no. 3, pp. 369–74, www.ncbi.nlm.nih.gov/pubmed/12791533

132 Alternatively, she could have . . . L. Westney et al., 'Evidence that gonadal hormone levels in amniotic fluid are decreased in males born to alcohol users in humans', *Alcohol and Alcoholism*, 1991, vol. 26, no. 4, pp. 403–407, www.ncbi.nlm.nih.gov/pubmed/1760051

132 Fathers with low sperm . . . A.G. Sutcliffe et al., 'Perturbations in finger length and digit ratio (2D:4D) in ICSI children', *Reproductive BioMedicine Online*, 2010, vol. 20, no. 1, pp. 138–43, www.ncbi.nlm.nih.gov/pubmed/20158999

133 Testosterone increases dopamine . . . E.J. Hermans et al., 'Effects of exogenous testosterone on the ventral striatal BOLD response during reward anticipation in healthy women', *Neuroimage*, 2010, vol. 52, no. 1, pp. 277–83, www.ncbi.nlm.nih.gov/pubmed/20398773

133 A normal-weight adult . . . D. Gallagher et al., 'How useful is body mass index for comparison of body fatness across age, sex, and ethnic groups?', *American Journal of Epidemiology*, 1996, vol. 143, no. 3, pp. 228–39, www.ncbi.nlm.nih.gov/pubmed/8561156

134 The results . . . J. de Vos et al., 'Meta analysis on the efficacy of pharmacotherapy versus placebo on anorexia nervosa', *Journal of Eating Disorders*, 2014, vol. 2, article no. 27, www.ncbi.nlm.nih.gov/pmc/articles/PMC4221720

135 At least in adults . . . L.P. Bodell & P.K. Keel, 'Current treatment for anorexia nervosa: efficacy, safety, and adherence', Psychology *Research and Behavior Management*, 2010, vol. 3: 91–108, www.ncbi.nlm.nih.gov/pmc/articles/PMC3218763

135 Of course, the primary . . . I. Eisler et al., 'Family and individual therapy in anorexia nervosa: a 5-year follow-up', *Archives of General Psychiatry*, 1997, vol. 54, no. 11, pp. 1025–30, jamanetwork.com/journals/jamapsychiatry/article-abstract/497962

136 We know that dopamine . . . That is exactly the theory underlying Family Therapy (Maudsley Approach) – nudging towards gradually greater intake – I am talking about the Maudsley approach here – probably worth saying so?
'The Maudsley Approach builds on evidence that family therapy approaches are superior to individual therapy approaches with younger patients. It involves the family right from the start of treatment and relies heavily on parent involvement in the re-feeding of the child with an eating disorder.' https://www.eatingdisorders.org.au/taking-the-first-step/types-of-treatment

136 So far the only . . . www.ncbi.nlm.nih.gov/pmc/articles/PMC3218763
From the review you cite: 'There has been much less research on the treatment of anorexia nervosa. Most of the studies suffer from small sample sizes and some from high rates of attrition. As a result, there is little evidence to support any psychological treatment, at least in adults. In adolescents the research has focused mainly on family therapy, with the result that the status of CBT in younger patients is unclear.' https://www.ncbi.nlm.nih.gov/pmc/articles/PMC2928448/

136 In that small trial . . . I. Eisler et al., 'A randomised controlled treatment trial of two forms of family therapy in adolescent anorexia nervosa: a five-year follow-up', *Journal of Child Psychology and Psychiatry*, 2007, vol. 48, no. 6, pp. 552–60, www.ncbi.nlm.nih.gov/pubmed/17537071

136 A drug containing . . . K. Lim et al., 'A systematic review of the effectiveness of medical cannabis for psychiatric, movement and neurodegenerative disorders', *Clinical Psychopharmacology and Neuroscience*, 2017, vol. 15, no. 4, pp. 301–312, www.ncbi.nlm.nih.gov/pmc/articles/PMC5678490

136 Nevertheless a small . . . A. Andries et al., 'Dronabinol in severe, enduring anorexia nervosa: a randomized controlled trial', *International Journal of Eating Disorders*, 2014, vol. 47, no. 1, pp. 18–23, www.ncbi.nlm.nih.gov/pubmed/24105610

136 And according to . . . K. Mickle, 'Can marijuana really help treat anorexia?', *Cosmopolitan*, 24 June 2015, www.cosmopolitan.com/health-fitness/news/a42398/marijuana-anorexia

137 The same 'journal' . . . K. Lim et al., 'A systematic review of the effectiveness of medical cannabis for psychiatric, movement and neurodegenerative disorders',

Clinical Psychopharmacology and Neuroscience, 2017, vol. 15, no. 4, pp. 301–312, www.ncbi.nlm.nih.gov/pmc/articles/PMC5678490
140 It was being used . . . I.A. Ramoutsaki et al., 'Pain relief and sedation in Roman Byzantine texts: *Mandragoras officinarum*, *Hyoscyamos niger* and *Atropa belladonna*, *International Congress Series*, 2002, vol. 1242, pp. 43–50, www.sciencedirect.com/science/article/pii/S0531513102006994
140 These morphine variants . . . H. Boecker et al., 'The runner's high: opioidergic mechanisms in the human brain', *Cerebral Cortex*, 2008, vol. 18, no. 11, pp. 2523–31, www.ncbi.nlm.nih.gov/pubmed/18296435
140 Long-distance runners . . . G. Kolata, 'Yes, running can make you high', *New York Times*, 27 March 2008, www.nytimes.com/2008/03/27/health/nutrition/27best.html
141 Self-harmers get . . . B. Stanley et al., 'Nonsuicidal self-injurious behavior, endogenous opioids and monoamine neurotransmitters', *Journal of Affective Disorders*, 2010, vol. 124, nos 1–2, pp. 134–40, www.ncbi.nlm.nih.gov/pmc/articles/PMC2875354
141 Two American doctors . . . G.M. Gould & W.L. Pyle, *Anomalies and Curiosities of Medicine*, Bell, New York, 1896
141 But some self-harmers . . . H. Arkowitz & S.O. Lilienfeld, 'Self-cutters may be seeking pain relief: people who intentionally hurt themselves are often seeking relief from pain', *Scientific American Mind*, 1 November 2013, www.scientificamerican.com/article/self-cutters-may-be-seeking-pain-relief
141 To a cutter . . . A.J. Edmondson et al., 'Non-suicidal reasons for self-harm: A systematic review of self-reported accounts', *Journal of Affective Disorders*, 2016, vol. 191, pp. 109–17, www.sciencedirect.com/science/article/pii/S0165032715307485
141 And the opioid rush . . . H. Blasco-Fontecilla et al., 'The addictive model of self-harming (non-suicidal and suicidal) behavior', *Frontiers in Psychiatry*, 2016, vol. 7, article no. 8, www.ncbi.nlm.nih.gov/pmc/articles/PMC4734209
142 The Growing Up in Australia . . . Australian Institute of Family Studies, *The Longitudinal Study of Australian Children Annual Statistical Report 2016*, AIFS, Melbourne, 2017, growingupinaustralia.gov.au/sites/default/files/lsac-asr-2016-book.pdf
143 This finding is . . . O.R. Simon et al., 'Characteristics of impulsive suicide attempts and attempters', *Suicide and Life-threatening Behavior*, 2001, vol. 32, suppl. 1, pp. 49–59, www.ncbi.nlm.nih.gov/pubmed/11924695
143 Testosterone drives a lack . . . T.R. Rice & L. Sher, 'Adolescent suicide and testosterone: Postnatal testosterone may be an important mediator of the association between prematurity and male neurodevelopmental disorders: a hypothesis', *International Journal of Adolescent Medicine and Health*, 2015, vol. 29, no. 4, article no. 20150058, www.degruyter.com/view/j/ijamh.2017.29.issue-4/ijamh-2015-0058/ijamh-2015-0058.xml
144 This led me to wonder . . . http://www.monitoringthefuture.org/pubs/monographs/mtf-vol1_2017.pdf
145 By the 1950s . . . N. Wade, 'Anabolic steroids: doctors denounce them, but athletes aren't listening', *Science*, 1972, vol. 176, no. 4042, pp. 1399–1403, science.sciencemag.org/content/176/4042/1399
146 In 1991 the US . . . H.G. Pope et al., 'Adverse health consequences of performance-enhancing drugs: an Endocrine Society scientific statement', *Endocrine Reviews*, 2014, vol. 35, no. 3, pp. 341–75, www.ncbi.nlm.nih.gov/pmc/articles/PMC4026349
146 Anabolic steroid . . . 'Steroid use', Child Trend Databank, December 2015, www.childtrends.org/wp-content/uploads/2012/04/92_appendix1.pdf
National Drug Strategy Household Survey 2016: detailed findings', Australian Institute of Health and Welfare, 28 September 2017, www.aihw.gov.au/reports/illicit-use-of-drugs/2016-ndshs-detailed/data

146 Offshore manufacturing . . . Australian Criminal Intelligence Commission, *Illicit Drug Data Report 2015–16*, ACIC, Canberra, 2017, acic.govcms.gov.au/sites/g/files/net1491/f/2017/06/illicit_drug_data_report_2015-16_full_report.pdf?v=1498019727
M. Dunn & V. White, 'The epidemiology of anabolic–androgenic steroid use among Australian secondary school students', *Journal of Science and Medicine in Sport*, 2011, vol. 14, no. 1, pp. 10–14, www.jsams.org/article/S1440-2440(10)00118-0/fulltext
http://www.fast-trackcities.org/sites/default/files/Australian%20Needle%20Syringe%20Program%20Survey%2020%20Year%20National%20Data%20Report%201995-2014.pdf

147 It may have nothing . . . G. Bolding et al., 'Use of anabolic steroids and associated health risks among gay men attending London gyms', *Addiction*, 2002, vol. 97, no. 2, pp. 195–203, onlinelibrary.wiley.com/doi/full/10.1046/j.1360-0443.2002.00031.x
I. Thiblin et al., 'Anabolic androgenic steroids and suicide', *Annals of Clinical Psychiatry*, 1999, vol. 11, no. 4, pp. 223–31, www.ncbi.nlm.nih.gov/pubmed/10596737

154 Hall helped found . . . A.W. Siege & S.H. White, 'The child study movement: early growth and development of the symbolized child', *Advances in Child Development and Behavior*, 1982, vol. 17, pp. 233–85, www.sciencedirect.com/science/article/pii/S0065240708603614
E.W. Bohannon, 'A study of peculiar and exceptional children', *Pedagogical Seminary*, 1896, vol. 4, no. 1, pp. 3–60, www.tandfonline.com/doi/abs/10.1080/08919402.1896.10532955?journalCode=vzps20

155 In 1904 . . . G.S. Hall, *Adolescence: Its Psychology and Its Relations to Physiology, Anthropology, Sociology, Sex, Crime, Religion and Education*, 2 vols, D. Appleton & Co., New York, 1904–05

155 He noted that . . . vol. I, p. xiii

155 Hall reported that . . . vol II, p. 77

155 He said that . . ..vol. II, p. 78

155 After noting that . . . vol. I, p. 404

155 He put this down . . . vol. I, p. 368

155 Hall even nailed . . . vol. II, p. 74

156 The kids of 1904 . . . vol. I, p. 361

156 He said a teenage girl . . . vol. I, p. 355

157 The massive inequities . . . T. Piketty, *Capital in the Twenty-First Century*, trans. A. Goldhammer, Belknap Press, Cambridge, Massachusetts, 2014 (first published in France, 2013).

157 In 1928, the first . . . J.B. Watson, *Psychological Care of Infant and Child*, W.W. Norton & Co., New York, 1928.

158 His advice to parents . . . Watson, *Psychological Care of Infant and Child*, p. 82.

159 Spock's 1946 book . . . B. Spock, *The Common Sense Book of Baby and Child Care*, Duell, Sloan and Pearce, New York, 1946.

159 It was an instant bestseller . . . E. Pace, 'Benjamin Spock, world's pediatrician, dies at 94', *New York Times*, 17 March 1998, archive.nytimes.com/www.nytimes.com/books/98/05/17/specials/spock-obit.html

160 By 1950 that figure . . . S. Tzvetkova & E. Ortiz-Ospina, 'Working women: What determines female labor force participation?', Our World in Data, 16 October 2016, ourworldindata.org/women-in-the-labor-force-determinants

160 Household appliances . . . T.V. de V. Cavalcanti & J. Tavares, 'Assessing the "engines of liberation": home appliances and female labor force participation',

Review of Economics and Statistics, 2008, vol. 90, no. 1, pp. 81–88, josetavares.pt/wp-content/uploads/2016/05/Engines-of-Liberation-RESTAT.pdf

160 He said it could . . . B. Spock, 'Managing young children: discipline', *Baby and Child Care*, 4th edn, Hawthorn Books, New York, 1976, Section 528, p. 373

160 He later said . . . B. Spock, *Child and Baby Care*, Bodley Head, London, 1958, pp. 57–60.

163 Spock later said of his work . . . E. Pace, 'Benjamin Spock, world's pediatrician, dies at 94', *New York Times*, 17 March 1998, archive.nytimes.com/www.nytimes.com/books/98/05/17/specials/spock-obit.html

164 Penelope Leach's 2 million–copy . . . P. Leach, *Your Baby and Child: From Birth to Age Five*, Michael Joseph, London, 1977.

164 The 30 hours a week . . . Reserve Bank of Australia, '4.4 Labour force by sex', *Australian Economic Statistics 1949–1950 to 1996–1997*, Occasional Paper no. 8, RBA, www.rba.gov.au/statistics/frequency/occ-paper-8.html
Australian Bureau of Statistics, 'Table 1. Labour force status by sex, Australia – trend, seasonally adjusted and original', *6202.0 – Labour Force, Australia*, ABS, Canberra, 2018, www.abs.gov.au/AUSSTATS/abs@.nsf/DetailsPage/6202.0Apr 2018?OpenDocument

164 Either as a cause . . . ABS, 'Births registered, summary statistics for Australia', *3301.0 – Births, Australia, 2016*, ABS, Canberra, 2017, www.abs.gov.au/AUSSTATS/abs@.nsf/allprimarymainfeatures/F41B99AB234B2074CA25792F00161838?opendocument
https://aifs.gov.au/facts-and-figures/births-australia/births-australia-source-data

165 These trends are . . . G. Livingston & D. Cohn, 'US birth rate falls to a record low; decline is greatest among immigrants', Pew Research Center Social and Demographic Trends, 29 November 2012, www.pewsocialtrends.org/2012/11/29/u-s-birth-rate-falls-to-a-record-low-decline-is-greatest-among-immigrants

165 The modern parent . . . C.D. Bowman, *Culture of American Families: A National Survey*, Institute for Advanced Studies in Culture, Charlottesville, Virginia, 2012, iasculture.org/research/publications/culture-american-families-national-survey

167 A recent nationally . . . C.D. Bowman, *Culture of American Families: A National Survey*, Institute for Advanced Studies in Culture, Charlottesville, Virginia, 2012, iasculture.org/research/publications/culture-american-families-national-survey

168 A recent study of . . . M. Iacovou & A. Sevilla, 'Infant feeding: the effects of scheduled vs. on-demand feeding on mothers' wellbeing and children's cognitive development', *European Journal of Public Health*, 2013, vol. 23, no. 1, pp. 13–19, www.ncbi.nlm.nih.gov/pmc/articles/PMC3553587

169 The science tells us . . . Gillespie, D. Taming Toxic People

171 You know the type . . . M. Krakovsky, 'Discredited "Mozart effect" remains music to American ears', 1 February 2005, Stanford Graduate School of Business, www.gsb.stanford.edu/insights/discredited-mozart-effect-remains-music-american-ears
J. Pietschnig et al., 'Mozart effect–Shmozart effect: a meta-analysis', *Intelligence*, 2010, vol. 38, no. 3, pp. 314–23, www.sciencedirect.com/science/article/pii/S0160289610000267?via=ihub

179 It's the same motivational . . . I. Lapowsky, 'Reward vs. punishment: what motivates people more?', Inc., 2 April 2013, www.inc.com/magazine/201304/issie-lapowsky/get-more-done-dont-reward-failure.html

180 It's from a collection . . . 'How Mr Rabbit was too sharp for Mr Fox', Uncle Remus, www.uncleremus.com/sharprabbit.html

183 The only thing . . . H.M. Sherrow, 'Adolescent male chimpanzees at Ngogo, Kibale National Park, Uganda have decided dominance relationships', *Folia Primatologica*, 2012, vol. 83, pp. 67–75, www.karger.com/Article/FullText/341168

188 This was back . . . P.J. Hilts, 'Tobacco chiefs say cigarettes aren't addictive', *New York Times*, 15 April 1994, www.nytimes.com/1994/04/15/us/tobacco-chiefs-say-cigarettes-aren-t-addictive.html

188 Smoking wasn't permitted . . . 'Tobacco advertising ban in Australia – fact sheet 252', National Archives of Australia, www.naa.gov.au/collection/fact-sheets/fs252.aspx

193 This is despite . . . See *Free Schools*

204 Don't fall for the iPad . . . C. Miller, 'Apple puts new 9.7-inch iPad to the test in "Homework" ad', 9to5 Mac, 27 March 2018, 9to5mac.com/2018/03/27/apple-education-ipad-homework-ad

204 The research on the use . . . Documented in *Free Schools*

204 A school without personal . . . 'Cyber security: enhanced design for schools', CyberHound, cyberhound.com/security
R.M. Gladden et al., *Bullying Surveillance among Youths: Uniform Definitions for Public Health and Recommended Data Elements*, National Center for Injury Prevention and Control, CDC and US Department of Education, Atlanta, Georgia, 2014, www.cdc.gov/violenceprevention/pdf/Bullying-Definitions-FINAL-a.pdf

208 The US Centers for Disease Control . . . R.M. Gladden et al., *Bullying Surveillance among Youths: Uniform Definitions for Public Health and Recommended Data Elements*, National Center for Injury Prevention and Control, CDC and US Department of Education, Atlanta, Georgia, 2014, www.cdc.gov/violenceprevention/pdf/Bullying-Definitions-FINAL-a.pdf

208 That definition is based . . . 'Dan Olweus', World Anti-bullying Forum2017, www.wabf2017.com/speaker/dan-olweus

209 A recent US survey . . . H. Luxenberg et al., *Bullying in US Schools, 2014 Status Report: Assessed Using Data Collected from the Olweus Bullying Questionnaire*, Hazelden Publishing, Center City, Minnesota, 2015, www.violencepreventionworks.org/public/document/bullying_2015_statusreport.pdf

210 Recent research that . . . J.H. Ryoo et al., 'Examination of the change in latent statuses in bullying behaviors across time', *School Psychology Quarterly*, 2015, vol. 30, no. 1, pp. 105–22, psycnet.apa.org/record/2014-33174-001
H.T.H. Leet al., 'Temporal patterns and predictors of bullying roles among adolescents in Vietnam: a school-based cohort study', *Psychology, Health and Medicine*, 2017, vol. 22, suppl. 1, pp. 107–21, www.tandfonline.com/doi/full/10.1080/13548506.2016.1271953?src=recsys

210 In this fluid social . . . H.T.H. Leet al., 'Temporal patterns and predictors of bullying roles among adolescents in Vietnam: a school-based cohort study', *Psychology, Health and Medicine*, 2017, vol. 22, suppl. 1, pp. 107–21, www.tandfonline.com/doi/full/10.1080/13548506.2016.1271953?src=recsys

211 his 1993 book . . . D. Olweus, *Bullying at School: What We Know and What We Can Do*, Wiley-Blackwell, Oxford, 1993.

211 Contrary to many . . . P.C. Rodkin et al., 'Heterogeneity of popular boys: antisocial and prosocial configurations', *Developmental Psychology*, 2000, vol. 36, no. 1, pp. 14–24, www.apa.org/pubs/journals/releases/dev-36114.pdf

212 Olweus's program is . . . M. Ttofi & D. Farrington, 'What works in preventing bullying: effective elements of anti-bullying programmes', *Journal of Aggression, Conflict and Peace Research*, 2009, vol. 1, no. 1, pp. 13–24, www.emeraldinsight.com/doi/abs/10.1108/17596599200900003
https://psyc525final.wikispaces.com/file/view/What+works+in+preventing+bullying.pdf

212 In a recent 210-school evaluation . . . S.P. Limber et al., 'Evaluation of the Olweus Bullying Prevention Program: a large scale study of US students in grades 3–11',

Journal of School Psychology, 2018, vol. 69, pp. 56–72, www.sciencedirect.com/science/article/pii/S0022440518300529
214 He's particularly dismissive . . . D. Olweus, 'Cyberbullying: an overrated phenomenon?', *European Journal of Developmental Psychology*, 2012, vol. 9, no. 5, pp. 520–38, www.tandfonline.com/doi/abs/10.1080/17405629.2012.682358
214 The latest US . . . L. Musu-Gillette et al., *Indicators of School Crime and Safety: 2017*, National Center for Education Statistics, US Department of Education, and Bureau of Justice Statistics, Office of Justice Programs, US Department of Justice, Washington DC, 2018, nces.ed.gov/pubsearch/pubsinfo.asp?pubid=2018036
215 The effect isn't massive . . . R.M. Kowalski & S.P. Limber 'Psychological, physical, and academic correlates of cyberbullying and traditional bullying', *Journal of Adolescent Health*, 2013, vol. 53, suppl. 1, pp. S13–20, www.sciencedirect.com/science/article/pii/S1054139X12004132
216 Consistent with this . . . R. Green et al., *Characteristics of Bullying Victims in Schools*, Research Report DFE-RR001, National Centre for Social Research, UK Department of Education, London, 2010, assets.publishing.service.gov.uk/government/uploads/system/uploads/attachment_data/file/182409/DFE-RR001.pdf E. Menesini & C. Salmivalli, 'Bullying in schools: the state of knowledge and effective interventions', *Psychology, Health and Medicine*, 2017, vol. 22, suppl. 1, pp. 240–53, www.tandfonline.com/doi/full/10.1080/13548506.2017.1279740
217 I suspect the tables . . . 'Overweight & obesity', Australian Institute of Health and Welfare, www.aihw.gov.au/reports-statistics/behaviours-risk-factors/overweight-obesity/overview
217 'Is Australia getting gayer – and how gay will we get?', Roy Morgan, 2 June 2015, www.roymorgan.com/findings/6263-exactly-how-many-australians-are-gay-december-2014-201506020136
217 In the most recent national polling . . . 'Is Australia getting gayer – and how gay will we get?', Roy Morgan, 2 June 2015, www.roymorgan.com/findings/6263-exactly-how-many-australians-are-gay-december-2014-201506020136
217 If that orientation is . . . E. Menesini & C. Salmivalli, 'Bullying in schools: the state of knowledge and effective interventions', *Psychology, Health and Medicine*, 2017, vol. 22, suppl. 1, pp. 240–53, www.tandfonline.com/doi/full/10.1080/13548506.2017.1279740
217 The Safe Schools program . . . 'Safe Schools: What is Safe Schools', Victoria Department of Education and Training, www.education.vic.gov.au/about/programs/Pages/safeschools.aspx - link40
218 The program is controversial . . . 'Safe Schools program downsized after campaign by right-wing MPs and Christian lobby groups', SBS News, 18 March 2016, www.sbs.com.au/news/safe-schools-program-downsized-after-campaign-by-right-wing-mps-and-christian-lobby-groups
218 A 2016 government review . . . W. Louden, 'Review of appropriateness and efficacy of the Safe Schools Coalition Australia program resources', 11 March 2016, docs.education.gov.au/system/files/doc/other/review_of_appropriateness_and_efficacy_of_the_ssca_program_resources_0.pdf
218 Even so, implementation . . . https://www.theaustralian.com.au/news/nation/safe-schools-victorias-det-cant-prove-homophobic-bullying/news-story/11b9fe2832a44e3cd39041a6d94566a0, 'Safe Schools: Victoria's DET can't prove homophobic bullying', Rebecca Urban, *The Australian*, 8 April 2017, Victorian education officials have conceded there is a lack of hard evidence on the rates of homophobic bullying in schools to justify the state government's decision to mandate the contentious Safe School program.

220 Being in a group . . . U. Frith & C. Frith, 'The social brain: allowing humans to boldly go where no other species has been', *Philosophical Transactions of the Royal Society of London B*, 2010, vol. 365, no. 1537, pp. 165–76, www.ncbi.nlm.nih.gov/pubmed/20008394

221 As a rule . . . J.M. Cohen, 'Sources of peer group homogeneity', *Sociology of Education*, 1977, vol. 50, no. 4, pp. 227–41, www.jstor.org/stable/2112497?origin=crossref&seq=1 - page_scan_tab_contents

223 Because this assessment . . . S.S. Horn, 'Group status, group bias, and adolescents' reasoning about the treatment of others in school contexts', *International Journal of Behavioral Development*, 2006, vol. 30, no. 3, pp. 208–18, journals.sagepub.com/doi/10.1177/0165025406066721

223 Year 8 girl's best friend . . . X.L. Jiang & A.H.N. Cillessen, 'Stability of continuous measures of sociometric status: a meta-analysis', *Developmental Review*, 2005, vol. 25, no. 1, pp. 1–25, www.sciencedirect.com/science/article/pii/S0273229704000395?via=ihub

224 Teens at the top . . . A.H. Cillessen & C. Borch, 'Developmental trajectories of adolescent popularity: a growth curve modelling analysis', *Journal of Adolescence*, 2006, vol. 29, no. 6, pp. 935–59, www.ncbi.nlm.nih.gov/pubmed/16860860?dopt=Abstract

A.H. Cillessen & C. Borch, 'Developmental trajectories of adolescent popularity: a growth curve modelling analysis', *Journal of Adolescence*, 2006, vol. 29, no. 6, pp. 935–59, www.ncbi.nlm.nih.gov/pubmed/16860860?dopt=Abstract

224 Teens at the bottom . . . A.H.N, Cillessen et al., 'Stability of sociometric categories', in A.H.N, Cillessen & W.M. Bukowski (eds), Recent Advances in the Measurement of Acceptance and Rejection in the Peer System, New Directions for Child and Adolescent Development, no. 88, Jossey-Bass, New York, pp. 75–93

224 Teens migrate to the top . . . M.R. Stone et al., 'We knew them when: sixth grade characteristics that predict adolescent high school social identities', *Journal of Early Adolescence*, vol. 28, no. 2, pp. 304–28, journals.sagepub.com/doi/10.1177/0272431607312743

225 Kids in this group . . . C. Sebastian et al., 'Social brain development and the affective consequences of ostracism in adolescence', *Brain and Cognition*, 2010, vol. 72, no. 1, pp. 134–45, www.ncbi.nlm.nih.gov/pubmed/19628323

226 This might sound . . . C.P. Lewis, 'The relation between extracurricular activities with academic and social competencies in school age children: a meta-analysis', PhD thesis, Texas A&M University, 2004, oaktrust.library.tamu.edu/handle/1969.1/2710

227 In one interesting study . . . G.L. Cohen & M.J. Prinstein, 'Peer contagion of aggression and health risk behavior among adolescent males: an experimental investigation of effects on public conduct and private attitudes', *Child Development*, 2006, vol. 77, no. 967–83, onlinelibrary.wiley.com/doi/10.1111/j.1467-8624.2006.00913.x

228 Teens are hopped . . . B.B. Averbeck, 'Oxytocin and the salience of social cues', *PNAS*, 2010, vol. 107, no. 20, pp. 9033–34, www.ncbi.nlm.nih.gov/pmc/articles/PMC2889126s

M. Pfundmair et al., 'Oxytocin promotes attention to social cues regardless of group membership', *Hormones and Behavior*, 2017, vol. 90, pp. 136–40, www.sciencedirect.com/science/article/pii/S0018506X16304056

228 A well-constructed status-based . . . N. Eisenberg & A.S. Morris, 'Moral cognitions and prosocial responding in adolescence', in R.M. Lerner & L. Steinberg (eds), *Handbook of Adolescent Psychology*, Wiley & Sons, Hoboken, New Jersey, 2004, pp. 155–88, psycnet.apa.org/record/2004-12826-006

J. Hoorn et al., 'Peer influence on prosocial behavior in adolescence', *Journal of Research on Adolescence*, 2016, vol. 26, pp. 90–100, onlinelibrary.wiley.com/doi/pdf/10.1111/jora.12173

228 As teen-driven, pro-social movements . . . J. Surowiecki, 'What happened to the Ice Bucket Challenge?', *New Yorker*, 25 July 2016, www.newyorker.com/magazine/2016/07/25/als-and-the-ice-bucket-challenge

229 In a recent series of studies . . . D. Albert et al., The teenage brain: peer influences on adolescent decision making', *Current Directions in Psychological Science*, 2013, vol. 22, no. 2, pp. 114–20, journals.sagepub.com/doi/abs/10.1177/0963721412471347

229 Similarly, an earlier study . . . M. Gardner & L. Steinberg, 'Peer influence on risk taking, risk preference, and risky decision making in adolescence and adulthood: an experimental study', *Developmental Psychology*, 2005, vol. 41. no. 4, pp. 625–35, www.ncbi.nlm.nih.gov/pubmed/16060809

232 In the United States . . . 'Welcome to the youth risk behaviors data portal', CDC, chronicdata.cdc.gov/browse?category=Youth+Risk+Behaviors

232 The numbers of children . . . Data for 1995: G.J. Gates & F.L. Sonenstein, 'Heterosexual genital sexual activity among adolescent males: 1988 and 1995', *Family Planning Perspectives*, 2000, vol. 32, no. 6, pp. 295–304. Data for 2002, 2006–10, and 2011–13: Child Trends' analyses of the National Survey of Family Growth, www.childtrends.org/wp-content/uploads/2013/12/95_Oral_Sex_1.pdf

232 We don't have stats for Australia . . . J.W. Toumbourou et al., 'Student survey trends in reported alcohol use and influencing factors in Australia', *Drug and Alcohol Review*, 2018, vol. 37, suppl. 1, pp. S58–66, www.ncbi.nlm.nih.gov/pubmed/29327387

233 Testosterone is the hormone . . . J.R. Udry et al., 'Serum androgenic hormones motivate sexual behavior in adolescent boys', *Fertility and Sterility*, 1985, vol. 43, no. 1, pp. 90–94, www.ncbi.nlm.nih.gov/pubmed/4038388

234 If your teen is one . . . M.A. Ott et al., 'Greater expectations: adolescents' positive motivations for sex', *Perspectives on Sexual and Reproductive Health*, 2006, vol. 38, no. 2, pp. 84–89, www.ncbi.nlm.nih.gov/pubmed/16772189

234 Teenage boys want sex . . . B.C. Campbell et al., 'Timing of pubertal maturation and the onset of sexual behavior among Zimbabwe school boys', *Archives of Sexual Behavior*, 2005, vol. 34, no. 5, pp. 505–16, www.ncbi.nlm.nih.gov/pubmed/16211472

234 Because the number . . . ABS, 'Data cubes', *3301.0 – Births, Australia, 2016*, ABS, Canberra, 2017, www.abs.gov.au/AUSSTATS/abs@.nsf/DetailsPage/3301.02016?OpenDocument

235 In the United States . . . 'STDs in adolescents and young adults', 2016 Sexually Transmitted Diseases Surveillance, CDC, www.cdc.gov/std/stats16/adolescents.htm

236 By the time most . . . L.Y. Hwang et al., 'Factors that influence the rate of epithelial maturation in the cervix of healthy young women', *Journal of Adolescent Health*, 2009, vol. 44, no. 2, pp. 103–10, www.ncbi.nlm.nih.gov/pmc/articles/PMC2662755

236 Any damage creates . . . V. Lee et al., 'Relationship of cervical ectopy to chlamydia infection in young women', *Journal of Family Planning and Reproductive Health Care*, 2006, vol. 32, no. 2, pp. 104–106, www.ncbi.nlm.nih.gov/pubmed/16824301

236 Between them they affect . . . ABS, 'Chlamydia notifications, Australia – 2001–2011(a): Bacterial STIs', *4102.0 – Australian Social Trends, Jun 2012*, ABS, Canberra, 2012, www.abs.gov.au/AUSSTATS/abs@.nsf/Lookup/4102.0Main+Features10Jun+2012 - Bacterial

236 Untreated, around 10–15 per cent . . . 'STDs & infertility', Sexually Transmitted Diseases (STDs), CDC, www.cdc.gov/std/infertility/default.htm

237 All of the primary STIs . . . 'STD risk and oral sex – CDC fact sheet', Sexually Transmitted Diseases (STDs), CDC, www.cdc.gov/std/healthcomm/stdfact-stdriskandoralsex.htm

239 In 1916, Margaret Sanger . . . For the 1920 edition, see M. Sanger, *What Every Girl Should Know*, United Sales Co., Springfield, Illinois, 1920, archive.lib.msu.edu/DMC/AmRad/whateverygirl1920.pdf

239 Pincus based his work . . . A.W. Makepeace, 'The effect of progestin upon the anterior pituitary', *American Journal of Obstetrics and Gynecology*, vol. 37, no. 3, pp. 457–59, www.ajog.org/article/S0002-9378(15)32567-9/fulltext

240 A woman can still . . . 'Effectiveness of family planning methods', CDC, www.cdc.gov/reproductivehealth/unintendedpregnancy/pdf/contraceptive_methods_508.pdf

240 In Australia, use of this type . . . http://www.roymorgan.com/findings/6542-new-era-of-womens-contraception-201511112207

240 The growth rates are similar . . . A.N. Rashed et al., 'Trends and patterns of hormonal contraceptive prescribing for adolescents in primary care in the UK', *Journal of Family Planning and Reproductive Health Care*, 2015, vol. 41, no. 3, pp. 216–22, www.ncbi.nlm.nih.gov/pubmed/25398724

240 In the United States . . . R.K. Jones, 'Beyond birth control: the overlooked benefits of oral contraceptive pills', Guttmacher Institute, November 2011, www.guttmacher.org/report/beyond-birth-control-overlooked-benefits-oral-contraceptive-pills

241 About 85 per cent . . . D.D. Lynn et al., 'The epidemiology of acne vulgaris in late adolescence', *Adolescent Health, Medicine and Therapeutics*, 2016, vol. 7, pp. 13–25, www.ncbi.nlm.nih.gov/pmc/articles/PMC4769025

242 Effectiveness of acne treatments . . . J. Ravenscroft, 'Evidence based update on the management of acne', *Archives of Disease in Childhood – Education and Practice*, 2005, vol. 90, pp. ep98–101, ep.bmj.com/content/90/4/ep98

242 In Australia, it can only . . . 'Penalties for prescribing and dispensing isotretinoin without authorisation', Queensland Health, August 2015, www.health.qld.gov.au/__data/assets/pdf_file/0022/444154/fs-isotretinoin-prescribing.pdf

242 About 80 per cent . . . D.D. Lynn et al., 'The epidemiology of acne vulgaris in late adolescence', *Adolescent Health, Medicine and Therapeutics*, 2016, vol. 7, pp. 13–25, www.ncbi.nlm.nih.gov/pmc/articles/PMC4769025

244 It works because . . . https://www.ncbi.nlm.nih.gov/pmc/articles/PMC3845679/

244 This can also cause . . . https://www.smr.jsexmed.org/article/S2050-0521(16)30022-1/pdf

244 A 2011 French study . . . A. Norton, 'Symptoms in teen years may foretell severe endometriosis', Reuters, 20 November 2010, www.reuters.com/article/us-symptoms-teen/symptoms-in-teen-years-may-foretell-severe-endometriosis-idUSTRE6AI5EV20101119
C. Chapron et al., 'Questioning patients about their adolescent history can identify markers associated with deep infiltrating endometriosis', *Fertility and Sterility*, 2011, vol. 95, no. 3, pp. 877–81, www.ncbi.nlm.nih.gov/pubmed/21071024

245 A huge long-term study . . . C.W. Skovlund et al., 'Association of hormonal contraception with depression', *JAMA Psychiatry*, 2016, vol. 73, no. 11, pp. 1154–62, jamanetwork.com/journals/jamapsychiatry/fullarticle/2552796

246 In Australia, for one in 25 . . . 'Is Australia getting gayer – and how gay will we get?', Roy Morgan, 2 June 2015, www.roymorgan.com/findings/6263-exactly-how-many-australians-are-gay-december-2014-201506020136

246 In addition to this . . . E.L. Meerwijk & J.M. Sevelius, 'Transgender population size in the United States: a meta-regression of population-based probability samples', *American Journal of Public Health*, 2017, vol. 107, no. 2, pp. e1–8, www.ncbi.nlm.nih.gov/pmc/articles/PMC5227946

247 We don't know what . . . B.L. Frankowski & Committee on Adolescence, 'Sexual orientation and adolescents', *Pediatrics*, 2004, vol. 113, no. 6, pp. 1827–32, pediatrics.aappublications.org/content/113/6/1827

247 We know from large numbers . . . M. Hines, 'Prenatal testosterone and gender-related behaviour', *European Journal of Endocrinology*, vol. 155, suppl. 1, pp. S115–21, www.eje-online.org/content/155/suppl_1/S115.full

248 A long line of studies . . . T. Grimbos et al., 'Sexual orientation and the second to fourth finger length ratio: a meta-analysis in men and women', *Behavioral Neuroscience*, 2010, vol. 124, no. 2., pp. 278–87, www.ncbi.nlm.nih.gov/pubmed/20364887

248 One study found that higher . . . A. Csathó et al., 'Sex role identity related to the ratio of second to fourth digit length in women', *Biological Psychology*, 2003, vol. 62, no. 2, pp. 147–56, www.ncbi.nlm.nih.gov/pubmed/12581689
M.H. McIntyre, 'Digit ratios, childhood gender role behavior, and erotic role preferences of gay men', *Archives of Sexual Behavior*, 2003, vol. 32, no. 6, pp. 495–96, www.ncbi.nlm.nih.gov/pubmed/14627046
C. Li et al., 'The relationship between digit ratio and sexual orientation in a Chinese Yunnan Han population', *Personality and Individual Differences*, 2016, vol. 101, pp. 26–29, www.sciencedirect.com/science/article/pii/S0191886916304044

249 The science is far . . . M. Hines, 'Prenatal testosterone and gender-related behaviour', *European Journal of Endocrinology*, vol. 155, suppl. 1, pp. S115–21, www.eje-online.org/content/155/suppl_1/S115.full

253 If we don't sleep . . . S. Banks & D.F. Dinges, 'Behavioral and physiological consequences of sleep restriction', *Journal of Clinical Sleep Medicine*, 2007, vol. 3, no. 5, pp. 519–28, https://www.ncbi.nlm.nih.gov/pmc/articles/PMC1978335/

253 Simply put, our brains work . . . M. Thomas et al., 'Neural basis of alertness and cognitive performance impairments during sleepiness. I. Effects of 24 h of sleep deprivation on waking human regional brain activity', *Journal of Sleep Research*, 2000, vol. 9, no. 4, pp. 335–52, www.ncbi.nlm.nih.gov/pubmed/11123521

253 Recent studies . . . D. Kaliyaperumal et al., 'Effects of sleep deprivation on the cognitive performance of nurses working in shift', *Journal of Clinical and Diagnostic Research*, 2017, vol. 11, no. 8, pp. C01–03, www.ncbi.nlm.nih.gov/pmc/articles/PMC5620757
D.J. Raidy & L.F. Scharff, 'Effects of sleep deprivation on auditory and visual memory tasks', *Perceptual and Motor Skills*, 2005, vol. 101, no. 2, pp. 451–67, www.ncbi.nlm.nih.gov/pubmed/16383080

254 Other research has shown . . . A. Williamson & A. Feyer, 'Moderate sleep deprivation produces impairments in cognitive and motor performance equivalent to legally prescribed levels of alcohol intoxication', *Occupational and Environmental Medicine*, 2000, vol. 57, no. 10, pp. 649–55, www.ncbi.nlm.nih.gov/pmc/articles/PMC1739867

254 Up to 15 per cent . . . Institute of Medicine (US) Committee on Sleep Medicine and Research, *Sleep Disorders and Sleep Deprivation: An Unmet Public Health Problem*, National Academies Press, Washington DC, 2006, www.ncbi.nlm.nih.gov/pubmed/20669438

254 From about three months . . . J. Ardura, 'Emergence and evolution of the circadian rhythm of melatonin in children', *Hormonal Research in Paediatrics*, 2003, vol. 59, no. 2, pp. 66–72, www.ncbi.nlm.nih.gov/pubmed/12589109

255 Even more powerfully . . . D.X. Tan et al., 'One molecule, many derivatives: a never-ending interaction of melatonin with reactive oxygen and nitrogen species?', *Journal of Pineal Research*, 2007, vol. 42, no. 1, pp. 28–42, www.ncbi.nlm.nih.gov/pubmed/17198536

255 At rest it burns one-fifth . . . R.J. Reiter et al., 'Neurotoxins: free radical mechanisms and melatonin protection', *Current Neuropharmacology*, 2010, vol. 8, no. 3, pp. 194–210, www.ncbi.nlm.nih.gov/pmc/articles/PMC3001213
D.X. Tan et al., 'One molecule, many derivatives: a never-ending interaction of melatonin with reactive oxygen and nitrogen species?', *Journal of Pineal Research*, 2007, vol. 42, no. 1, pp. 28–42, www.ncbi.nlm.nih.gov/pubmed/17198536

255 There are a lot of free radicals . . . L. Xie et al, 'Sleep drives metabolite clearance from the adult brain', *Science*, 2013, vol. 342, no. 6156, pp. 373–77, www.ncbi.nlm.nih.gov/pmc/articles/PMC3880190

255 It has similar effects . . . S.R. Pandi-Perumal et al., 'Physiological effects of melatonin: role of melatonin receptors and signal transduction pathways', *Progress in Neurobiology*, 2008, vol. 85, no. 3, pp. 335–53, www.ncbi.nlm.nih.gov/pubmed/18571301
T. Uz et al., 'The regional and cellular expression profile of the melatonin receptor MT1 in the central dopaminergic system', *Molecular Brain Research*, 2005, vol. 136, nos 1–2, pp. 45–53, www.ncbi.nlm.nih.gov/pubmed/15893586

255 Because of this . . . C. de Bodinat et al., 'Agomelatine, the first melatonergic antidepressant: discovery, characterization and development', *Nature Reviews Drug Discovery*, 2010, vol. 9, no. 8, pp. 628–42, www.ncbi.nlm.nih.gov/pubmed/20577266
S. Comai & G. Gobbi, 'Unveiling the role of melatonin MT2 receptors in sleep, anxiety and other neuropsychiatric diseases: a novel target in psychopharmacology', *Journal of Psychiatry and Neuroscience*, 2014, vol. 39, no. 1, pp. 6–21, www.ncbi.nlm.nih.gov/pubmed/23971978

255 We don't know . . . J.M. Siegel, 'Why we sleep: the reasons that we sleep are gradually becoming less enigmatic', *Scientific American*, November 2003, pp. 92–97, at web.archive.org/web/20081203071459/http://www.semel.ucla.edu/sleepresearch/sciam2003/sciamsleep.pdf

256 There are two distinct phases . . . V.V. Vyazovskiy & A. Delogu, 'NREM and REM sleep: complementary roles in recovery after wakefulness', *Neuroscientist*, 2014, vol. 20, no. 3, pp. 203–19, journals.sagepub.com/doi/full/10.1177/1073858413518152

257 In particular, the huge increases . . . M.H. Hagenauer et al., 'Adolescent changes in the homeostatic and circadian regulation of sleep', *Developmental Neuroscience*, 2009, vol. 31, no. 4, pp. 276–84, www.ncbi.nlm.nih.gov/pmc/articles/PMC2820578
M.H. Hagenauer et al., 'Adolescent changes in the homeostatic and circadian regulation of sleep', *Developmental Neuroscience*, 2009, vol. 31, no. 4, pp. 276–84, www.ncbi.nlm.nih.gov/pmc/articles/PMC2820578

258 We're particularly sensitive . . . B. Wood et al., 'Light level and duration of exposure determine the impact of self-luminous tablets on melatonin suppression', *Applied Ergononomics*, 2013, vol. 44, no. 2, pp. 237–40, www.ncbi.nlm.nih.gov/pubmed/22850476

258 Lying in bed looking . . . J. Schmerler, 'Q&A: why is blue light before bedtime bad for sleep?', *Scientific American*, 1 September 2015, www.scientificamerican.com/article/q-a-why-is-blue-light-before-bedtime-bad-for-sleep

260 Our ability to cope . . . E. van der Helm & M.P. Walker, 'Overnight therapy? The role of sleep in emotional brain processing', *Psychological Bulletin*, 2009, vol. 135, no. 5, pp. 731–48, www.ncbi.nlm.nih.gov/pmc/articles/PMC2890316

265 According to recent research . . . http://www.pewresearch.org/fact-tank/2018/03/14/about-a-quarter-of-americans-report-going-online-almost-constantly/ft_18-03-15_constantusers_oneinfour/

274 She had three or four . . . 'Divorce in Australia source data', Australian Institute of Family Studies, aifs.gov.au/facts-and-figures/divorce-australia/divorce-australia-source-data

275 Suddenly there was a huge market . . . J. May, 'Who listens to the baby whisperer?', *Sydney Morning Herald*, 2 September 2013, www.smh.com.au/lifestyle/who-listens-to-the-baby-whisperer-20130902-2t10r.html

277 It could even be . . . 'Snapshot of Australia: 2016 Census data summary', ABS, 28 June 2017, www.abs.gov.au/ausstats/abs@.nsf/Lookup/by Subject/2071.0~2016~Main Features~Snapshot of Australia, 2016~2 http://www.ausstats.abs.gov.au/ausstats/free.nsf/0/C6162D97641789C6CA257880008240B2/$File/1966%20Census%20-%20Volume%202%20Population%20-%20Related%20Characteristics%20-%20Part%205%20Families%20and%20Households.pdf

282 But, perversely . . . S. Berger, 'Gen Z is the loneliest generation, survey reveals, but working can help', CNBC Make It, 2 May 2018, www.cnbc.com/2018/05/02/cigna-study-loneliness-is-an-epidemic-gen-z-is-the-worst-off.html

ACKNOWLEDGEMENTS

None of this would be possible without my wife, Lizzie. Not this book, and not the kids we experimented on to come up with the advice it dispenses. As with every book I have ever written, Lizzie has been an integral part of making sure it not only happens but passes muster when the common-sense filter is applied. Her support, criticism and intelligence has once again been vital, and I am eternally grateful for all of that, as well as the fact she bothered to produce six kids just to try this stuff out on.

Lizzie isn't the only parent who contributed to this book. My publisher, Ingrid Ohlsson, normally just bangs heads at publishing houses to make sure my ideas make it into print. But this time she did much more than that. This time she passionately lent her experience as a parent of teenaged kids and helped convince a large group of other parents to share their stories. The book is based on science but is informed by the experiences of real-life parents and teens. Besides Ingrid and Lizzie, Virginia Birch, Natasha Bita, Lisa Cassimatis, Ben Caunt, Brianne Collins, Katie Crawford, Anthony Gribble, Sean Lipsett, Heidi Middleton, and more than a few others (who would prefer not to be named, lest their kids hunt them down) all gave generously of their time in helping me collect stories, strategies and tactics from the frontline of gen Z parenting. Their on-the-ground experience was useful beyond measure.

Senior Editor Ariane Durkin did her usual sterling job of making sure my handmade pile of research and thought bubbles actually turned into the magnificent book you have just read. And Nicola Young brought her usual persistent desire for extreme accuracy to the task of copyediting and fact-checking. It is reassuring indeed to know that the evidence presented here has made it through the eagle-eyed scrutiny of these two very experienced editors.

Daniel New once again put together a fabulous cover, but it wouldn't have been possible without our ridgy-didge gen Z models, Max Cheetham and Claudia Birch (and of course their respective parents, Tracey Cheetham and Virginia Birch, for letting them do it).

Last and probably least, my agent, Frank Stranges, a parent of teens himself, again played no perceptible part in proceedings but will still, no doubt, expect to be paid.

INDEX

E

F

R